KT-379-423

UML

IN A NUTSHELL

A Desktop Quick Reference

UML
IN A NUTSHELL

A Desktop Quick Reference

Sinan Si Alhir

O'REILLY®

Beijing · Cambridge · Farnham · Köln · Paris · Sebastopol · Taipei · Tokyo

UML in a Nutshell

by Sinan Si Alhir

Copyright © 1998 O'Reilly & Associates, Inc. All rights reserved.
Printed in the United States of America.

Published by O'Reilly & Associates, Inc., 101 Morris Street, Sebastopol, CA 95472.

Editor: Andy Oram

Production Editor: Paula Carroll

Production Service: Argosy

Printing History:

September 1998: First Edition.

Nutshell Handbook, the Nutshell Handbook logo, and the O'Reilly logo are registered trademarks of O'Reilly & Associates, Inc. The relationship between the image of the domestic short-hair cat and the topic of UML is a trademark of O'Reilly & Associates. Many of the designations used by manufacturers and sellers to distinguish their products are claimed as trademarks. Where those designations appear in this book, and O'Reilly & Associates, Inc. was aware of a trademark claim, the designations have been printed in caps or initial caps.

While every precaution has been taken in the preparation of this book, the publisher assumes no responsibility for errors or omissions, or for damages resulting from the use of the information contained herein.

ISBN: 1-56592-448-7   [4/02]
[M]

Table of Contents

Part II: Using the Unified Modeling Language

Part III: The Unified Modeling Language Quick Reference

Preface

Overview

"Knowledge and human power are synonymous," once said the great philosopher Francis Bacon. However, based on experience within today's global markets, he would probably say, "The ability to capture, communicate, and leverage knowledge to solve problems is human power." This raises the question of how exactly one can best capture, communicate, and leverage knowledge, especially within the world of systems engineering. Could the answer to this question be the Unified Modeling Language (UML)?

The UML is a modeling language for specifying, visualizing, constructing, and documenting the artifacts of a system-intensive process. It was originally conceived by Rational Software Corporation and the three prominent methodologists in the information systems and technology industry, Grady Booch, James Rumbaugh, and Ivar Jacobson (the Three Amigos). The language has gained significant industry support from various organizations via the UML Partners Consortium and has been submitted to and approved by the Object Management Group (OMG) as a standard.

The UML represents the evolutionary unification of the three most prominent methodologists' experience with other industry engineering best practices. It is a general-purpose, broadly applicable, tool-supported, industry-standardized modeling language. It applies to a multitude of different types of systems, domains, and methods or processes.

UML in a Nutshell is a quick reference to the Unified Modeling Language (UML) version 1.1.

This book is for managers and professionals who seek a broad understanding of what the UML is and is not, and for practitioners (engineers) and professionals who seek a detailed understanding of every part of the UML, including the syntax and semantics of the language and how to apply it to solve problems.

This book consolidates the authoritative UML documentation and specification into a holistic and integrated quick reference. It does not simply describe the subject, but provides the foundation for the subject from a practitioner's perspective. This book is not exclusively for methodologists, managers, analysts, developers, or programmers, but rather is for *all* types of individuals who apply knowledge to solve problems and develop solutions or systems (business, software, hardware, etc.).

This book also goes beyond the standard to show how the UML may be applied in the context of problem solving and the application of knowledge. This book will be most useful to you after you've learned the UML. It is holistic in that it covers every aspect of the UML, integrated in that it shows how all the elements of the UML are cooperatively used, and organized in a quick reference format so that you can consult it. However, this book can also help you learn the UML. It contains a simple yet complete principle-focused and technique-oriented tutorial that introduces the essentials of the UML.

Why This Book?

Working within the business and technology industry in applying object orientation, I was very aware of the issues surrounding nonstandard methods and notation. So when the thoughts of prominent methodologists in the industry started to converge toward a unified standard, I eagerly began applying the results. As I and the business and technology industry began to apply the UML from its earliest version (Unified Method), I saw that the industry was sold on the hype of the UML rather than its real benefits; that is, everyone is trying to sell the UML *standard* without really contemplating what the UML is and how to apply the UML to maximize a return on investment. Most people think it is a good thing to comply with a standard, but very few can truly articulate why!

After utilizing the UML on various projects, I started to realize that the UML is significantly more than a standard or another modeling language. It is a paradigm, philosophy, revolution, and evolution of how we approach problem solving and systems.

Furthermore, most books on the subject focus on the technology that applies (or adheres to) the UML rather than looking at the impact the UML itself has on systems development. These books directly tie the UML to some implementation language (Java, C++, etc.); however, very few, if any, are able to move beyond the notation to the concepts and their true value. This book confronts the problem that users think the UML is just for drawing diagrams, when it is really meant for capturing the knowledge and semantics behind the diagrams.

You will find that the text is pretty compressed in many places. For example, I say that the UML is a language. That's obvious, you may reply. However, don't take for granted what such a statement really means: A language is used for communication. Various practitioners with experience in the object-oriented world classify the UML as just another notation simply because the official UML documentation and most books on the subject emphasize notation rather than the holistic view of the UML. One needs to look beyond the notation and look at what constitutes a notation, why it is used, and how it is best applied.

It is often said that the English language is the world's universal language; now it is virtually certain that the UML will be the information systems and technology world's universal language.

This book, just like every other book ever written, is a snapshot of thoughts in time. If you discover errors in the text, please let me know. The UML will most likely have evolved since the writing of this book; however, this book captures the fundamental concepts that drive this evolution. Therefore, the book should remain valuable to you. Readers who would like to contact me to ask questions or to discuss this book, the UML, object orientation, or other related topics are very welcome to do so at the e-mail address salhir@earthlink.net or to visit my World Wide Web site home page at *http://home.earthlink.net/~salhir.*

Contents

This book consists of three sections or parts and 16 chapters.

Part I, "Introducing the Unified Modeling Language," presents the overall context in which the UML may be applied.

- Chapter 1, *Introduction,* introduces the goals, scope, and formal documentation of the UML, and its history and evolution.

- Chapter 2, *The Big Picture,* introduces the context for understanding and applying the UML. This includes the key concepts underlying the UML. The chapter explores the concepts of problems, solutions, problem solving, life cycles, development cycles and phases, iteration cycles and phases, domains or spaces, systems, architectures, models, architectural views, diagrams, languages, paradigms, artifacts, activities, and heuristics.

- Chapter 3, *Object Orientation,* presents the object-oriented paradigm that forms the basis for the UML. This chapter introduces some of the key concepts and constructs of object orientation. It explores real-world concepts, implementation-world concepts, the function-driven paradigm, the data-driven paradigm, the object-oriented paradigm, and key concepts independent of any implementation language.

Part II, "Using the Unified Modeling Language," presents an integrated view of the UML and how all its constituent parts (diagrams) interact to facilitate its use.

- Chapter 4, *A Unified Modeling Language Tutorial,* presents a tutorial introducing the different diagrams and elements of the UML.

- Chapter 5, *The Unified Modeling Language,* presents an overview of the constituent parts of the UML, how they relate to one another, and how they contribute to a method or process utilizing the UML. This chapter brings together problems, solutions, and problem-solving concepts into a unified view of the UML.

Part III, "The Unified Modeling Language Quick Reference," presents a detailed view of the UML constituents in a quick reference format.

- Chapter 6, *Diagramming and Model Organization,* presents information on diagramming and model organization. This is general information on diagramming and modeling in the UML.

- Chapter 7, *Class and Object Diagrams*, presents information on class and object diagrams. These diagrams are concerned with the static structure of a system, or how it is organized rather than how it behaves.

- Chapter 8, *Use Case Diagrams*, presents information on use case diagrams. These diagrams are concerned with the functions provided by a system to external entities.

- Chapter 9, *Sequence Diagrams*, presents information on sequence diagrams. These diagrams are concerned with the dynamic structure of a system, or how it behaves rather than how it is structured. The chapter focuses on communication between elements within a system.

- Chapter 10, *Collaboration Diagrams*, presents information on collaboration diagrams. Like sequence diagrams, these are concerned with the dynamic structure of a system, or how it behaves rather than how it is structured. The chapter focuses on relationships between communicating elements within a system.

- Chapter 11, *Statechart Diagrams*, presents information on statechart diagrams. These diagrams are concerned with the dynamic structure of a system, or how it behaves in response to external stimuli.

- Chapter 12, *Activity Diagrams*, presents information on activity diagrams. These diagrams are concerned with the dynamic structure of a system, or how it behaves in response to internal processing.

- Chapter 13, *Component Diagrams*, presents information on component diagrams. These diagrams are concerned with the organization of and dependencies among implementation components.

- Chapter 14, *Deployment Diagrams*, presents information on deployment diagrams. These diagrams are concerned with the configuration of processing resource elements and the mapping of implementation components onto them.

- Chapter 15, *Extension Mechanisms*, presents information on extension mechanisms. These mechanisms are used to customize and extend the UML.

- Chapter 16, *The Object Constraint Language*, presents information on the Object Constraint Language. This language is used for expressing constraints and rules on model elements.

The appendix contains references to notable resources on the World Wide Web and various books that may be of interest.

The book makes extensive use of bulleted lists. Although unusual (even unique), the style is suited to the book's purpose and subject in many ways. The information you need to know about each feature falls into several different categories— visual appearance, rule vis-a-vis other features, rules—and is thus easiest to absorb in bite-sized pieces. Furthermore, by comparing the bullets under different paragraphs you can quickly see the ways in which similar features differ.

The UML notation is presented in example-like diagram templates. These diagrams depict all possible parts and options of the notation, and the text indicates which constructs are required or optional as well as any other important information.

Ellipses in the diagram templates indicate that information is repeated. These diagrams are not simply generic templates, since I would have to invent a whole complex language in order to show what's optional and what's required. Furthermore, these diagrams are not strict examples, since there would be too many examples required to depict all possible options. Rather, they are templates exemplifying the concepts.

The book does not contain any source code because focus is given to the modeling language independent of any translation to a specific implementation. Rather than show you how to translate a system to a specific implementation, I show you how to view a system and determine what the right system is to solve a problem.

How to Contact Us

We have tested and verified the information in this book to the best of our ability, but you may find that features have changed (or even that we have made mistakes!). Please let us know about any errors you find, as well as your suggestions for future editions, by writing to:

O'Reilly & Associates, Inc.
101 Morris Street
Sebastopol, CA 95472
1-800-998-9938 (in the U.S. or Canada)
1-707-829-0515 (international/local)
1-707-829-0104 (FAX)

You can also send us messages electronically. To be put on the mailing list or request a catalog, send email to:

info@oreilly.com

To ask technical questions or comment on the book, send email to:

bookquestions@oreilly.com

We have a web site for the book, where we'll list errata and any plans for future editions. You can access this page at:

http://www.oreilly.com/catalog/umlnut/

For more information about this book and others, see the O'Reilly web site:

http://www.oreilly.com

Acknowledgments

There are a number of individuals who made this work possible. It is not only I who deserve credit, but rather those who had to live with me, who demonstrated an abundance of encouragement, patience, understanding, and had to sacrifice a part of themselves to let me accomplish this endeavor.

I thank God for making everything possible, and I thank my teachers for making this real: My father Saad, who taught me the meaning of success by exemplifying it as my mentor and role model; my mother Rabab, who taught me that being analytical without emotion provides only a limited view of the world and its wonder; my wife Milad, who taught me that reason without passion is insufficient to bring fulfillment; my brother Ghazwan, who taught me to be pragmatic; my brother Phillip, who taught me to be idealistic; and my daughter Nora, who continuously teaches me the truths I failed to learn from my own childhood.

I would also like to thank my mentors, Dr. Carl Victor Page and Dr. George C. Stockman, for teaching me that the theoretical and abstract realm of computer science and the practical and real life of a computer professional are not disjoint, but intersect to establish a foundation for good solutions to complex real-world problems.

I would also like to thank Tim O'Reilly for giving me the opportunity to do this book; my editor, Andy Oram, for his effort and understanding and for showing me the true fabric that makes O'Reilly and Associates and *In a Nutshell* books a success; and all the staff at O'Reilly and Associates for their work in bringing this book to life. I would also like to thank the following reviewers for their feedback: Jeff Estefan, Dr. Brian Henderson-Sellers, and Kevin Jameson.

I will not forget any of you, and I only ask that you please remember me.

PART I

Introducing the Unified Modeling Language

This section presents the overall context in which the UML may be applied.

Chapter 1, *Introduction*, introduces the goals, scope, and formal documentation of the UML, and its history and evolution.

Chapter 2, *The Big Picture*, introduces the context for understanding and applying the UML.

Chapter 3, *Object Orientation*, presents the object-oriented paradigm that forms the basis for the UML.

CHAPTER 1

Introduction

This chapter introduces the goals, scope, and formal documentation of the Unified Modeling Language (UML), along with its history and evolution. Upon reading this chapter, you will understand:

- The scope and goals of the UML, and the various issues it attempts to address.
- What documents formally define and establish the UML.
- The historical evolution of the UML.

This chapter introduces some of the key motivations behind the UML. I start by introducing the UML's goals and scope. I then briefly identify the formal documents that define the UML. You should reference these documents for detailed information beyond this book. I then review the history of how the UML came to be.

What Is the Unified Modeling Language?

The Unified Modeling Language

The Unified Modeling Language (Figure 1-1) is a language that unifies the industry's best engineering practices for modeling systems. The UML

- Is a *language*. It is not simply a notation for drawing diagrams, but a complete language for capturing knowledge (semantics) about a subject and expressing knowledge (syntax) regarding the subject for the purpose of communication.
- Applies to *modeling* and systems. Modeling involves a focus on understanding (knowing) a subject (system) and capturing and being able to communicate this knowledge.
- Is the result of *unifying* the information systems and technology industry's best engineering practices (principles, techniques, methods, and tools).
- Is used for specifying, visualizing, constructing, and documenting systems.
- Is used for expressing the artifacts of a system-intensive process.

3

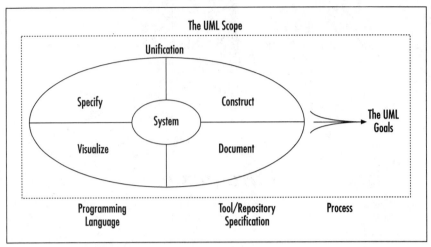

Figure 1-1: The Unified Modeling Language

- Is based on the object-oriented paradigm.

- Is a modeling language for specifying, visualizing, constructing, and documenting the artifacts of a system-intensive process.

- Is an evolutionary general-purpose, broadly applicable, tool-supported, industry-standardized modeling language.

- Applies to a multitude of different types of systems, domains, and methods or processes.

- Enables the capturing, communicating, and leveraging of strategic, tactical, and operational knowledge to facilitate increasing value by increasing quality, reducing costs, and reducing time-to-market while managing risks and being proactive in regard to ever-increasing change and complexity.

- Was originally conceived by Rational Software Corporation and the Three Amigos.

  - Grady Booch's work has involved the use of Ada and the application of data abstraction and information hiding with an emphasis on iterative software development and software architecture. He has been influential in disseminating object orientation. He is the inventor of the Booch method, as expressed in his book *Object-Oriented Analysis and Design*.

  - James Rumbaugh's work has involved various topics concerning research and development within the context of complex algorithms and data structures. He coauthored the Object Modeling Technique (OMT) with Mike Blaha, Bill Premerlani, Fred Eddy, and Bill Lorensen.

  - Ivar Jacobson's work has involved the application of object orientation to the context of business reengineering and the industrialization of software development. He is often known as the father of use cases. He is the inventor of the Object-Oriented Software Engineering (OOSE) method, as expressed in his book *Object-Oriented Software Engineering: A Use Case Driven Approach*.

- Is supported by the UML Partners Consortium (Rational Software Corporation, Microsoft Corporation, Hewlett-Packard Company, Oracle Corporation, Sterling Software, MCI Systemhouse Corporation, Unisys Corporation, ICON Computing.

Unification

Unification creates a single, consistent system from the most prominent methods (at the modeling language level) within the industry. Unification

- Involves uniting the modeling languages of the following methods:

  - Grady Booch's method: A design- and construction-oriented approach supporting excellent expressiveness for engineering-intensive systems.

  - James Rumbaugh and associates' Object Modeling Technique (OMT) method: An analysis-oriented approach supporting excellent expressiveness for data-intensive systems.

  - Ivar Jacobson's Object-Oriented Software Engineering (OOSE) method: A use-case-oriented approach supporting excellent expressiveness for business engineering and requirements analysis.

- Incorporates other methods and the best engineering practices to capture lessons learned.

- Occurs across types of systems (software and nonsoftware), domains (business versus software), and development phases (requirements, analysis, design, implementation, testing, and deployment).

- Involves modeling language semantics and syntax, not development processes.

- Addresses contemporary and future development issues.

The UML Goals

The goals of the UML are to

- Be a ready-to-use expressive visual modeling language that is simple and extensible.

- Have extensibility and specialization mechanisms for extending, rather than modifying, core concepts.

  - Formalize a core set of concepts that constitute the object-oriented paradigm. Extensions will not require reimplementation of the core object-oriented paradigm (analysis and design) concepts in order to be applicable to a broad set of applications. Instead, practitioners can extend this core set of concepts based on varying interpretations without having to repeatedly redefine the fundamental concepts.

  - Allow adding new concepts and notation beyond the core.

  - Allow variant interpretations of existing concepts when there is no clear consensus.

  - Allow specialization of concepts, notation, and constraints for particular domains.

- Be implementation independent (programming language).

- Be process independent (development).

- Encourage the growth of the object-oriented tools market.

- Support higher-level concepts (collaborations, frameworks, patterns, and components).

- Address recurring architectural complexity problems (physical distribution and distributed systems, concurrency and concurrent systems, replication, security, load balancing, and fault tolerance) using component technology, visual programming, patterns, and frameworks.

- Be scalable.

- Be widely applicable (general purpose and powerful) and usable (simple, widely accepted, evolutionary).

- Integrate the best engineering practices.

The UML Scope

The scope of the UML encompasses

- Fusing the concepts of Booch, OMT, and OOSE.

- Focusing on a standard modeling language (common semantics and then common notation) and not a standard process.

- Incorporating the object-oriented community's consensus on core modeling concepts.

- Providing sufficient notation to address contemporary modeling issues directly and economically.

- Providing sufficient semantics to address the following issues directly and economically:

  - Contemporary modeling issues

  - Future modeling issues (specifically related to component technology, distributed computing, frameworks, and executability)

  - Model interchange among tools

  - Repository interfaces (to modeling artifacts) among tools

- Providing extensibility mechanisms to address the following issues directly and economically:

  - Current deviations within the object-oriented community

  - Extending the UML for individual projects

  - Future modeling approaches (on top of the UML)

What the UML Is Not

The UML is not

- A visual programming language, but a visual modeling language.

  - A programming language communicates an implementation or solution.

- – A modeling language communicates a model (or conceptualization or specification).
- A tool or repository specification, but a modeling language specification.
  - – A tool or repository specification specifies a tool's or repository's interface, storage, run-time behavior, and so forth.
  - – A modeling language specification specifies modeling elements, notation, and usage guidelines.
- A process, but enables processes.
  - – A process provides guidance regarding the order of activities, specification of artifacts to be developed, direction of individual developer and team tasks (or activities), and monitoring and measuring criteria of project artifacts and activities.
  - – Processes are organization, culture, and domain specific and dependent.
  - – The UML enables and promotes (but does not require nor mandate) a use-case-driven, architecture-centric, iterative, and incremental process that is object oriented and component based.

What Constitutes the Unified Modeling Language?

The UML Definition

The UML is defined by a set of documents (Figure 1-2) from Rational Software Corporation and the Object Management Group. The UML definition

- Is expressed by the following documents (the UML-defining artifacts):
  - – UML Semantics
  - – UML Notation Guide
  - – UML Extension for the Objectory Process for Software Engineering
  - – UML Extension for Business Modeling
- Uses the Object Constraint Language (OCL) defined by the Object Constraint Language specification document.
- May be obtained from Rational Software Corporation or the Object Management Group via the World Wide Web (see the references section)

The UML Semantics Document

The UML semantics document constitutes the single, common, definitive, formal, comprehensive, and precise specification of the UML (called the *inside view*). The UML semantics document

- Is primarily used by tool vendors; however, it may be used by practitioners since it is the definitive definition of the UML.
- Specifies the UML's layered architecture, organization (using packages), and defined modeling elements.

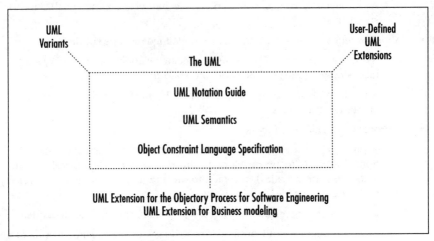

Figure 1-2: The UML Definition

- Includes the following inside-view information for a given UML package:
    - Overview: General introduction
    - Abstract syntax: Concept definitions, relationships, and constraints expressed using the UML's graphical notation and English prose
    - Well-formedness rules: Rules and constraints expressed using English prose and the OCL
    - Semantics: Meanings expressed using English prose
    - Standard elements: Applicable standard extension mechanisms
    - Notes: Other commentary
- Also contains appendices on the standard elements and the UML glossary.
- Enables the development of complex systems, consistent usage of the UML, and tool interchange

The UML Notation Guide

The UML Notation Guide constitutes the notational or visual representation of the UML and provides examples (called the *outside view*). The UML Notation Guide

- Is primarily used by practitioners applying the UML
- Specifies the UML's diagrams and their modeling elements
- Includes the following outside-view information for each modeling element:
    - Semantics: Summarizes the UML semantics.
    - Notation (concrete syntax): Explains the notational representation (forward mapping to notation).
    - Presentation options: Describe options in presenting modeling information.

- Style guidelines: Suggest stylistic markers and options.

- Examples: Provide notation samples.

- Mapping: Explains the mapping of the notation to the semantics document (reverse mapping from notation).

• Enables the use of the UML.

The UML Extension Documents

The UML extension documents provide user-defined extensions (using extension mechanisms). These documents

• Extend the UML to the objectory process for software engineering.

• Extend the UML to business modeling.

A *UML extension* is a set of extensions (stereotypes, tagged values, and constraints) that extend, customize, or tailor the UML for a specific domain or process.

A *UML variant* is a semantically well-defined language (expressed as a metamodel) based on (and built on top of) the UML metamodel. It specializes the UML but does not change the UML terms or redefine their meanings.

The Object Constraint Language

The Object Constraint Language (OCL) is a formal, easily readable and writable, nonprogramming, implementation-independent language. The OCL

• Is used for expressing typed, pure, side-effect-free (precise and unambiguous) constraints and expressions.

• Is used for attaching constraints and other expressions to the UML models and modeling elements (or objects).

• Is used to specify the well-formedness rules of the UML within the UML semantics document.

• Is formally specified in the Object Constraint Language specification document, which provides the following information: Connection with the UML semantics, basic values and types, objects and properties, collection operations, predefined OCL types, and the grammar for the OCL.

The Evolution of the Unified Modeling Language

Fragmentation

The historical period between the mid-1970s and the mid-1990s (Figure 1-3) was characterized by fragmentation.

• Software proved to have strategic, tactical, and operational value for organizations.

• Techniques for controlling and automating the production of software were sought in order to increase value by increasing quality, reducing costs, and

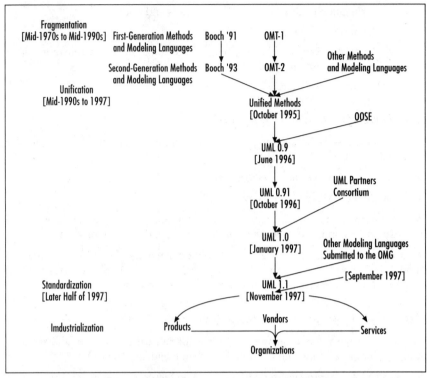

Figure 1-3: The Evolution of the Unified Modeling Language

reducing time-to-market while managing risks and being proactive concerning ever-increasing change and complexity.

- Various techniques and methods emerged to capture, communicate, and leverage technical and business artifacts and knowledge; within the software world, the modern reuse movement was born.

- Object-oriented modeling languages began to appear between the mid-1970s and the late 1980s.

- The number of modeling languages and methods increased from less than 10 to more than 50 between 1989 and 1994. These are known as *first-generation methods.*

- "Method wars" were perpetuated because practitioners had trouble finding satisfaction in using any one modeling language. There was no clearly leading modeling language, but many similar modeling languages with minor differences in overall expressive power. They all shared a set of commonly accepted concepts, but expressed them differently.

- Lack of agreement discouraged new users (due to the cost of use) and vendors (due to the cost of support) from entering the object-oriented tools and methodology market.

- Users longed for a broadly supported general-purpose modeling language.

- New iterations of first-generation methods began to appear that incorporated each other's techniques during the mid-1990s. These are known as *second-generation methods.*

- The following prominent methods emerged: Booch '93 (from Booch '91), OMT-2 (from OMT-1), and OOSE.

Unification

The historical period between the mid-1990s and 1997 (Figure 1-3) was characterized by unification.

- Jim Rumbaugh joined Grady Booch at Rational Software Corporation to unify their methods in October 1994.

- Grady Booch and Jim Rumbaugh released version 0.8 of the Unified Method (as the UML was then called) in October 1995.

- Ivar Jacobson and his Objectory Company joined Rational Software Corporation to merge his method in the fall of 1995. The three methodologists became known as the Three Amigos.

- The basis of the Three Amigos' unification effort concerning the UML included the following:

  - Since their independent methods were evolving toward one another, they could continue the evolution by unifying their semantics and notation.

  - By unifying their semantics and notation, they could bring stability to the object-oriented marketplace and promote the use of object orientation via a mature modeling language.

  - By collaborating, they could improve their earlier methods and build on lessons learned while addressing problems that their earlier methods insufficiently addressed.

- The goals of the Three Amigos' unification effort concerning the UML were, among others, to

  - Enable the modeling of systems, not just software systems, using the object-oriented paradigm and concepts.

  - Couple conceptual as well as executable artifacts.

  - Address scalability issues involving complex mission-critical systems.

  - Be usable by both humans and machines.

- The unification approach used by the Three Amigos involved trade-offs regarding the following issues:

  - Binding the problem. What is the scope of the language? Should it address requirements gathering? (Yes.) Should it address visual programming? (No.)

  - Balancing expressiveness and simplicity. Expressiveness involves a balance between minimalism and overengineering. Simplification involves removing existing elements that did not work in practice, adding more effective elements from other methods, and inventing new elements only when existing elements are not available. If the language is too simple, the number of problems it may address becomes limited. If the language is too complex, its usability becomes hindered.

- Being sensitive to the installed base of methods. Introducing too much new notation will only cause unnecessary confusion. Not introducing (and unifying) notation will miss the opportunity to engage a broader set of users.

- Identify and incorporate underlying fundamental semantic concepts, agreeing on the importance and consequences of these concepts, building a meta-model to precisely describe these concepts, building a notation connected to the abstract syntax of these concepts, and organizing these concepts across abstraction layers, levels of complexity, and domains.

- The Three Amigos released version 0.9 of the UML in June 1996, and version 0.91 in October 1996. They invited, received, and incorporated feedback from the general community during 1996.

- Organizations began to see the strategic strength of the UML during 1996.

- The Object Management Group's Object Analysis and Design Task Force issued a Request for Proposal (RFP) regarding establishing standards for tools that support object-oriented analysis and design; it was aimed at defining semantics and a metamodel standard for object-oriented technology.

- The OMG's request provided the catalyst for organizations to join forces and jointly respond.

- Rational Software Corporation formed the UML Partners Consortium.

- The UML Partners collaborated and released a well-defined, expressive, powerful, and generally applicable version 1.0 of the UML that was submitted to the OMG (as an initial RFP response) in January 1997. Other organizations also submitted separate RFP responses to the OMG.

- The result achieved by the Three Amigos' unification effort included the following:

  - It ends many of the (inconsequential) differences between modeling languages of previous methods.

  - It unifies many perspectives among different kinds of systems (business versus software), development phases (requirements, analysis, design, implementation, testing, and deployment), and internal concepts.

  - It introduces new concepts, including extensibility mechanisms (stereotypes, tagged values, and constraints), threads and processes, distribution and concurrency, patterns and collaborations, activity diagrams for business modeling, refinement for levels of abstraction, interfaces and components, and a constraint language.

  - It unifies the Booch, OMT, OOSE, and other object-oriented methods (at the modeling language level) with object-oriented and computer science practices from the object-oriented field and community of ideas. By removing unnecessary differences in notation and terminology that obscure underlying similarities, the UML is an evolutionary modeling language that is more expressive yet cleaner, more unified, and more holistically integrated than its predecessors.

Standardization

The historical period of standardization (Figure 1-3) began in the latter half of 1997 and had the following highlights:

- Others who submitted responses to the OMG joined the UML Partners to contribute their ideas and produce version 1.1 of the UML during 1997.

- The UML Partners collaborated and released a more clear and updated version 1.1 of the UML that was submitted to the OMG (as a revised RFP response) for consideration and adoption as a standard in September 1997.

- The following constitute the differences (and changes) between UML version 1.0 and UML version 1.1:

  - Increased formalism in defining the UML and eradicating ambiguities.

  - Improved structural packaging.

  - Increased unification of collaboration and interaction semantics and of relationship semantics.

  - Increased simplification of the class, type, and interface semantics model.

  - Incorporation of extensions (model management semantics, including models and subsystems and use case semantics).

  - Improved mapping of notation to semantics.

Industrialization

The historical period of industrialization (Figure 1-3) started during standardization and flourished once the OMG adopted the UML. Some of its highlights and characteristics are as follows:

- The UML was adopted by the OMG on November 17, 1997.

- The UML definition is readily available and evolving.

- Industry organizations and vendors embraced the UML.

- Products and services for the UML emerged and will continue to do so.

- Products (tools, books, etc.) will incorporate the usage of the UML.

- Services (training, mentoring, consulting, etc.) will promote and support the use of the UML.

The UML's success will be measured by its appropriate use on successful projects. The UML does not guarantee project success, but does enable practitioners to focus on delivering business value using a consistent, standardized, and tool-supported modeling language.

CHAPTER 2

The Big Picture

This chapter introduces the context for understanding and applying the UML. After reading this chapter, you will understand the following:

- An overall view of problems, solutions, and problem solving.
- Life-cycle concepts, including development cycles and phases and iteration cycles and phases.
- Problem and solution concepts, including domains or spaces, systems, architectures, models, architectural views, diagrams, and languages.
- Problem-solving concepts, including paradigms, artifacts, activities, and heuristics.

This chapter introduces some of the key concepts underlying the UML. I start by introducing the whole notion of problem solving, which involves how an effort is distributed over a life cycle in order to solve a problem. I then introduce the details of how we understand problems and solutions. I also introduce the details of how we understand problem-solving processes.

Problems, Solutions, and Problem Solving

Organizations produce and deliver products and services that address customer needs and requirements. Requirements may be characterized as *problems*. Products and services that address requirements are characterized as *solutions*. To deliver valued solutions (maximum quality and minimum cost within the minimum time), organizations must capture (acquire), communicate (share), and leverage (utilize) knowledge. The value of a solution is determined by the quality of the product or service, the cost of the product or service, and the time needed to produce the product or deliver the service. These producer-consumer relationships exist at all levels within the professional world: Organizations solve problems for their customers, employees solve problems for their employers, doctors solve problems for their patients, and so forth. Within these types of relationships, knowledge is the determining factor of success.

Organizations use technology to disseminate and communicate information so that their employees can solve business problems. Technology is only a tool; without people knowing how to apply it and actualize its potential, it is useless. Because the business world and technology world are in constant flux, we are required to manage increasing complexity within our ongoing efforts. However, we ought not to forget that technology is only a means to an end rather than the end in itself.

Projects are problem-solving efforts. They involve understanding or conceptualizing a problem, solving the problem, and implementing or realizing the solution. The people or organizational entities involved in a project are known as *stakeholders*. Some stakeholders are the ones for whom the problem is solved. They are responsible for contributing their knowledge to understand the problem and verify the solution. Other stakeholders are responsible for contributing their knowledge to implement the solution. The results of a project are know as *deliverables* or *work products*. They are the products or services that solve a problem. Projects, fundamentally, formalize the "work hard and hope for the best" approach to problem solving.

The UML is a language that facilitates the following:

- Specifying, visualizing, understanding, and documenting problems.
- Capturing, communicating, and leveraging knowledge in problem solving.
- Specifying, visualizing, constructing, and documenting solutions.

However, the UML does not prescribe any particular problem-solving approach. Rather, it is very flexible and customizable to fit any approach.

Programs are collections of problem-solving efforts (or projects). They are coordinated and related so that each project may benefit from the work of other projects in the program. One of the critical criteria necessary for achieving this objective is communication. If communication is possible across projects, it may be more likely that work and knowledge will be readily shared and work effort reduced. The role of the UML is to enable and facilitate such communication.

Consider an organization that is having trouble optimally allocating its employees to various projects. It desires an information system for maintaining employee and project information. The solution should provide the capability to allocate employees to projects based on their skills and where they may be best utilized. In addressing this problem, an overall approach must address how we will understand or conceptualize the problem, derive a solution to the problem, and implement or realize the solution. This approach will determine how we view the problem (paradigm) for the purpose of understanding it and how we view the resulting solution (paradigm) for the purpose of realizing it. We will apply our knowledge of the situation and other rules of thumb (heuristics) gained from other experiences to derive the solution (artifacts). Our effort will be organized (life cycle) as a series of (possibly concurrent) steps (activities) so that it may be managed to develop the resulting information system. We examine these constructs in the section "Problem Solving."

The problem occurs within a business context (domain or space). The solution must be realized to fit within the organization's information technology infrastructure (domain or space). The business problem (system) must be fully understood in terms of the requirements of the business, and the information system must be fully understood in terms of how it meets those requirements. The resulting information system must also be organized (architecture) to fit into the organization's technology infrastructures. As we conceptualize the problem and work toward realizing the solution, we will capture knowledge (models) about the business problem and information system, make decisions (architectural views) about how we will address different issues, and should be able to depict and communicate this information (diagrams). We examine these constructs in the section "Problems and Solutions."

Methods specify how to conduct problem-solving efforts. They specify an overall problem-solving approach and its components. They specify how problems and solutions are viewed in relation to a problem-solving approach; this is known as a method's *descriptive* aspect since it describes how knowledge is captured and communicated regarding a problem and solution. Methods also specify a problem-solving approach to be used to solve the problem and derive a solution; this is known as a method's *prescriptive* aspect since it prescribes how knowledge is leveraged to solve a problem. Methods specify descriptively how problems and solutions are viewed, and prescriptively how the problem-solving effort may be actualized.

Processes are realizations of methods. They use a method's problem-solving approach to solve a problem and realize a solution. Processes are specified by methods; this is known as a process's *static* aspect since it is a description of how a problem may be solved. Processes apply methods within projects to solve problems; this is known as a process's *dynamic* aspect.

Since projects can be very complex, methods should be used to provide an infrastructure for the problem-solving process. They should be considered as suggestions and recommendations that organize and facilitate the problem-solving process rather than being considered rigid and inflexible rules that restrict the art of problem solving. A *methodology* is a taxonomy, or well-organized collection, of related methods; therefore, a method may be part of a methodology.

To understand how the UML can be used to facilitate problem solving, a deeper understanding of what really constitutes problems, solutions, and problem solving is required. Such an understanding will enable you to analyze a problem and determine what parts of the UML may be best applied to facilitate deriving the solution to the problem.

Problems are often referred to as *as-is* situations since they represent the current conditions; solutions are similarly referred to as *to-be* situations since they represent the target conditions we are trying to reach. See Figure 2.1.

A situation that does not cause difficulty may still be treated as a problem in order to understand it; however, the solution is nothing more than an understanding of the situation. This results in determining the characteristics, rather than the requirements, of the situation and provides a purely descriptive view of the situation without any descriptive or prescriptive view of a solution. This is often done when a solution to a problem exists, and the existing solution needs to be understood or evaluated.

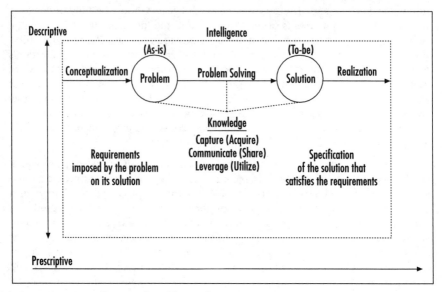

Figure 2-1: Overall View of Problem Solving

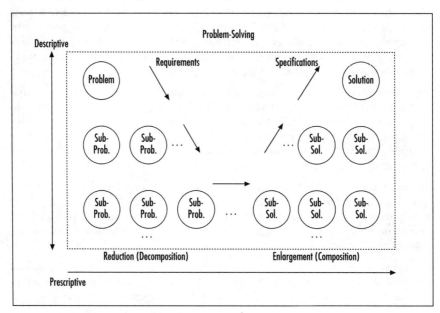

Figure 2-2: Detailed View of Problem Solving

Problem solving (Figure 2-2) involves efforts or processes that cooperatively solve problems. Such efforts include the following:

- Conceptualizing and representing the problem in some malleable and communicable form. This allows the problem to be represented in some language so that it may be manipulated and communicated to others.

- Determining the requirements imposed by the problem on its solution, that is, the requirements caused by the problem that its solution must satisfy.

- Attaining a description of the problem by addressing the following questions: What is the problem? What are the requirements of the problem that its solution must satisfy? Within a project, if these questions can be minimally answered with a sufficient level of detail, the effort has attained a descriptive view of the problem.

- Identifying or specifying the solution that satisfies the requirements imposed by the problem.

- Attaining a description of the solution by addressing the following questions: What is the solution? What are the specifications of the solution that satisfies the requirements imposed by the problem? Within a project, if these questions can be minimally answered with a sufficient level of detail, the effort has attained a descriptive view of the solution.

If a solution cannot be identified for a problem, the requirements imposed by the problem on its solution are grouped, classified, and organized into subordinate problems that are solved concurrently. A superordinate problem may be recursively reduced or decomposed into subordinate problems. Subordinate problems may be solved concurrently, and the solution to the original problem may be recursively enlarged or composed from subordinate solutions. The reduction process continues until all the subordinate problems are solved, and the enlargement process continues until the solution to the original problem is derived. Because this process is recursive, the descriptive view is used to discover the prescriptive view. Furthermore, decomposition allows a great deal of concurrent and parallel problem solving so that the whole process is expedited.

Problem solving continues as follows:

- Attaining a prescription of the steps within the solution that solves the problem by addressing the following question: How does the solution, in turn, have its requirements (or subordinate problems) satisfied? Within a project, if these questions can be minimally answered with a sufficient level of detail, the effort has attained a prescriptive view of the solution.

- Realizing the representation of the solution in some concrete and usable form.

Knowledge is the overriding component that must be captured (acquired), communicated (shared), and leveraged (utilized) to facilitate this process. The total knowledge involved in such an effort may be segmented into groups, where each group is associated with some part of the effort (conceptualization, problem, solution, problem solving, or realization) at any given point in time. This association signifies when the knowledge elements influence the effort; that is, when the knowledge elements were acquired, shared, or utilized within the problem-solving effort.

Intelligence is the ability to conduct the problem-solving process by organizing knowledge in a taxonomy and strategically applying knowledge via a problem-solving effort in order to derive a solution.

Life Cycle

Problem-solving approaches are organized (life cycles) to offer a management perspective and a development perspective. The two perspectives enable the effort to be managed and performed. The life cycle will be discussed again in Chapter 5 as it relates to the UML.

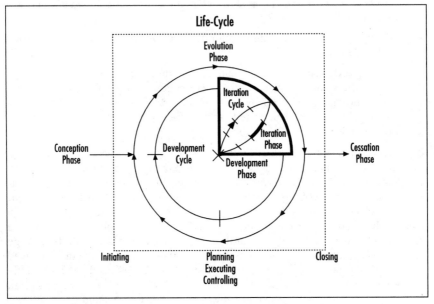

Figure 2-3: Life Cycle

Life cycles (Figure 2-3) can be broken down as follows.

- A *life cycle* is a collection of phases that divide an effort into several more manageable and controllable subordinate efforts.

- Each phase within a life cycle is a discrete part of a single flow of logic to solve a problem. Each phase

    - Has inputs, or items that will be acted on. This addresses what is manipulated in the phase.

    - Has entry criteria for entering or initiating the phase.

    - Requires the application of principles, techniques, and tools to the inputs to generate the outputs. This addresses how something is manipulated and who is responsible for doing the manipulation.

    - Has outputs, or items that result from the phase's effort.

    - Has exit criteria for exiting or closing the phase. This results in a review of the resulting work products and, often, a decision whether to continue or abandon the overall effort.

- The conception phase involves recognizing a problem or opportunity and committing to solving the problem.

- The evolution phase includes multiple evolutionary cycles of initiating, planning, executing, controlling, and closing an effort.

  - Initiating involves recognizing that an evolution cycle is required in addressing a new or existing problem.

  - Planning involves designing and maintaining a scheme to accomplish the solving of the problem.

  - Executing involves coordinating resources for carrying out the plan and solving the problem.

  - Controlling includes monitoring and measuring progress so that corrective measures may be taken when necessary.

  - Closing involves formalizing acceptance of the current cycle and the solution to the problem for which the cycle was initiated.

The evolution phase consists of one or more development cycles (evolution cycles), where each development cycle includes a single effort distributed among the constituents of the development cycle. It encompasses the evolution of a product as it grows and matures throughout its existence.

- A development cycle

  - Consists of development phases.

  - Distributes effort among its development phases.

  - Encompasses one evolutionary generation of a product in its life-cycle evolution.

  - Occurs the first time in response to a problem and produces a solution or product.

  - Occurs multiple times thereafter to help an existing solution or product evolve.

  - Is triggered by the occurrence of a problem and the need for a solution or by changes in a problem and the need for evolution in an existing solution. These changes may include changes in stakeholder requirements, underlying technology, and organizational competitiveness.

  - May slightly overlap with its predecessor or successor development cycles. The start of the current development cycle may slightly overlap with the end of the previous development cycle, and the end of the current development cycle may slightly overlap with the start of the next development cycle.

  - Produces a product generation.

- A development phase

  - Consists of iteration cycles.

  - Distributes effort among its iteration cycles.

  - Encompasses one evolutionary phase of a product in its development-cycle evolution.

- Is triggered by the start of a new development cycle or the completion or near completion of the previous development phase within a development cycle.

- May slightly overlap with its predecessor or successor development phases. The start of the current development phase may slightly overlap with the end of the previous development phase, and the end of the current development phase may slightly overlap with the start of the next development phase.

- Synchronizes the development-oriented elements and management-oriented elements via milestones, that is, points in a development cycle where critical decisions must be made and key goals achieved.

- An iteration cycle
  - Consists of iteration phases.
  - Distributes effort among its iteration phases.
  - Encompasses one evolutionary iteration of a product in its development-phase evolution.
  - Is triggered by the start of a new development phase or the completion or near completion of the previous iteration cycle within a development phase.
  - May slightly overlap with its predecessor or successor iteration cycles. The start of the current iteration cycle may slightly overlap with the end of the previous iteration cycle, and the end of the current iteration cycle may slightly overlap with the start of the next iteration cycle.
  - Produces a product release. This is a subset of a complete product generation.

- An iteration phase
  - Consists of activities or tasks.
  - Distributes effort among its activities or tasks.
  - Encompasses one evolutionary increment of a product in its iteration-cycle evolution.
  - Is triggered by the start of a new iteration cycle or the completion or near completion of the previous iteration phase within an iteration cycle.
  - May slightly overlap with its predecessor or successor iteration phases. The start of the current iteration phase may slightly overlap with the end of the previous iteration phase, and the end of the current iteration phase may slightly overlap with the start of the next iteration phase.

- The *cessation phase* involves recognizing that a solution is no longer required and terminating the application of the solution in an orderly manner.

- A great deal of concurrency and parallelism occurs within a life cycle; thus the overall process is expedited as an effort or project is distributed over a development cycle.

Development Cycles and Phases

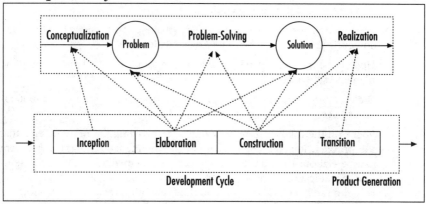

Figure 2-4: Focus of Development Phases within a Development Cycle

Development cycles and phases (Figure 2-4) have the following characteristics:

- Each development cycle consists of four phases (inception, elaboration, construction, and transition) and results in a product generation. This view of the life cycle is often called the *management perspective* since it provides high-level indicators of a project's progress.

- The inception (initiating) development phase usually uses one iteration cycle and involves the following activities:

  - Specify and delimit scope, objectives, and requirements.

  - Establish a business case or rationale, including specifying the vision, specifying success criteria, assessing risks, estimating time and cost, and specifying a plan.

  - Focus on understanding or forming a notion of the problem and the rationale for solving it (scoping and business case).

- The elaboration (planning) development phase usually uses one iteration cycle and involves the following activities:

  - Elaborate the specification of the effort from the previous phase.

  - Baseline and completely delimit scope, objectives, and requirements.

  - Baseline the business case by solidifying the vision, solidifying success criteria, and mitigating the highest risks. Baseline the plan with a schedule.

  - Distribute the requirements among multiple iteration cycles within the construction phase.

  - Focus on understanding or forming a notion of the problem to determine the requirements that the problem imposes on its solution (requirements capture and requirements analysis), establishing and verifying the foundation for the overall solution (architectural design), and distributing the requirements among the iteration cycles of the construction development phase (planning).

- The construction (executing) development phase usually uses more than one iteration cycle and involves the following activities:

  - Update the business case by managing ongoing risks and maintaining the plan and schedule.

  - Build and develop the effort's products by performing the multiple iteration cycles.

  - Focus on the following: understanding or evolving the requirements that the problem imposes on its solution (requirements) so that the problem can be elaborated and the solution can be specified, elaborating the solution specification (analysis), updating the foundation for the overall solution (architectural design) and the foundation required to support the specific solution (detailed design) for the iteration cycle requirements, generating the solution (implementation) for the iteration cycle requirements, verifying the solution (validation and integration) for the iteration cycle requirements, and providing or integrating (or delivering) the solution (deployment) or a subset thereof.

- The transition (closing) development phase usually uses one iteration cycle and involves the following activities:

  - Deploy the effort's ultimate product or solution to the problem.

  - Assess and classify the effort's interim products.

  - Focus on providing and integrating or delivering the solution (deployment).

Iteration Cycles and Phases

Iteration cycles and phases (Figure 2-5) have the following characteristics:

- Each iteration cycle consists of two support components (management and support) and six development components (requirements, analysis, design, implementation, validation, and deployment). It results in a product release. This view of the life cycle is often called the *development perspective* since it provides low-level indicators of a project's progress.

- The management (controlling) phase involves managing the overall iteration cycle.

- The support (controlling) phase involves supporting the needs and requirements of the stakeholders participating in the iteration cycle; this includes development environment support and configuration, standards definition, and guidelines.

- Within the elaboration (planning) development phase, the following iteration phases apply:

  - The requirements (requirements capture) and analysis (requirements analysis) phases involve understanding or forming a notion of the problem to determine the requirements of the solution and distributing the require-

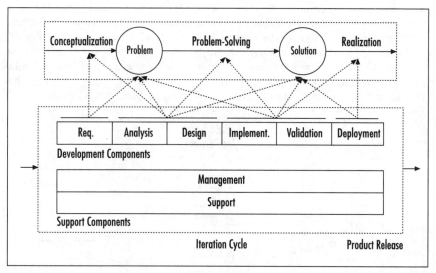

Figure 2-5: Focus of Iteration Phases within an Iteration Cycle

ments among iteration cycles of the construction development phase (planning).

– The design (architectural design) phase involves establishing and verifying the foundation for the overall solution.

• Within the construction (executing) development phase, the following iteration phases apply:

– The requirements phase involves understanding or elaborating the requirements the problem imposes on its solution so that the problem can be elaborated and the solution can be specified.

– The analysis phase involves elaborating the solution specification. This phase hinges on the application of knowledge.

– The design phase involves updating the foundation for the overall solution (architectural design) and the foundation required to support the specific solution (detailed design) for the iteration cycle requirements. This phase hinges on the application of knowledge.

– The implementation phase involves generating the solution for the iteration cycle requirements.

– The validation (and integration) phase involves verifying the solution for the iteration cycle requirements.

– The deployment phase involves providing and integrating or delivering the solution or a subset thereof.

Problems and Solutions

Problems and solutions (Figure 2-6) occur within a context (domain or space). The problem (system) must be understood in order to be solved. The solution (system) to a problem must be understood in order to be constructed and used. The solution must be organized (architecture) in order to facilitate its realization and adhere to the various constraints of the context in which it will be realized. To solve the problem, appropriate knowledge about the problem and solution must be captured (models), organized around decisions regarding the problem and solution (architectural views), and depicted (diagrams) using some language that enables it to be communicated and leveraged in the problem-solving process.

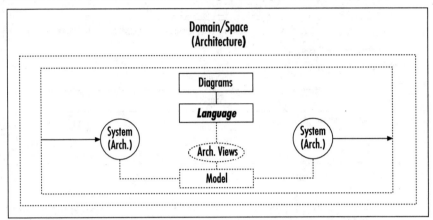

Figure 2-6: Problems and Solutions

Domains or Spaces

Domains or spaces (Figure 2-7) are organized collections of related components in a self-contained situation or area of interest. These components are called *domain* or *space elements*. They

- Are also known as contexts.

- Have a set of terms forming a vocabulary that facilitates communication regarding the components within the domain.

- Have a set of concepts forming ideas or notions associated with components within the domain and giving meaning to the communications regarding the components of the domain.

- Have a definitive and delimiting boundary defining the context of scope for the domain. This identifies an inner realm where every component inside the boundary is within the context and every component outside the boundary is in an outer realm or some other context.

- Have no purpose. That is, the components that constitute a domain are not organized to accomplish a set of objectives, but are incidentally organized together for some other reasons or basis. Often, the components of a domain are organized together simply because they relate to the same subject of the domain.

- May represent real or abstract situations.

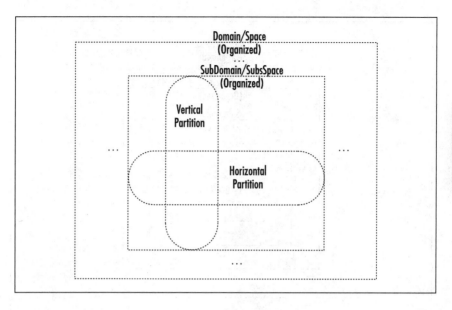

Figure 2-7: Domains or Spaces

- May be recursively decomposed into multiple domains called *subordinate domains*. These subordinate domains may be considered topics of interest within the domain's subject.

- May be decomposed, segmented, and viewed vertically or in vertical partitions of components as multiple areas of interest and concerns.

- May be decomposed, segmented, and viewed horizontally or in horizontal partitions of components as crossing multiple areas of interest and concerns. These partitions reveal progressively more detailed information with depth.

- May be the subject of multiple bodies of knowledge, where each body of knowledge may have different content yet is derived by focusing on the same domain.

- Represent contexts or frameworks in which problems and solutions exist and are addressed.

The UML is domain independent. It may be utilized within domains to facilitate problem solving, and across domains to facilitate the reuse of knowledge. In developing information systems, domains are the contexts in which problems exist and solutions are realized.

Systems

Systems (Figure 2-8) are organized collections of interacting and connected components cooperating to accomplish a purpose. These components are called *system elements*. Systems

- Are contexts that have a purpose, goal, or responsibility. Systems may be treated as contexts if their purposefulness is not utilized or is simply ignored, and contexts may be treated as systems by introducing a purpose. Contexts

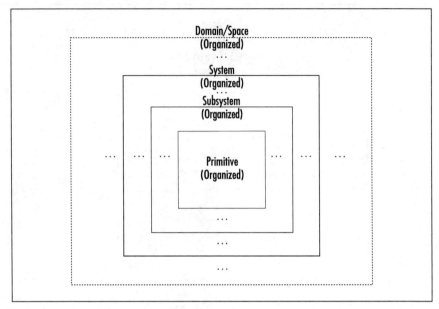

Figure 2-8: Systems

and systems are the same, differing only when treated or manipulated on the basis of their purpose or on the basis of having a purpose.

- Must have a purpose or set of purposes. That is, they are organized to accomplish a set of objectives, and are essentially organized by virtue of their objectives or goals.

- May represent real or abstract purposeful entities.

- May be recursively decomposed into multiple systems called *subordinate systems* (or *subsystems*).

- When fully decomposed, consist of primitive system elements that are not further decomposable.

- May be the subject of multiple bodies of knowledge, where each body of knowledge may have different content yet is derived by focusing on the same system.

- Represent problems and solutions that exist and are addressed within a context.

The UML is system independent. It may be utilized to address different types of systems, including hardware systems, software systems, and human interaction systems. In developing information systems, systems are the realized solutions to problems.

Architectures

Architectures (Figure 2-9) are schemes involving the structural and behavioral organization of systems within contexts. Architectures

- Have an inward focus on systems.

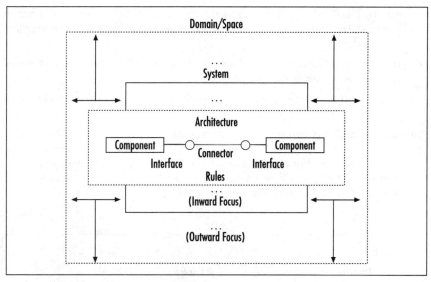

Figure 2-9: Architectures

- Have an outward focus on contexts.

- Include components and their interfaces. These are systems and subordinate systems. The components are called *architectural elements.*

- Include connectors that integrate and connect other components via their interfaces. These connectors are also called *architectural elements.*

- Include rules and constraints governing the assembly of components and connectors.

- Include rules and constraints governing the interactions among components and connectors.

- Involve the arrangement of components connected via connectors in order to satisfy some purpose.

- May be recursively decomposed into multiple architectures called subordinate architectures. Each component and connector may be recursively decomposed into successively smaller components and connectors.

- May be decomposed, segmented, and viewed in vertical partitions of components as subordinate architectures of interest.

- May be decomposed, segmented, and viewed in layered horizontal partitions of components that cross subordinate architectures of interest.

- When fully decomposed, consist of primitive components and primitive connectors that are not further decomposable. The primitive components and primitive connectors correspond to primitive system elements.

- May be classified as forms or ready-made patterns that solve recurring architectural problems. These patterns capture significant knowledge that may be reused.

- May be classified as architectural styles that reference a collection of forms or patterns. These styles are used to impose a degree of uniformity on architecture selection.

- Involve the organization of problems and solutions. They are very well suited for managing overwhelming complexity.

- Represent the internal organization of problems, solutions, and the contexts in which they exist and are addressed.

The UML is architecture-centric. It supports the organization of systems within domains. Organizational mechanisms address and attempt to minimize the complexity that arises from changes to systems. In developing information systems, a well-organized system allows changes to the system to be less time consuming and less costly than an unorganized system does.

Models

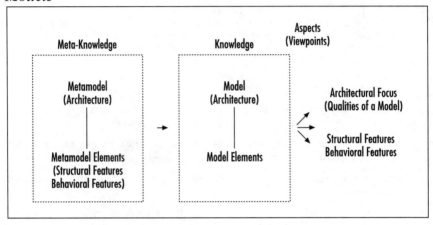

Figure 2-10: Models

Models (Figure 2-10) are complete abstractions of systems or contexts. Models

- Are complete or semantically closed; that is, comprehending and interpreting the contents of a model does not require the introduction of other information from outside the model.

- Are abstract or "fictitious" constructs that represent systems or contexts as the given subject of a model.

- Utilize abstraction to focus on the relevant details of a system while ignoring insignificant details. This defines a boundary of a system relative to the perspective of a viewer.

- Are blueprints of systems used for system construction and renovation.

- Are used to understand and manage complexity within systems.

- Are used for communication and assurance of architectural soundness.

- May be recursively decomposed into multiple models called *subordinate models*.

- When fully decomposed, consist of model elements that are primitive and not further decomposable.

- Have elements as atomic constituents. Model elements are complete abstractions of system elements or context elements. They

  - Are defined by modeling elements. Metamodels are models that define the modeling elements (metamodel elements) that may be used within derived models. Models are instances, occurrences, or configurations of metamodels that contain model elements. Model elements are instances, occurrences, or configurations of modeling elements (metamodel elements).

  - Capture features or characteristics of system elements.

  - Capture the structural features of system elements, that is, the static or structural features of system elements.

  - Capture the behavioral features of system elements, that is, the dynamic or behavioral features of system elements and interactions or collaborations among system elements.

  - May be relationships that relate other elements within models.

- May be viewed via a small set of holistic but nearly independent and non-overlapping aspects. Aspects are dimensions of modeling that emphasize particular qualities of a model. The following aspects exist for any model:

  - The structural model aspect emphasizes the static, or structural, features of the model elements within a model.

  - The behavioral model aspect emphasizes the dynamic, or behavioral, features of the model elements and interactions or collaborations among model elements within a model.

- May be expressed at different levels of fidelity or accuracy.

- May be reference models that describe all possible configurations of their model elements. Architectures are subsets of reference models. Implementations are products that result from implementing specified architectures.

- Have an architecture when treated as systems whose purpose is to capture a complete abstraction of other systems.

- Capture knowledge regarding a system or context.

- Represent knowledge of problems, solutions, and the contexts in which they exist and are addressed.

The UML enables capturing and leveraging knowledge to facilitate problem solving. Knowledge cannot explicitly be viewed; however, it can be demonstrated. A demonstration of knowledge occurs in the application of knowledge to derive a solution to a problem. This is known as intelligence.

Architectural Views

Architectural views (Figure 2-11) are abstractions of models. Architectural views

- Are perspectives through which models may be represented or projected as diagrams.

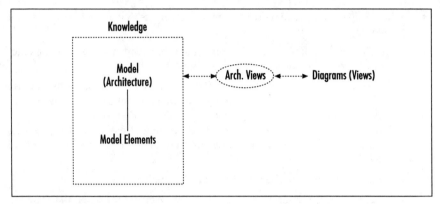

Figure 2-11: Architectural Views

- Organize perspectives or views of models around specific sets of concerns particular to different stakeholders involved in the problem-solving effort. A set of concerns establishes an architectural focus.

- Enable the extraction of architecturally significant elements of a model via different viewpoints or perspectives. Architecturally insignificant elements of a given perspective are omitted for that perspective. A set of aspects of a model that addresses an architectural focus establishes a viewpoint.

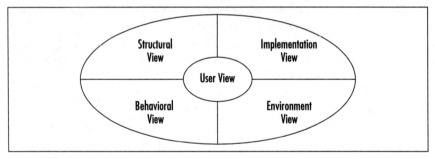

Figure 2-12: Model Views

- Include the following model views (Figure 2-12) regarding models of problems and solutions:

  - The *user model view* encompasses a problem and solution from the perspective of those individuals whose problem the solution addresses. This view presents the goals and objectives of the problem owners and their requirements of the solution.

  - The *structural model view* encompasses the static, or structural, aspects of a problem and solution.

  - The *behavioral model view* encompasses the dynamic, or behavioral, aspects of a problem and solution and interactions or collaborations among problem and solution elements.

- The *implementation model view* encompasses the structural and behavioral aspects of the solution's realization.

- The *environment model view* encompasses the structural and behavioral aspects of the domain in which a solution must be realized.

- May be extended to include other views of models (such as interface, security, and data).

- Are quite often referred to as models because they ultimately map back to a subset of a whole model.

- Map models to types of diagrams.

- Organize knowledge within a model around decisions concerning the knowledge and subject. These decisions further constrain the knowledge and future decisions.

The UML supports the user model view, structural model view, behavioral model view, implementation model view, and environment model view to facilitate the organization of knowledge within problem solving.

Diagrams

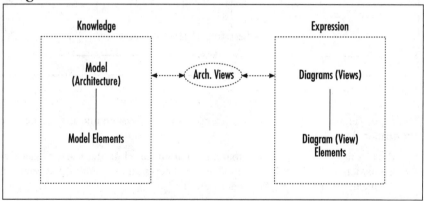

Figure 2-13: Diagrams

Diagrams (Figure 2-13) are graphical projections of sets of model elements. Diagrams

- Are connected graphs of arcs (or paths) and vertices (or nodes).

- Render architectural views or subsets of architectural views of a model pictorially or graphically.

- Are collections of graphical constructs with visual relationships.

- Are concrete and real constructs describing models.

- Are blueprints of models described via architectural views.

- Have view elements that are textual or graphical projections of collections of model elements.

- Are used to communicate model content or knowledge.

- Depict knowledge within a model in a communicable form.
- Are also called models because they render models or are the visual representation of models.

The UML enables communication of knowledge to facilitate problem solving by supporting a multitude of diagrams organized around architectural views.

Languages

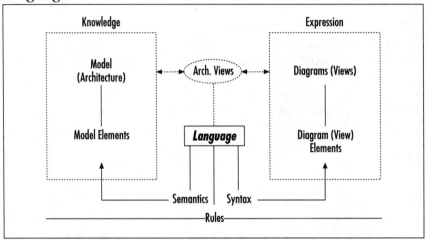

Figure 2-14: Languages

Languages (Figure 2-14) are means for expressing and communicating content or information. Languages

- Have concepts and semantics that are communicated. In the UML, model elements define the fundamental modeling concepts and semantics that establish the meaning or content of communication.
- Have a notation or syntax used to render semantics for communication. Syntactic elements represent semantic elements. In the UML, the notation or visual rendering of model elements provides the syntax and establishes the expression of the semantics for communication.
- Have rules or guidelines expressing idioms of usage and how syntactical constructs are combined in forming the content of communication. The UML captures various guidelines or idioms of usage and best practices.
- Map one or more model elements to one or more diagram elements.
- Such as the UML govern how knowledge within a model is depicted so that it can be communicated.

Problem Solving

Problem solving (Figure 2-15) requires being able to view the problem (paradigm) for the purpose of understanding it, and being able to view the resulting solution (paradigm) for the purpose of realizing it. The problem-solving process involves leveraging knowledge to derive the solution (artifacts) to the problem through a series of (possibly concurrent) steps (activities) in which knowledge is applied and various tools are utilized. Furthermore, knowledge and rules of thumb (heuristics) gained from other problem-solving efforts may be used.

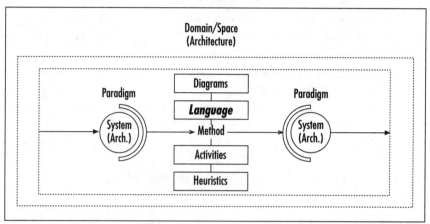

Figure 2-15: Problem Solving

Paradigms

Paradigms are organized, self-contained collections of related components that form the bases for models. These components are called *paradigm elements*. Paradigms

- Define a set of terms forming a vocabulary.

- Define a set of concepts forming ideas or notions associated with subjects.

- Establish the foundation for metamodels by defining the modeling elements that may be used in modeling. They define the terms and concepts that may be used within models.

- Form the foundation for languages and methods. The UML is founded on the object-oriented paradigm and may be used by different methods.

- Establish concepts and associated terms that are fundamental, essential, and universally accepted truths or maxims (principles) within the paradigm. These concepts form the foundation upon which other concepts are built and through which systems are modeled, viewed (perceived, understood, and interpreted), and manipulated.

- Represent how a method approaches, views, and models problems, solutions, and the contexts in which they exist and are addressed.

The UML is founded on the object-oriented paradigm. This enables the UML to be flexible for use by a multitude of methods across various domains concerning various types of systems. The object-oriented paradigm also offers other benefits for managing change and complexity.

Artifacts

Artifacts are work products or deliverables resulting from efforts. Artifacts

- Are specified or described by methods.
- Are realized or constructed within processes.
- Must have an order in which they are created.
- Must have stakeholders responsible for producing them and others responsible for accepting (or rejecting) them.
- Are expressed in languages such as the UML. This expression enables the realization of the solution to a problem.
- Become assets if they may be reapplied or reused in the same context but with different systems or across different contexts and systems.
- Represent the interim and ultimate products (solution) as specified by a method and realized by a process.

The UML diagrams are artifacts that facilitate problem solving. They organize and depict required information for realizing a solution to a problem.

Activities

Activities are efforts or collections of tasks directed at producing or developing artifacts. Activities

- Are specified and partially or tentatively ordered by methods.
- Are realized within processes.
- Must have associated stakeholders who conduct or perform the tasks.
- Must have associated artifacts that they develop (create, modify, etc.).
- Must address both technical and managerial (human) issues related to an effort.
- Must be treated as sets of recommendations and must be customized to the context in which they are applied.
- Establish or recommend tasks and techniques in order to accomplish objectives. *Tasks* specify thinking, performing, and reviewing actions to meet the goals of an activity. *Techniques* provide the means for performing tasks. They are based on principles and may be supported by tools.
- Represent subordinate efforts within projects and are specified by a method and realized by a process.

Because the UML does not prescribe a method or process, it does not specify particular activities.

Heuristics

Heuristics are empirical or experience-based guidelines or rules of thumb. Heuristics

- Facilitate the application of methods as processes.

- Include best practices and lessons learned from experience.

- Represent the knowledge gained from other experiences as well as knowledge gained from previous applications of methods.

The UML encompasses the industry's best engineering practices for problem solving. These practices are realized in the overall organization of the UML and the various diagrams it provides.

CHAPTER 3

Object Orientation

This chapter presents the object-oriented paradigm that forms the basis for the UML. After reading this chapter, you will understand the following:

- Real-world concepts; this is where problems are conceptualized.

- Implementation-world concepts; this is where solutions are realized.

- The function-driven, data-driven, and object-oriented paradigms and how they relate to one another.

- Fundamental object-oriented paradigm concepts.

This chapter introduces some of the key concepts and constructs of object orientation. Some of these concepts may be new to you if you have only become familiar with object orientation through an implementation language such as C++ or Java. I start by introducing the object-oriented view of the real world, and the fundamental concepts of objects and classes. I then introduce links and associations, which represent relationships among objects. I also introduce scenarios and interactions, which determine how objects interact and make use of one another.

Worlds

The world we all live in is impenetrably complex; to solve our problems we must reduce the important parts of each problem to elements we can manipulate. Our representational constructs are mental notions or ideas that represent something within a particular world or domain. Fundamentally, anything we are able to think about is a representational construct. Our way of simplifying the world so we can create and manipulate representational constructs is called a paradigm; in this chapter we examine the object-oriented paradigm and two others.

Solving a problem involves manipulating representational constructs from the problem domain and the solution domain to derive a representation of the desired solution. Realizing a solution involves mapping those representational constructs of the solution onto the solution world, that is, constructing the solution. The use of representational constructs is a very natural process that often occurs subtly and sometimes unconsciously in problem solving.

A paradigm determines the possible types of representations utilized in problem-solving efforts. The actual representations are determined by the problem being solved and the solution being derived. A language allows us to express these representations. Once expressed, they can be communicated to others so that we can solve problems within teams. A paradigm ought to consist of all constructs required to address a diverse multitude of problems and to derive a solution that may be realized using a diverse multitude of mechanisms.

Consider the example in Chapter 2, in which an organization desires an information system to better utilize employees on projects. In solving the problem, representational constructs from the problem domain must be identified and elaborated; this includes representing employees, projects, and organizational groups (departments, teams). Representational constructs from the solution domain must also be identified so that they can be utilized to realize the resulting information system; this includes representing mechanisms for storing information (databases) and mechanisms for processing information (programs). Considering this problem, we must be able to represent "things," including the following:

- People (resources) or employees
- Projects
- Organizational groups (departments, teams)

We must be able to represent what composes these things, including the following:

- A person's name, social security number, employee number, etc.
- A project's tasks or activities, resources requirements and assignments, deadlines, etc.

We examine the concept of a thing and its composition in the section "Objects and Classes."

We must be able to represent relationships among things, including the following:

- People assigned to projects
- People belonging to organizational groups
- Projects managed by people (managers) within organizational groups

We examine relationships in the section "Links and Associations."

We must be able to represent interactions among things, including the following:

- People moving among projects
- People moving among organizational groups

We examine interactions in the section "Scenarios and Interactions."

Considering a solution to this problem, we must be able to represent a system and its components or elements as "things." We must be able to represent what constitutes these components, and how they are related to one another. We must be able to represent how these components cooperatively function or interact to provide the desired functionality. These may be some of the many aspects that must be captured and manipulated to solve the problem. Furthermore, the information system must be tailored to address the needs of the organization.

To understand how the UML can be used to support problem solving, an understanding of the representational constructs provided by the UML is required. Such an understanding will enable you to deliberate on a problem and utilize the representational constructs provided by the UML to facilitate deriving the solution to the problem.

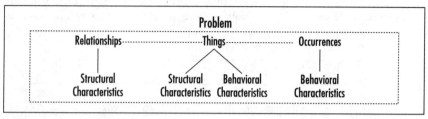

Figure 3-1: Real World

The real world (Figure 3-1) is the domain encompassing problems, solutions, and problem-solving efforts. The real world

- Is where problems must be conceptualized as input.

- Is where problem solving occurs.

- Is where solutions must be realized as output.

- Consists of things or entities that have a purpose or role within a problem or solution. Things can be classified as follows:

    - Concrete (real) entities have real existence in the world. They can be identified as existing independent of their perceiver.

    - Conceptual (abstract) entities do not have real existence in the world. They represent concrete entities, or can be attributed to concrete or other conceptual entities. They do not exist independent of their perceiver and are introduced into a situation to facilitate understanding.

Things, whether concrete or conceptual, have the following types of characteristics or features:

    - Structural characteristics determine what a thing "knows" in order to sustain its purpose. These characteristics determine the possible states of an entity, that is, the conditions that an entity may attain at any time during its existence. Within a problem, these characteristics include datalike elements and express datalike requirements of a problem or a solution.

    - Behavioral characteristics determine the activities a thing "does" in order to achieve or sustain its purpose. These characteristics determine the possible behaviors of an entity, that is, the actions and reactions that an entity may perform at any time during its existence. Within a problem, these characteristics include algorithmlike elements and express processlike requirements of a problem or a solution.

- Consists of relationships among entities. *Relationships* are conceptual or concrete constructs that connect or associate two or more other entities. They may be treated as structural characteristics shared among multiple entities that have a relationship with one another.

- Consists of occurrences or dynamic characteristics within entities and among related and unrelated entities. *Occurrences* are conceptual or concrete constructs that involve something that happens within an entity or among two or more other entities. These events or incidents transpire as a result of entities sustaining their responsibilities. Dynamic characteristics determine how groups of entities interact and communicate based on their roles within domains. Occurrences may be treated as behavioral characteristics shared among multiple entities that participate or interact with one another.

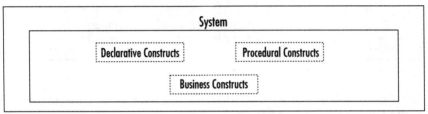

Figure 3-2: Solution Worlds

Solution worlds (Figure 3-2) are systems that solve problems and involve realization or implementation constructs. These are mechanisms that are used to implement solutions to problems. They include declarative constructs, procedural constructs, and business constructs.

Declarative Constructs

Declarative constructs represent the problem a system is to solve, and the solution once the problem is solved. These constructs

- Are data oriented; that is, they focus on datalike elements (information) within problems and solutions.
- Capture information regarding problems and solutions.
- Are often realized as data sections within programs or processes, tables within database management systems or file systems, and data stores within information systems.

The realization of declarative constructs involves the following:

- Data constructs that represent information.
- Variables that represent values that may be manipulated.
- Data types that determine the possible values and operations applicable for a variable.
- Primitive data types, which are existing or predefined data types.
- Complex data types, which are new or user-defined data types.
- Scope that determines the accessibility of a variable.

These constructs constitute half of the technology aspect of a solution.

Procedural Constructs

Procedural constructs manipulate and transform the problem into the solution. These constructs

- Are process oriented; that is, they focus on algorithmlike elements that manipulate problems and derive solutions.

- Capture processes for transforming or deriving a solution from a problem.

- Are often realized as code sections within programs or processes, stored procedures within database management systems or file systems, and processes within information systems.

The realization of procedural constructs involves the following:

- Code constructs that represent actions and activities.

- Subprograms that represent manipulators that manipulate data constructs. Subprograms consist of statements or expressions using sequential, conditional, and repetitive logic to express how data constructs are manipulated. They are also known as functions and procedures.

- Parameters, which are variables used to pass information to a subprogram or used to receive information from a subprogram. A subprogram declares formal parameters in which it receives and may return data. The expressions invoking the subprogram supply actual parameters and values to pass to the subprogram and variables to receive information passed back from the subprogram.

- Input parameters, which are used to pass information to a subprogram.

- Output parameters, which are used to receive information from a subprogram. They may send and receive information in variables.

- Return parameters, which are used only to receive information from a subprogram. They may only receive information in variables; that is, they don't send any information to a subprogram.

- Preconditions, which are conditions that must be true when a subprogram is invoked.

- Postconditions, which are conditions that must be true when a subprogram is finished executing.

- Scope that determines the accessibility of a subprogram by other subprograms. Global scope means it is accessible from anywhere within a system. Local scope means it is accessible from within another subprogram.

- Implemented systems, which are a collection of subprograms that invoke one another to accomplish some purpose for the end user.

These constructs constitute the other half of the technology aspect of a solution.

Business Constructs

Business constructs exist within a business context in which the solution is realized. These constructs include the following:

- Workers, who are people or teams, within organizations, that have responsibility for doing some set of activities.

- Work units, which are work products that are manipulated by workers participating in activities.
- Workflows, which are sequences of activities or relevant pieces of work, within an organization, that involve workers and work units. Workflows are the means through which value is derived for other workers or customers and clients.

These constructs constitute the human and organizational aspect of a solution.

Paradigms

The following paradigms are common:

- The *function-driven paradigm* focuses on behavioral and dynamic characteristics of a problem to derive the solution.
- The *data-driven paradigm* focuses on structural characteristics of a problem to derive the solution.
- The *object-oriented paradigm* focuses on problem concepts as a whole to derive the solution.

Function-Driven Paradigm

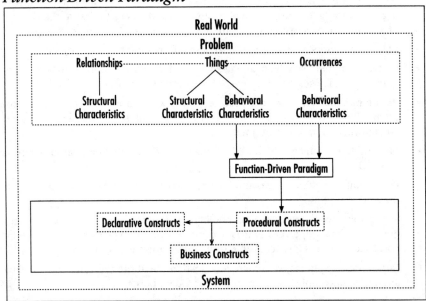

Figure 3-3: Function-Driven Paradigm

The function-driven paradigm (Figure 3-3) drives problem-solving efforts by emphasizing processlike elements of problems. Such approaches to problem solving are classified as function-centric. This paradigm

- Facilitates the following problem-solving approach to realize solutions (systems):

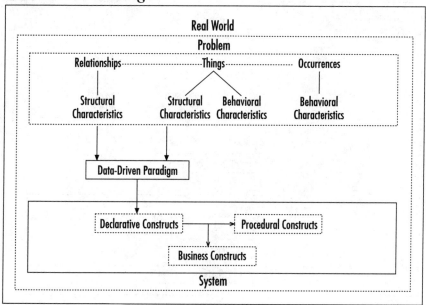
- Identify processes within the problem. Process-oriented elements of problems are regarded as primary in facilitating and driving problem-solving efforts.

- Identify data manipulated by processes. Data-oriented elements of problems are regarded as secondary in facilitating problem-solving efforts.

- Decompose or partition and elaborate processes to further understand the problem and solution. Elaboration consists of specifying the inputs and outputs of processes and reducing processes into subordinate processes.

- Derive a solution from this decomposition by satisfying process-oriented requirements of the problem with procedural constructs and then supporting declarative constructs.

- Utilize an architecture based on process decomposition rather than data decomposition.

• Is more suitable for domains in which problems are more process intensive. This includes most real-time systems where there are more process elements than data elements involved in a system.

Data-Driven Paradigm

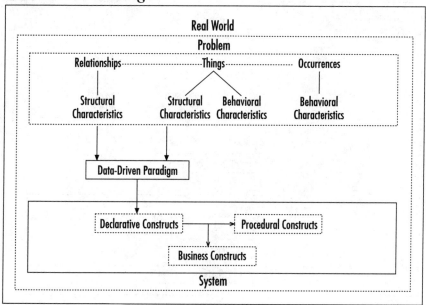

Figure 3-4: Data-Driven Paradigm

The data-driven paradigm (Figure 3-4) drives problem-solving efforts by emphasizing datalike elements of problems. Such approaches to problem solving are classified as data-centric. This paradigm

• Facilitates the following problem-solving approach to realize solutions (systems):

- Identify data within the problem. Data-oriented elements of problems are regarded as primary in facilitating and driving problem-solving efforts.

- Identify processes that manipulate data. Process-oriented elements of problems are regarded as secondary in facilitating problem-solving efforts.

- Decompose or partition and elaborate data to further understand the problem and solution. Elaboration consists of specifying relationships among data elements and reducing data elements into subordinate data elements.

- Derive a solution from this decomposition by satisfying data-oriented requirements of the problem with declarative constructs and then supporting procedural constructs.

- Utilize an architecture based on data decomposition rather than process decomposition.

• Is more suitable for domains in which problems are more data intensive. This includes most business or database systems where there are more data elements than process elements involved in a system.

Object-Oriented Paradigm

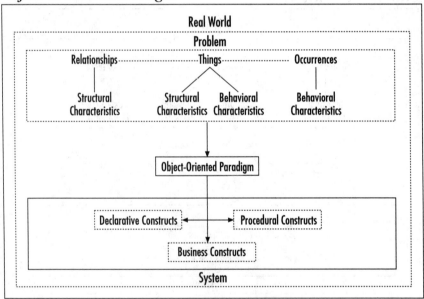

Figure 3-5: Object-Oriented Paradigm

The object-oriented paradigm (Figure 3-5) drives problem-solving efforts by emphasizing processlike and datalike elements of problems as complete units. Such approaches to problem solving are classified as concept-centric because they focus on both the processlike and datalike elements that constitute a given concept. This paradigm

• Focuses on understanding real-world concepts in terms of the composition, relationships, and interactions of entities.

- Provides intrinsic mechanisms for packaging datalike elements and process-like elements together to represent real-world concepts. These mechanisms mimic the naturally occurring scheme where entities have structural characteristics, behavioral characteristics, and dynamic characteristics.

- Provides intrinsic mechanisms for organizing real-world concepts into representations and extending representations of real-world concepts without having to change existing representations. These mechanisms mimic the naturally occurring scheme of how entities evolve over time.

- Facilitates the following problem-solving approach to realize solutions:

  - Identify and elaborate entities within the problem and solution.

  - Identify and elaborate relationships within the problem and solution.

  - Identify and elaborate occurrences within the problem and solution.

  - Regard some real-world concepts as essential to domains in which problems and solutions exist.

  - Regard other real-world concepts as incidental to domains in which problems and solutions exist.

  - Regard concepts as essential or incidental. The paradigm does not primarily focus on process-oriented elements or data-oriented elements; rather, it focuses on concepts as a whole.

  - Decompose or partition and elaborate concepts to further understand the problem and solution. Elaboration consists of elaborating structural characteristics, behavioral characteristics, and dynamic characteristics.

  - Derive a solution from this decomposition by satisfying real-world requirements with realization constructs.

  - Utilize an architecture based on real-world concept decomposition.

Comparing Paradigms

A comparison of the function-driven, data-driven, and object-oriented paradigms reveals the following.

- An ideal paradigm aspires to

  - Facilitate communication among stakeholders involved in a problem-solving effort.

  - Facilitate the creation and utilization of assets to deliver value and increase productivity and consistency.

  - Facilitate the management of change and complexity.

- The function-driven paradigm and data-driven paradigm have the following characteristics:

  - They extract realization constructs from within the problem domain. Stakeholders are forced to communicate using realization concepts; thus, communications may be hindered by being biased toward realization concepts. This often results in a technology-focused solution to a problem rather than the best business solution that is supported by technology.

- They focus on process-oriented or data-oriented characteristics of the real world to drive problem-solving efforts. Artifacts become problem specific and skewed with a process-oriented or data-oriented emphasis; thus, artifacts are tightly coupled with the specific problem and are not likely to be dramatically exploited in other efforts requiring a different emphasis. Furthermore, attempts to reuse artifacts require extrinsic packaging, organizing, and extending mechanisms (library systems, component management systems, etc.) to mechanize the reuse process.

- With a bias toward realization concepts and no intrinsic mechanisms for reuse, changes in requirements have a tendency to dramatically increase complexity within a system. Changes that require a shift in focus between data-oriented and process-oriented elements may cause extensive modifications in an existing system, thus increasing the complexity of the system. The severity of such changes can be very costly and time consuming.

- The object-oriented paradigm has the following characteristics:
  - It focuses on real-world concepts rather than realization constructs. Communications among stakeholders are more natural and focused on the real-world problem to be solved and its solution. This often establishes the foundation for a business-oriented solution that is supported by technology.

  - It focuses on real-world concepts rather than realization constructs. A foundation for reuse among multiple efforts is established. By providing intrinsic packaging mechanisms, representational constructs may be classified and organized by their purpose rather than how they are realized; thus, knowledge is packaged for the possibility of opportunistic reuse. By providing intrinsic organizing and extending mechanisms, emphasis is placed on the systematic reuse of artifacts across multiple problem-solving efforts and domains.

  - It focuses on real-world concepts and applying intrinsic mechanisms for packaging, organizing, and extending representational constructs. Solutions are more readily accommodating to change. Since the emphasis is on real-world concepts, changes in real-world concepts can be more readily realizable in solutions. Since real-world concepts are quite stable and don't change adversely (that is, the processes and procedures that involve these real-world entities do change, but the entities evolve rather than adversely change), solutions and the representational constructs they utilize are more stable and less likely to require adverse changes. As technology changes, the knowledge about real-world concepts may be reapplied using new technology to generate updated solutions. This minimizes the effort required to rediscover what was previously learned, but not captured in a reusable form, about the problem when it was originally solved using existing technology. Furthermore, intrinsic packaging mechanisms aid in managing the impact of changes on solutions by localizing modifications around representational constructs. This has the potential to deliver tremendous value.

- The object-oriented paradigm empowers organizations to gain a competitive advantage by delivering value (increasing quality, reducing costs, reducing time to market) while managing complexity and change via the creation and use of assets.

Object Orientation

The object-oriented paradigm (Figure 3-6) focuses on abstractions that are closely associated with their real-world counterparts.

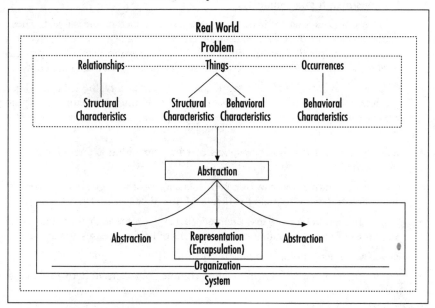

Figure 3-6: Object Orientation

Abstraction

Abstraction involves the formulation of representations concerning a subject in a world. Abstraction

- Involves the following steps:
    - Identifying the subject.
    - Constructing a representation of the subject.
- Establishes a level of detail at which attention and concentration are focused regarding the subject. This level of detail has the following properties:
    - It can be further elaborated to other levels of detail. At higher levels of abstraction, there is less granularity and detail regarding the subject. At lower levels of abstraction, there is more granularity and detail regarding the subject.
    - It establishes a level of detail at which stakeholders can communicate using a common perspective.
    - It constrains decisions regarding the subject to the particular level of detail, thus avoiding premature decisions and commitments.

- Focuses on similarities and differences among a set of identified particular examples or entities so that a representation can be formulated. This involves the following properties of abstraction:

    - Similarities among entities are combined into a single representational construct for the entities.

    - Differences among entities are separated into multiple representational constructs for the entities.

- Focuses on extracting intrinsic essential characteristics of the subject. These characteristics are necessary and sufficient to distinguish a given entity at a given level of detail from all other entities at the same level. This process involves identifying an entity and establishing a boundary around the entity.

- Focuses on avoiding extrinsic incidental characteristics of the subject. These characteristics are either not necessary for representing and manipulating the subject for a given purpose (problem solving) or may belong at a different level of abstraction.

- May be used to focus on the aspects of what something is and what it does while avoiding how it is realized.

- May be declarative, or data oriented, focusing on the logical or conceptual properties of data rather than the details of how data is actualized.

- May be procedural, or process oriented, focusing on the logical or conceptual properties of processes rather than the details of how processes are actualized.

- Facilitates understanding complex problems.

- Facilitates simplifying and manipulating complex problems to derive solutions.

Encapsulation

Encapsulation involves the packaging of representations concerning a subject in a world. Encapsulation

- Focuses on packaging datalike elements and processlike elements together as they occur within concepts themselves in their world.

- Mimics the naturally occurring scheme where entities have structural characteristics, behavioral characteristics, and dynamic characteristics.

- Focuses on the internal architecture of representational constructs or the architecture of a single representational construct.

- Focuses on enabling representational constructs to be self-contained.

- Utilizes modularity, which is the purposeful partitioning of representational constructs to manage size and complexity.

- Utilizes information hiding, which is the appropriate hiding of detail to facilitate abstraction. Information hiding distinguishes between the following aspects of a representational construct or entity:

    - A *specification* describes what an entity is and what an entity does. It is a declarative description used to define interfaces through which communication with the entity may occur. This involves specifying the outside view of the entity.

- An *implementation* describes how an entity is realized. It is a declarative description used to define how the entity may be realized. This involves specifying the inside view of the entity.

Information hiding facilitates abstraction by partitioning what we know into levels of detail. A level of detail is not concerned with how much of the specification or implementation is discovered and captured; rather, it is concerned with a level of abstraction for describing the inside and outside view of an entity.

- Utilizes localization, which is the physical grouping of logically related constructs to maintain unity among related constructs. Localization facilitates the following:

  - Increased cohesion, or maximizing intradependencies within an entity. Cohesion is a measure of how parts of a whole are logically related to each other and the overall whole. Higher cohesion indicates that changes will more likely be localized. This is maximized by the use of modularity.

  - Decreased coupling, or minimizing interdependencies among multiple entities. Coupling is a measure of the strength of the connections between parts. Tighter coupling among representational constructs indicates that changes will less likely be localized to a single construct since one construct knows more about the implementation of another construct. This is minimized by adhering to and using interfaces.

- Enables representational constructs to communicate and interact together via interfaces without establishing interdependencies among their implementations.

- Enables the localization and containment of changes.

- Is used to combat complexity and localize the impact of changes.

Organization

Organization involves the relating and reusing of representations concerning a subject in a world. Organization

- Enables new representations to be variations of existing representations.

- Focuses on evolutionary relationships as they occur among concepts in a world.

- Mimics the naturally occurring scheme of how entities evolve over time.

- Focuses on the external architecture among representational constructs, or the architecture among multiple representational constructs.

- Focuses on classifying representations into higher or lower levels of abstraction.

- Enables the evolution of existing representational constructs.

- Is used to combat complexity and support the reusability of representational constructs.

Objects and Classes

Objects and classes (Figure 3-7) abstract *entities* from the problem world or solution world.

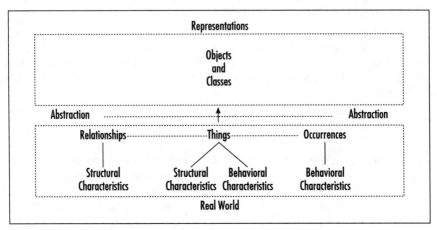

Figure 3-7: Objects and Classes

Objects

Objects (Figure 3-8) are well-defined representational constructs of concrete or conceptual entities.

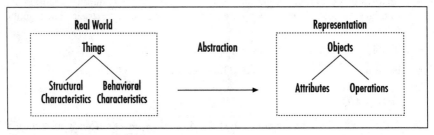

Figure 3-8: Objects

Objects

• Encapsulate structural characteristics known as *attributes*. Attributes

   – Are representational constructs of structural characteristics of entities.

   – Determine the possible states of an object.

   – Are extracted from a domain using declarative, or data-oriented, abstraction.

   – May be of a simple or complex data type. Simple data types are not reducible to any subordinate parts. Complex data types are conglomerates reducible to subordinate parts.

- May be single valued or multi-valued. Single-valued attributes resolve to one value. Multi-valued attributes resolve to a collection or set of values.
- Encapsulate behavioral characteristics known as *operations*. Operations
  - Are representational constructs of behavioral characteristics of entities.
  - Determine the possible behaviors of an object.
  - Are extracted from a domain using procedural, or process-oriented, abstraction.
  - Have a signature consisting of a name, input parameters, output parameters, and possibly return parameters.
  - Are invoked in response to receiving a message.
- May be active or passive.
  - *Active* objects have a thread of control or may initiate activity. They may take the initiative to request services from other objects.
  - *Passive* objects do not have a thread of control and may not take the initiative to request services from other objects unless they receive control from an active object.
- May be persistent or transient. *Persistent* objects exist after their creator has ceased to exist. *Transient* objects exist only during the time that their creator exists.
- May be referenced, that is, denoted in some manner.
- Have identity. All objects are unique and distinguishable from other objects. They may be compared for the following:
  - Pure identity, yielding true for the same object.
  - Shallow equality, yielding true for objects with the same attribute values.
  - Deep equality, yielding true for objects with the same attribute values recursively within their subordinate parts.
- Participate in relationships.
- Participate in occurrences.
- Have semantics, that is, meaning or purpose within a problem or solution.
- May be complex and reducible into subordinate objects, or may be primitive and irreducible.
- Are instances of classes. They are said to *instantiate* classes. The relationship between an object and its class is known as an *is-a* relationship.

Classes

Classes (Figure 3-9) are descriptions of objects or a set of objects with a common implementation. Classes

- Are concerned with the implementation of uniform structural characteristics and behavioral characteristics.

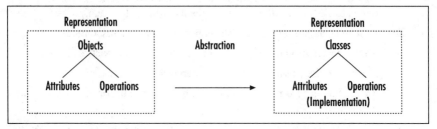

Figure 3-9: Classes

- Have an intensional notion or capability. This is the ability of a class to define a pattern for objects of the class. A class determines the structure and behavior of these objects.

- Have an extensional notion or capability. This is the ability of a class to create objects of the class. The class is known as an *object factory*. The extensional capability is also the ability of a class to maintain references to all objects of the class. The objects of a class are known as the class's *extent*.

- Encapsulate structural characteristics called attributes. They

  - Are implemented by the class.

  - May be associated with objects of a class. That is, each object has its own value. These are known as *object attributes* and have a scope that affects an individual object.

  - May be associated with the class as a whole. That is, all objects of a class share a value. These are known as *class attributes* and have a scope that affects all objects of the class.

- Encapsulate behavioral characteristics called operations. They

  - Are implemented by the class as methods or subprograms.

  - Are known as *services* offered by the class (or objects of the class).

  - May be associated with objects of a class. That is, they may be applied on objects of the class. These are known as *object operations* and have instance or object scope.

  - May be associated with the class as a whole. That is, they may be applied on the class itself. These are known as *class operations* and have class scope.

  - May be classified as *abstract*. That is, they may specify an interface but no implementation. When a class has one or more abstract operations, it may not have any instances. Once all abstract operations have an implementation provided by a subclass, the subclass may have instances. When a class has all operations defined, it is classified as *concrete*. By making an operation abstract, the class may use the operation; however, the implementation of the operation is delayed until a subclass provides a method. Subclasses are discussed in the section "Generalizations."

- Define the accessibility of attributes and operations from outside an object of a class. The following accessibility criteria may be associated with characteristics:

- *Public* accessibility means characteristics are accessible from outside an object.

- *Protected* accessibility means characteristics are not accessible from outside an object. They are like private characteristics when accessed from outside an object of a class.

- *Private* accessibility means characteristics are not accessible from outside an object.

- May have an introspective protocol or mechanism through which attributes and operations may be discovered by other objects, and an intercessory protocol or mechanism through which attributes and operations may be added, deleted, or modified by other objects.

- May be parameterized; that is, may require parameters in order to become a defined class that is capable of instantiation. The parameters are bound to actual values to create a real class. Parameterized classes are known as *template classes* or *generic classes*.

- May allow their objects to be statically or dynamically classified. Static classification disallows objects from changing their classes. Dynamic classification allows objects to change their classes.

- May allow their objects to be singly or multiply classified. Single classification disallows objects from belonging directly to more than one class. Multiple classification allows objects to belong directly to more than one class.

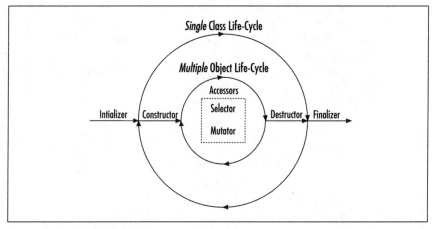

Figure 3-10: Life Cycle of Classes and Objects

- Have a life cycle (Figure 3-10) that is shared with their objects. This life cycle is depicted by the following types of operations:

- *Initializer operations* are class operations that are implicitly utilized to initialize a class. They are invoked when the first object of the class is created.

- *Constructor operations* are class operations that create or construct objects of the associated class.

- Accessors known as *selector operations* provide an interface for "getting" information about and from within an object or class.

- Accessors known as *mutator operations* provide an interface for "setting" information about and within an object or class. Mutator operations also involve the general behavior of the object or class.

- *Destructor operations* are class operations that destroy objects of the associated class.

- *Finalizer operations* are class operations that are implicitly utilized to uninitialize a class. They are invoked when the last object of the class is destroyed.

- Participate in relationships.

- Participate in occurrences.

- Define an implementation for their objects.

- May be complex and reducible into subordinate classes or may be primitive and irreducible.

Types

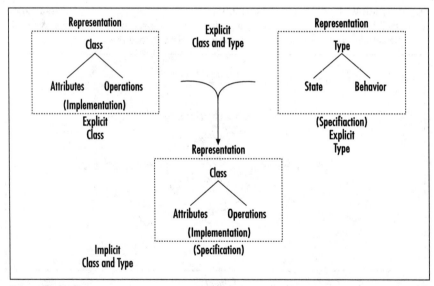

Figure 3-11: Types

Types (Figure 3-11) are descriptions of objects or a set of objects with a common specification or interface. Types

- Are concerned with the specification of uniform structural characteristics and behavioral characteristics.

- Encapsulate structural characteristics called attributes. They

  - Are specified by the type.

- May be object attributes or class attributes.
- Encapsulate behavioral characteristics called operations. They
  - Are specified by the type.
  - May be object operations or class operations.
- Define the accessibility of attributes and operations from outside an object or class using the same accessibility criteria as classes.
- Participate in relationships.
- Participate in occurrences.
- Define a specification or one or more interfaces for classes.
- May be complex and reducible into subordinate types or may be primitive and irreducible.
- May be explicitly related to classes. That is, the class of an object may be distinguished from the type of an object. This involves a class receiving an interface from a type and providing an implementation for the interface.
- May be implicitly related to classes. That is, the class of an object implicitly includes its type. This is accomplished via the class's intensional notion and involves a class defining an interface and providing an implementation.

Links and Associations

Links and associations (Figure 3-12) abstract *relationships* among entities within the problem world or solution world.

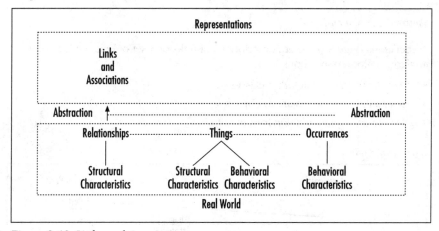

Figure 3-12: Links and Associations

Links

Links (Figure 3-13) are well-defined representational constructs of concrete or conceptual entities that relate other entities. Links

- Are objects that relate other objects.
- Are dependent on all of the objects they relate.

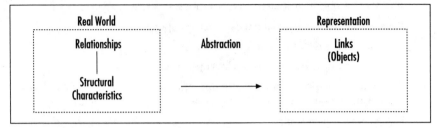

Figure 3-13: Links

- Are not part of any of the objects they relate.
- May be binary, ternary, or higher order. That is, they may relate two, three, or more than three other objects.
- Are instances of associations. They are said to instantiate associations. The relationship between a link and its association is known as an *is-a* relationship.

Associations

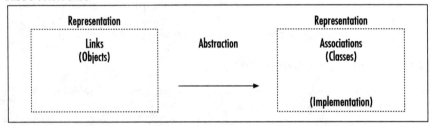

Figure 3-14: Associations

Associations (Figure 3-14) are descriptions of links or a set of links with a common implementation. Associations

- Are classes that relate other classes.
- Are to links as classes are to objects.
- Define an implementation for their links.

Aggregations

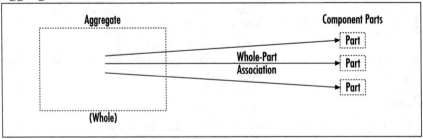

Figure 3-15: Aggregations

Aggregations (Figure 3-15) are associations and links specifying a whole-part relationship. Aggregations

- Are known as *has-a* relationships.

- Are abstractions of concrete or conceptual whole-part relationships among entities.

- Involve aggregates or wholes that are connected to their component parts.

- Involve component parts that exist independent of their aggregates.

- Specify that aggregates "loosely" contain component parts. The relationship is "loose" because there are no other semantics associated with the relationship.

- Are transitive; that is, if *A* is a part of *B* and *B* is a part of *C*, *A* is a part of *C*.

- Are antisymmetric; that is, if *A* is a part of *B*, *B* is not a part of *A*.

Compositions

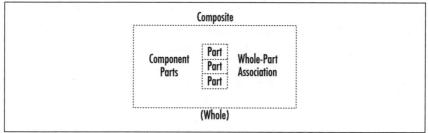

Figure 3-16: Compositions

Compositions (Figure 3-16) are aggregations with strong ownership and coincident lifetime constraints. These are also known as *composite aggregations*. Compositions

- Are known as *contains-a* relationships.

- Are abstractions of concrete or conceptual whole-part relationships with ownership and coincident lifetime constraints among entities.

- Specify that composites or aggregates own their component parts.

- Specify that the component parts may only have one owner.

- Specify that component parts exist or live and die with their composite owner.

- Specify that composites "tightly" contain component parts. The relationship is "tight" because there are semantics other than aggregation associated with the relationship. That is, parts live and die with their owners.

Generalizations

Generalizations (Figure 3-17) are associations specifying a taxonomic relationship. Generalizations

- Are known as *is-a-kind-of* relationships.

- Relate more general representational constructs and more specific representational constructs. These constructs include entities, classes, and types.

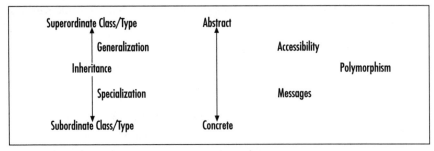

Figure 3-17: Generalizations

- Enable new constructs to be derived from existing constructs.

- Involve existing classes and types known as *superclasses* (superordinate classes) and *supertypes* (superordinate types). These classes and types are also called *ancestors* or *base constructs*. They have the following characteristics:

  - Types provide existing specifications or interfaces.

  - Classes provide existing implementations.

- Involve new classes and types known as *subclasses* (subordinate classes) and *subtypes* (subordinate types), also called *descendent* or *derived* classes and types. They have the following characteristics:

  - They acquire the characteristics of their superclasses and supertypes.

  - They can add characteristics including attributes and operations.

  - They can redefine operations.

- Indicate that more specific constructs are derived from more general constructs.

- Are called *specializations* to indicate that more specific constructs are derived from more general constructs.

- Utilize *inheritance* as the sharing mechanism through which more specific constructs acquire the characteristics (attributes, operations, methods, and associations) of more general constructs. Inheritance has the following characteristics:

  - Subtyping enables inheritance of specifications or interfaces. This is known as *interface inheritance* and establishes an interface hierarchy.

  - Subclassing enables inheritance of implementation. This is known as *implementation inheritance* and establishes an implementation hierarchy.

  - In single inheritance, a more specific construct receives characteristics from one or more general constructs, resulting in a treelike hierarchy.

  - In multiple inheritance, a more specific construct receives characteristics from multiple general constructs, resulting in a latticelike hierarchy.

  - Inheritance is transitive; that is, if *A* is a subclass of *B* and *B* is a subclass of *C*, *A* is a subclass of *C*. If *A* is a subtype of *B* and *B* is a subtype of *C*, *A* is a subtype of *C*.

- Inheritance is antisymmetric; that is, if *A* is a subclass of *B* and *B* is a subclass of *A*, *A* and *B* are the same class. If *A* is a subtype of *B* and *B* is a subtype of *A*, *A* and *B* are the same type.

- Inheritance enables substitution; that is, a subclass instance may be substituted where a superclass instance is required, and a subtype instance may be substituted where a supertype instance is required. The reverse is not true, however: a superclass cannot be substituted for a subclass.

- Inheritance enables inclusion; that is, a subclass instance, is a superclass instance, and a subtype instance is a supertype instance.

- Inheritance enables specialization; that is, a subclass instance is a superclass instance with more specific information, and a subtype instance is a supertype instance with more specific information.

- May be used to create abstract classes or concrete classes.

  - Abstract classes are incompletely implemented; that is, the class has interfaces without implementations. Abstract classes may not have any instances.

  - Concrete classes are completely specified and completely implemented; that is, the class has implementations for all interfaces. Concrete classes may have instances.

- Affect the life cycle for classes and types in the following manner during instantiation of an object:

  - Initializer operations are invoked from most general to most specific.

  - Constructor operations are invoked from most general to most specific.

  - Destructor operations are invoked from most specific to most general.

  - Finalizer operations are invoked from most specific to most general.

- Affect the accessibility of attributes and operations from outside an object, class, or type in the following manner:

  - Public accessibility means that characteristics are accessible when inherited by more specific constructs.

  - Protected accessibility means that characteristics are accessible when inherited by more specific constructs. They are like public characteristics when inherited.

  - Private accessibility means that characteristics are not accessible when inherited by more specific constructs.

  More specialized constructs may further restrict the accessibility of inherited characteristics.

- Involve *polymorphism* (meaning "many forms"), that is, the ability of an interface to have many implementations.

- Involve *overloading;* that is, the ability of an operation to have the same name, different signatures, different implementations, and possibly different semantics within the same class or different classes. It enables the same message to invoke different operations within the same class or different classes. The invoked operation is determined by statically considering the signature of the message. This is also known as *ad hoc polymorphism*.

- Involve *parametric polymorphism,* that is, the use of parameterized classes and types. The invoked operation is a generic function that is dependent on the class or type of the arguments used in the operation invocation. These functions are known as generic functions or templates.

- Involve *pure polymorphism,* that is, the ability of an operation to have the same name, same signature, different implementations, and possibly different semantics within different classes. This involves *overriding,* that is, the ability of a subclass to specialize an inherited operation by redefining the implementation of the operation but not its specification. It enables the same message to invoke different operations within different classes based on the class of the object on which the operation is invoked. The invoked operation is determined by dynamically searching the inheritance hierarchy. The actual implementation of an operation is found by searching the class of the object on which the operation is applied. If no implementation is found, the class's superclasses are searched; this process continues until an implementation is found. This is known as *inclusion polymorphism* or *polymorphism by inheritance*. The operations are said to be *virtual.*

- Involve *delegation,* that is, the ability of an object or class to issue a message to another object or class in response to a message.

Scenarios and Interactions

Scenarios and interactions (Figure 3-18) abstract *occurrences* among entities within the problem world or solution world.

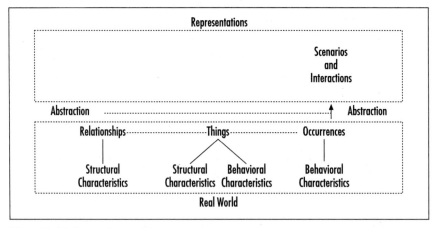

Figure 3-18: Scenarios and Interactions

Scenarios

Scenarios (Figure 3-19) are well-defined representational constructs of concrete or conceptual entities that are conduits for a sequence of message exchanges among other entities.

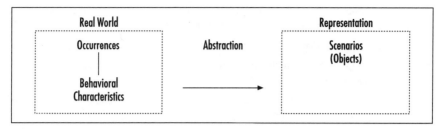

Figure 3-19: Scenarios

Scenarios

- Are objects that are conduits for a sequence of message exchanges among other objects.

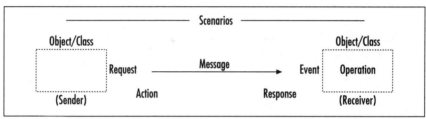

Figure 3-20: Message Exchanges

- Are concerned with a specific sequence of message exchanges (Figure 3-20). The specific sequence involves messages and actions between a sender (client) object or class and a receiver (supplier or server) object or class in the following manner:

  - The sender sends a message (operation or signal) or request to the receiver. The message is an instance of a message class and conveys information with the expectation that the receiver will act or perform some activity.

  - The receiver receives the message as an event and responds by performing an activity. The event is an instance of an event class. The response involves the invocation of an operation that is carried out by the operation's implementation or method.

  - Synchronous communication involves the sender waiting for the receiver to respond. The sender calls the receiver, and the event generated is a call event. If the receiver is not an active object, the sender must pass control to the receiver and wait for the receiver to respond and send control back to the sender.

  - Asynchronous communication involves the sender not waiting for the receiver to respond. The sender signals the receiver (or raises the signal), and the event generated is a signal event. The receiver must be an active object, and both the sender and receiver continue processing.

  - This manner of interaction may continue.

Fundamentally, the sender is said to apply an operation on the receiver by sending a message that invokes the appropriate operation within the receiver.

Within an interaction

- Messages focus on the communication of information and requests for some activity.
- Events focus on the occurrence of receiving a message. These may be call events or signal events.
- Operations focus on specifying a service that is offered.
- Methods focus on the implementation of a service.

- Are dependent on all of the objects involved in the sequence of message exchanges.

- Are not part of any of the objects involved in the sequence of message exchanges.

- May be binary, ternary, or higher order. That is, they may involve two, three, or more than three other objects.

- Are instances of interactions.

Interactions

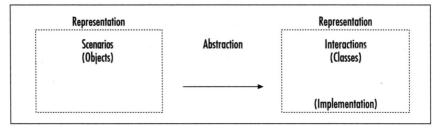

Figure 3-21: Interactions

Interactions (Figure 3-21) are descriptions of scenarios or a set of scenarios with a common implementation. Interactions

- Are classes that are conduits for a set of message exchange sequences among other classes.

- Are concerned with a set of message exchange sequences.

- Are to scenarios as classes are to objects.

- Are divided into two constructs:

    - *Sequences* focus on the messages exchanged among objects (classes) within scenarios.

    - *Collaborations* focus on the messages exchanged among objects (classes) and their links (associations) within scenarios.

Variations and Summary

Variations of the Object-Oriented Paradigm

An in-depth analysis of object-oriented paradigms (Figure 3-22) reveals the following points.

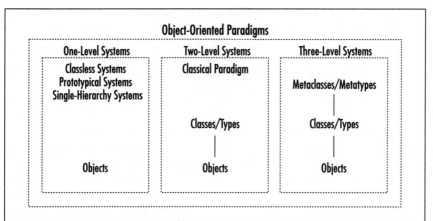

Figure 3-22: Object-Oriented Paradigms

- The following aspects of the object-oriented paradigm establish the foundation for various semantic variations or interpretations of the paradigm:
  - Definition and interpretation of the concepts that constitute the paradigm.
  - Application and utilization of the paradigm.
  - Closure and extensibility of the paradigm.

  All object-oriented paradigms must encompass and support the pillars (first principles) of object orientation
  - Abstraction as an identification principle.
  - Encapsulation as an organizing principle.
  - Inheritance as a sharing principle.
  - Polymorphism as a sharing principle.

- To distinguish among variations of the object-oriented paradigm, the following classification based on the distinct levels of instantiation may be utilized:
  - One-level systems, known as classless systems, prototypical systems, or single-hierarchy systems, stipulate that all objects are classes and all classes are objects. An instance is created by copying another object.
  - Two-level systems, known as classical object orientation, involve objects that are instances of classes and types. This is the most common interpretation of the object-oriented paradigm.
  - Three-level systems involve objects that are instances of classes and types, and classes and types that are instances of metaclasses and

metatypes. Metaclasses are classes whose instance are classes. Metatypes are types whose instance are types.

– *n*th-level systems involve *n* levels of instantiation.

- The UML utilizes a three-level system that includes an extension mechanism for metamodel access and customization. The UML may also be used for working with one-level systems and two-level systems.

- The object-oriented paradigm is reducible to the function-driven paradigm or the data-driven paradigm. That is, while using the object-oriented paradigm, activities can be skewed to independently leverage function-driven concepts or data-driven concepts in a given problem-solving approach. Therefore, because the UML is based on the object-oriented paradigm, it may be used to facilitate and express artifacts within a function-driven approach, a data-driven approach, or an object-oriented approach. This is possible because the object-oriented paradigm is a convergence of the other two paradigms.

- Applying the object-oriented paradigm within a problem-solving effort does not imply any specific constraints on the realization of the solution. That is, using the object-oriented approach does not imply that a realization toolset must be object oriented or support the paradigm. An object-oriented system may be implemented using declarative constructs and procedural constructs using an object-oriented toolset or a non-object-oriented toolset. This is possible because the object-oriented paradigm is a convergence of the other two paradigms and may be mapped to tools implementing the other paradigms.

Summary of the Object-Oriented Paradigm

The object-oriented paradigm (Figure 3-23) is summarized in the following.

- The real world consists of concrete and conceptual entities, including things, relationships, and occurrences that have a purpose, structural characteristics, and behavioral characteristics.

- The first level of abstraction within the object-oriented paradigm consists of representational constructs of concrete and conceptual entities.

  – Objects are abstracted entities that encapsulate state and behavior.

  – Links are abstracted relationships among objects.

  – Scenarios are abstracted message exchanges among objects.

- The second level of abstraction within the object-oriented paradigm consists of a set of representational constructs.

  – Classes are descriptions of a set of objects with common attributes, operation implementations, semantics, associations, and interactions.

  – Types are descriptions of a set of objects with common attributes, operation interfaces, semantics, associations, and interactions.

  – Associations are descriptions of a set of links with common attributes, operation implementations, semantics, associations, and interactions.

  – Interactions are descriptions of a set of scenarios with common message exchange sequences, classes, and associations.

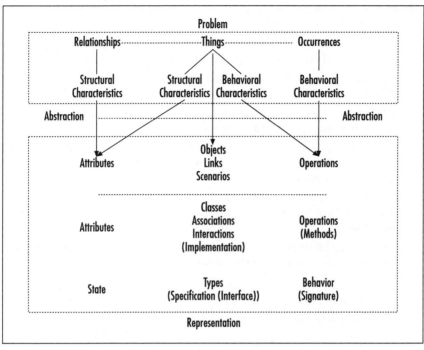

Figure 3-23: Summary of the Object-Oriented Paradigm

- Objects may be combined to build larger or more involved components. This has become known as the *component-oriented paradigm.*

Society of Objects

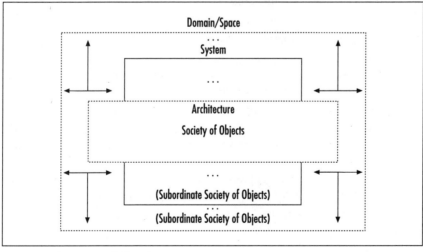

Figure 3-24: Society of Objects

The impacts of the object-oriented paradigm on the notion of a system (Figure 3-24) are summarized in the following.

- A *society* is an organized collection of entities joined together for some purpose. The evolution of a society is the summation of the evolution of its entities.

- A society may be recursively decomposed into multiple societies called subordinate societies (or subsocieties).

- When fully decomposed, a society consists of primitive society elements, or objects that are not further decomposable.

- Using the object-oriented paradigm, the architecture of a system within a domain consists of a society of objects and links that interact to achieve the goals of the society.

- Societies of objects that are focused on specific domains and provide appropriate interfaces for adaptability within other societies of objects are known as *frameworks.*

- Objects may be combined to build larger or more involved components. This has become known as the component-oriented paradigm.

- Objects
    - Are abstracted from a world or domain.
    - Live within a society of objects.
    - Encapsulate knowledge in attributes and encapsulate skills in operations.
    - May be classified based on common implementations or interfaces.
    - May inherit characteristics from their ancestors.
    - Communicate via messages.
    - Cooperate in interactions to accomplish complex tasks.
    - Make requests of other objects by sending messages.
    - Fulfill requests made by other objects when receiving messages.
    - Perform operations in response to requests.
    - May respond differently to the same request. That is, they respond in their own manner as long as the response is semantically consistent with other object's responses to the same message.
    - Need not disclose exactly how they respond to requests.
    - May not express exactly how they want other objects to respond to requests. They may express only what they are requesting other objects to do, not how it should be done.
    - May determine the appropriate response when requests are received. That is, they are not bound to predetermined responses.

The UML is used to specify, visualize, construct, and document a society of objects that are organized to achieve some purpose.

PART II

Using the Unified Modeling Language

This section presents an integrated view of the UML and how its constituent parts (diagrams) interact to facilitate its use.

Chapter 4, *A Unified Modeling Language Tutorial,* presents a tutorial on the UML.

Chapter 5, *The Unified Modeling Language,* presents an overview of the constituent parts of the UML, how they relate to one another, and how they contribute to a method or process utilizing the UML.

CHAPTER 4

A Unified Modeling Language Tutorial

This chapter presents a tutorial on the UML. I start with the example briefly mentioned in Chapter 2 and Chapter 3, and examine this problem using the various UML diagrams. This brief tutorial will introduce you to the different diagrams and elements of the UML. The tutorial is not intended to prescribe a particular process for developing models, but provides a learning mechanism by starting with small and intuitive models that are elaborated using the UML. The complete details of each diagram type are found in the reference chapters.

The Unified Modeling Language Diagrams

The UML defines nine types of diagrams: class, object, use case, sequence, collaboration, statechart, activity, component, and deployment diagrams. All of these diagrams are based on the principle that concepts are depicted as symbols and relationships among concepts are depicted as paths (lines) connecting symbols, where both of these types of elements may be named. The example of Chapter 2 and Chapter 3 involved an organization that desires an information system to better utilize employees (resources) on projects.

Use Case Diagrams

Use case diagrams describe the functionality of a system and users of the system. These diagrams contain the following elements:

- *Actors*, which represent users of a system, including human users and other systems.

- *Use cases*, which represent functionality or services provided by a system to users.

Figure 4-1 shows a Resource Manager actor who uses the functionality of the system to manage resources, a Project Manager actor who uses the functionality of the system to manage projects, a System Administrator actor who is responsible for

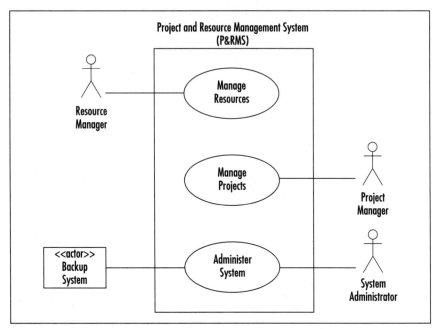

Figure 4-1: High-Level Use Case Diagram

administrative functions of the system, and a Backup System actor that houses backup data for the system. The large rectangle represents the boundary of the system. The name of the system appears above the rectangle. The stick person icon represents an actor who is a human user. The Backup System rectangle icon represents an actor that is another system.

The name of the Backup System actor is preceded by an "<<actor>>" string. This string is called a *stereotype* and indicates that the Backup System is an actor. This stereotype and the stick person icon are equivalent. The stick person icon is usually used to represent humans, whereas the "<<actor>>" string is usually used to represent systems. The ellipses represent use cases. The lines connecting actors and use cases indicate that the actors use or participate in the functionality provided by the use cases. This line is called a *communicates* relationship.

Figure 4-2 elaborates the Manage Resources use case by detailing the functionality a Resource Manager actor expects of the system.

Resource managers may add, remove, or update skills information. Because a skill must be found in the system database before it may be removed or updated, a Find Skill use case is utilized. The arrows from the Remove Skill use case and the Update Skill use case to the Find Skill use case are labeled with a "uses" stereotype to indicate that the Find Skill use case is called or included in the Remove Skill use case and the Update Skill use case. This arrow is called a *uses* relationship.

Resource managers may also add, remove, or update resource information. The Remove Resource and Update Resource use cases utilize a Find Resource use case.

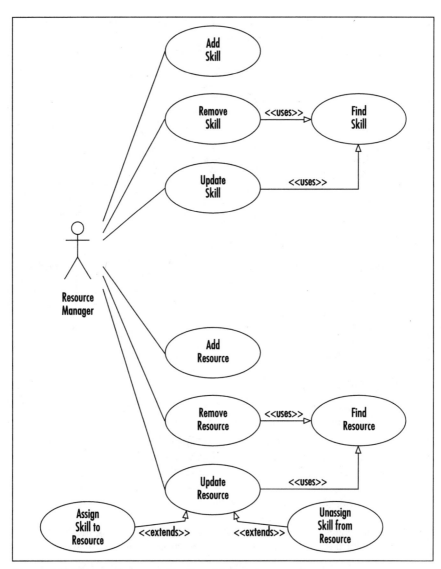

Figure 4-2: Manage Resources Use Case Diagram

Resource managers may assign a skill to a resource or unassign a skill from a resource while updating resource information. An Assign Skill to Resource use case and an Unassign Skill from Resource use case are utilized to depict this functionality. The arrows from these use cases to the Update Resource use case are labeled with an "extends" stereotype to indicate that these use cases are options from the Update Resource use case. This arrow is called an *extends* relationship. Use it when you want to make functionality optional to a use case.

Figure 4-3 elaborates the Manage Projects use case by detailing the functionality a Project Manager actor expects of the system. The elements are similar to Figure 4-2.

Find Project is required by the Remove Project and Update Project use cases, so they are connected by a uses relationship. A number of other use cases are optionally invoked by Update Project, so they are connected to it by an extends relationship.

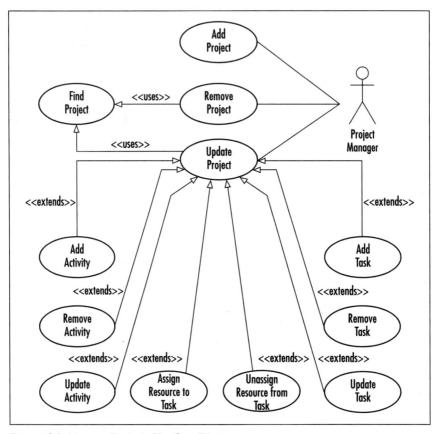

Figure 4-3: Manage Projects Use Case Diagram

Figure 4-4 elaborates the Administer System use case by detailing the functionality a System Administrator actor and Backup System actor expect of the system.

System administrators may start up the system, shut down the system, back up data to the Backup System actor, or restore data from the Backup System actor. Because backing up data is very common before a system is shut down, the Back Up Data use case is a connected option to the Shut Down System use case through an extends relationship. Because restoring data is very common after a system is started up, the Restore Data use case is a connected option to the Start Up System use case through an extends relationship. Because the Backup System actor is involved only in backing up or restoring data and is not directly involved in starting up or shutting down the system, the Backup System actor communicates only with the Restore Data use case and Back Up Data use case. The Back Up Data use case uses the combined functionality of a Back Up Project Data use case and a Back Up Resource Data use case. The Restore Data use case uses the

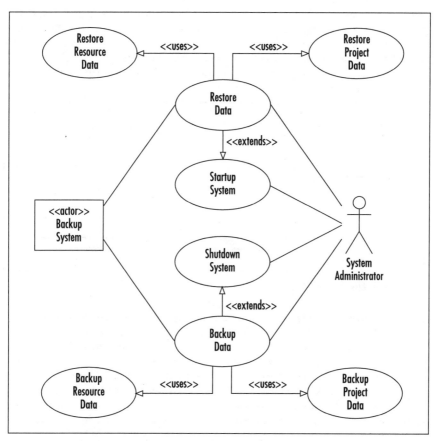

Figure 4-4: Administer System Use Case Diagram

combined functionality of a Restore Project Data use case and a Restore Resource Data use case.

Use cases are usually described in a textual document that accompanies the use case diagram. The combination of these use case diagrams and their supporting documentation is known as a *use case model*.

Use case diagrams are described in greater detail in Chapter 8.

Class Diagrams

Class diagrams describe the static structure of a system, or how it is structured rather than how it behaves. These diagrams contain the following elements:

- *Classes*, which represent entities with common characteristics or features. These features include attributes, operations, and associations.

- *Associations*, which represent relationships that relate two or more other classes where the relationships have common characteristics or features. These features include attributes and operations.

Figure 4-5 shows that the system is concerned with projects, activities, tasks, and resources. The rectangles represent these concepts or classes. The figure also shows that projects are related to activities, activities are related to tasks, and tasks are related to resources. The paths represent relationships or associations. Each class must have a name within the rectangle, and each association may have a name attached.

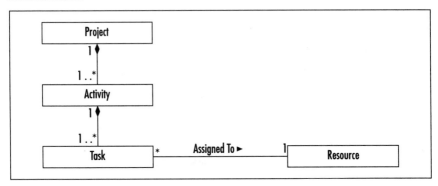

Figure 4-5: High-Level Project Class Diagram

Projects, activities, and tasks are all efforts of work. A project consists of activities, and activities consist of tasks. A project does not have any hours associated with it, but activities and tasks have hours indicating the duration required to do the work. Activities have associated deliverables or work products, whereas tasks have associated resources for doing the work. The filled diamond attached to the Project class of the association between the Project class and the Activity class indicates that the project contains activities and that if the project is removed, so are its associated activities. A similar relationship holds between the Activity class and the Task class.

Thus, the filled diamond is used to indicate a *composition* relationship. If activities could exist without being associated with a project or a project could be removed without having to remove its activities, the diamond may be hollow. Such a hollow diamond is used to indicate an *aggregation* relationship rather than a composition relationship.

Projects contain one or more activities. The "1..*" string attached to the Activity class of the association between the Project class and the Activity class indicates that one or more activities are involved in the relationship. This is called the *multiplicity* of the Activity class within the relationship. The multiplicity specifies how many objects of the class are associated with a single object of the other class in the association. An activity may be associated with only one project.

The "1" string attached to the Project class of the association between the Project class and the Activity class indicates that only one project is involved in the relationship. The multiplicity indicators on this association specify that each project must have one or more activities, and each activity may only belong to a single project. The association between the Activity class and the Task class specifies that each activity must have one or more tasks, and each task may only belong to a single activity.

Resources may be assigned zero or more tasks. The "*" string attached to the Task class of the association between the Task class and the Resource class indicates that zero or more tasks are involved in the relationship. Each task may only be assigned to one resource. Note the difference between the "1..*" multiplicity, which requires at least one instance, and the "*" multiplicity, which permits zero as an option. The "1" string attached to the Resource class of the association between the Task class and the Resource class indicates that only one resource is involved in the relationship.

The association name has a small arrow indicating the direction in which to read the association name. If no arrow is attached, associations are read from left to right and top to bottom. In this case, the arrow is not required. The association between the Task class and the Resource class specifies that zero or more tasks are associated with a single resource, and each resource may be associated with zero or more tasks.

Figure 4-6 shows that zero or more resources may be associated with zero or more skills. Thus, any number of resources may have the same skill. Because we want to maintain information about the relationship between a resource and a skill, a Resource-Skill class is used. The dashed line connecting the Resource-Skill class to the actual path indicates that the class maintains information about the relationship. This class is called an *association class*. Association classes are used to maintain information about the relationship rather than the objects involved in the relationship.

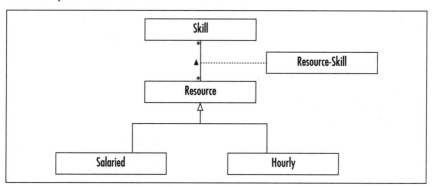

Figure 4-6: High-Level Resource Class Diagram

There are two kinds of resources, salaried and hourly. The arrows from the Salaried class and the Hourly class to the Resource class indicate that the Salaried class and the Hourly class inherit or receive all the characteristics of the Resource class. This also indicates that whenever a Resource class object is used, a Salaried class object or Hourly class object may be used in its place. The Resource class is reused by the Salaried class and Hourly class. This arrow is called a *generalization* relationship. In object-oriented languages, the term *inheritance* is often used instead of generalization relationship, and the particular relationship between the Resource class and the others would be called an *is-a-kind-of* inheritance.

Figure 4-7 details Figure 4-5 by defining what constitutes projects, activities, and tasks. Projects have a name, description, and a start date. The compartment below the name represents the *attributes* of the class. Attributes are *structural features* of the class, that is, information about the class. The name attribute will hold a string value, the description attribute will hold a string value, and the start date attribute will hold a date value. The attributes are all inaccessible outside the class, as indicated by the preceding "-" visibility character. This is known as *private* visibility.

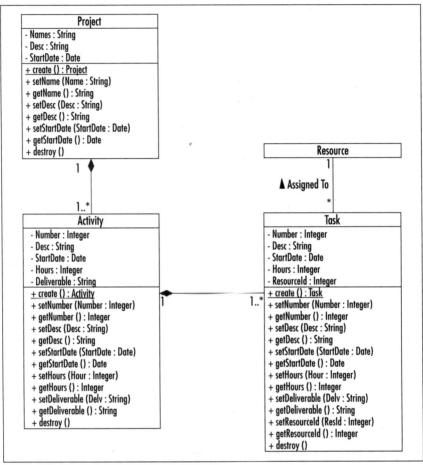

Figure 4-7: Detailed Project Class Diagram

Projects must provide services for setting and getting the values of their attributes. The compartment below the attribute compartment represents the *operations* of the class. Operations are *behavioral features* of the class, that is, the services (often known as *methods* in object-oriented languages) provided by the class. Thus, the setName operation requires a string parameter to set the value of the Name attribute, and the getName operation returns the value of the Name attribute. There are operations for setting and getting the values of all of the attributes.

The Project class must also provide services for creating and destroying objects of the class. The "create" operation is used to create an object of the class. This operation requires no arguments and returns a Project. This operation is known as a *constructor* operation. Because the operation is applied to the class rather than an object of the class, it is underlined. The "destroy" operation is used to destroy objects of the class. This operation requires no parameters and does not return anything. This operation is know as a *destructor* operation. The operation may be applied to an object of the Project class just like the other operations. All of these operations are accessible outside the class, as indicated by the preceding "+" visibility character. This is known as *public* visibility.

When we want to make an attribute or operation inaccessible outside a class, but accessible to classes with a generalization relationship to the class, we use *protected* visibility. Protected visibility is indicated by a preceding "#" character.

Activities have a number to describe the order in which they are done within a project, a description, a start date, the number of hours they require, and the deliverable product that results from the activity. The Activity class provides appropriate operations for setting and getting the values of these attributes, and operations for creating and destroying objects of the class.

Tasks have a number to describe the order in which they are done within an activity, a description, a start date, the number of hours they require, and an identification number of the resource who is responsible for the task. The Task class provides appropriate operations for setting and getting the values of these attributes, and operations for creating and destroying objects of the class.

Because activities and tasks are very similar, with the only distinction being that activities have an associated deliverable and tasks have an associated resource, a Work Effort class is used as a base from which to define activities and tasks. Figure 4-8 shows that a Work Effort class represents everything common to activities and tasks, whereas the Activity class and the Task class have a generalization relationship to the Work Effort class. The Work Effort class is reused to define the Activity class and the Task class.

Figure 4-9, which is part of this chapter's hypothetical system, details Figure 4-6 by defining what constitutes skills and resources. Skills have two attributes: a name and a description. The Skill class provides appropriate operations for setting and getting the values of these attributes, and operations for creating and destroying objects of the class.

Resources have a name. The Resource class provides appropriate operations for setting and getting the values of this attribute, and operations for creating and destroying objects of the class. Salaried resources have an associated salary, and hourly resources have an associated hourly rate. The Salaried class and Hourly class also provide similar operations.

The information maintained about the relationship between a resource and a skill includes the proficiency of the resource and the years experience the resource has with the skill. The Resource-Skill class has a Prof attribute that may have the values of Expert or Novice, and a YearsExpr attribute for representing the number of years of experience. The class also provides appropriate operations for setting and getting the values of these attributes, and operations for creating and destroying objects of the class.

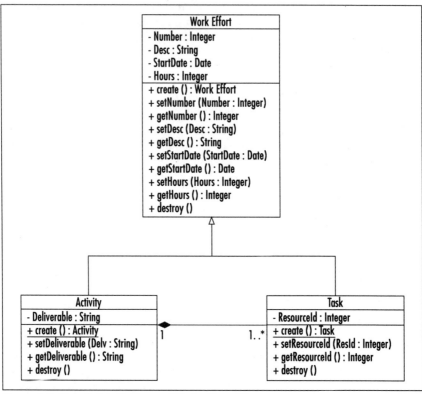

Figure 4-8: Detailed Activities and Tasks Class Diagram

Figure 4-10 details Figure 4-9 by defining how the relationship between skills and resources will be implemented. The Resource-Skill class must provide the capability to associate any number of resources with any number of skills.

We introduce the Identifiable class as an abstract class that simply provides an identification integer. The class is specified as abstract by including the constraint string "abstract" in curly braces following the class name. *Abstract classes* cannot have instances; they merely provide attributes and services shared by the classes that inherit them.

The Skill class and the Resource class both inherit the characteristics of the Identifiable class; that is, objects of these classes are now identifiable via their Id attribute. The Resource-Skill class stores the Id attributes of the associated Resource class object and Skill class object pairs. The SkillId attribute of the Resource-Skill class stores the Id attribute of the associated Skill class object, and the ResourceId attribute of the Resource-Skill class stores the Id attribute of the associated Resource class object. Because we now know enough detail about how the Resource-Skill class maintains information about the association, the association may be refined.

To determine if a particular resource has a particular skill, the Resource class object and a SkillId attribute value of the Resource-Skill class are used to find the

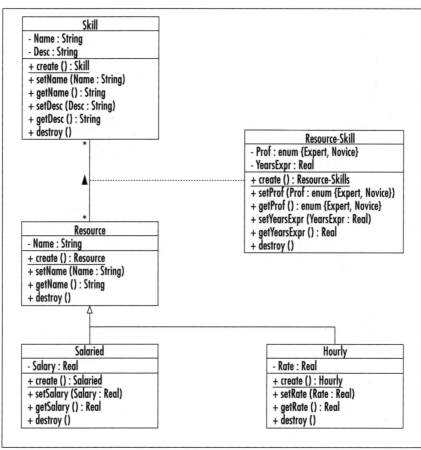

Figure 4-9: Detailed Resource Class Diagram

associated Skill class object. The SkillId attribute of the Resource-Skill class is attached, as a small rectangle, to the Resource class to indicate that a Resource class object and a SkillId value are used to partition or select zero or one Skill class object. The SkillId attribute attached to the Resource class is called a *quali-fier*. The multiplicity on the association is changed to "0..1" to specify that pairing a Resource class object and a qualifier value may or may not select a Skill class object. That is, not every Resource class object must be associated with a Skill class object. There are situations where a particular resource simply does not have an associated skill.

This collection of class diagrams is used to understand the system's structure. They are elaborated with more and more detail until they can be virtually implemented. Classes, associations, attributes, and operations are usually described in a textual document that accompanies the class diagrams. The combination of these class diagrams and their supporting documentation is known as a *class model*. This model is often referred to as an *object model* because it represents the possible configurations of objects within the system.

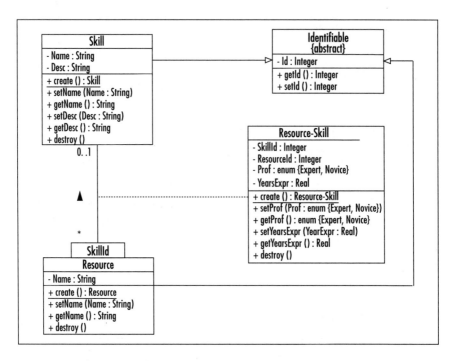

Figure 4-10: Detailed Skills and Resources Class Diagram

Class diagrams are described in greater detail in Chapter 7.

Object Diagrams

Object diagrams describe the static structure of a system at a particular time. Whereas a class model describes all possible situations, an object model describes a particular situation. Object diagrams contain the following elements:

- *Objects*, which represent particular entities. These are instances of classes.

- *Links*, which represent particular relationships between objects. These are instances of associations.

Figure 4-11 shows a project named "Human Resource System Development" that consists of three activities. The first activity is named "Scope" and consists of two tasks. The first task is named "Review," and the second task is named "Scope." As you can see, the same name can be assigned to two different elements (here, an activity and a task) without confusion in the UML.

The second activity is named "AnalysisDesign" and consists of two tasks. The first task is named "Analysis," and the second task is named "Design." The third activity is named "Implementation" and consists of three tasks. The first task is named "Code," the second task is named "Test," and the third task is named "Deploy." The rectangles in this diagram represent objects, and the paths represents links. The object names are underlined and indicate the class of the object. Each object has actual values for their attributes.

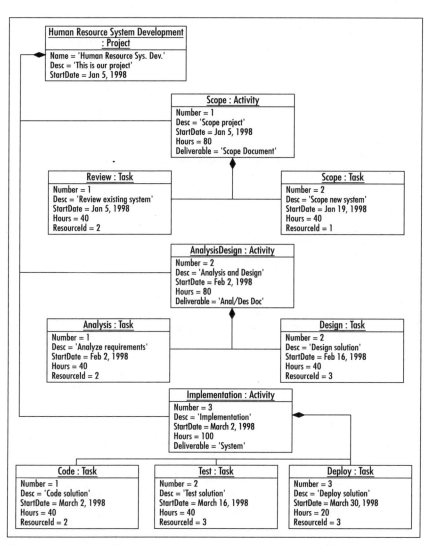

Figure 4-11: Project Object Diagram

All the multiplicity rules identified in the class diagram are adhered to; that is, each task belongs to only one activity, each activity contains one or more tasks, each activity belongs to one project, and each project contains one or more activities.

Figure 4-12 shows resources and their skills. To understand the connections, follow the lines from each Resource class object to the related Skill class object. Each Resource class object represents a person in this figure, and the attributes of each person's skills are shown in the Resource-Skill class objects connected by a dotted line to the relationships to Skill class objects.

For instance, Andy has three years' experience in gathering requirements, three years' experience in doing analysis and design, and seven years' experience in

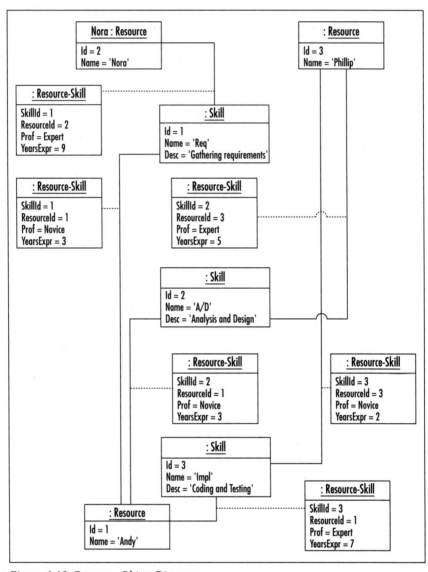

Figure 4-12: Resource Object Diagram

coding and testing. Andy is represented as an object. Notice that the object has no name, but is identified by its attributes. Such an object is called an *anonymous object.* This emphasizes the idea that an object need not be identified by its name, but instead may be identified by its characteristics (here, Id and Name). A name is useful if we want to refer to an object independent of the values of its characteristics. Each of Andy's skills are objects of the Skill class, and each relationship between the object representing Andy and his skills has an associated Resource-Skill class object.

Phillip has two years' experience in coding and testing, and five years' experience in doing analysis and design. Notice that the Skill class objects are shared between the Resource class objects, but the information about the relationships is actually maintained within Resource-Skill class objects.

Nora has nine years' experience in gathering requirements. Notice that the Resource class object representing Nora is named "Nora." This is optional.

Object diagrams are often used to validate the class model of a system. If we discover an object diagram that invalidates the class model, we must either change the class model or determine that the object diagram is invalid. For example, Figure 4-13 shows a project named "Payroll System Development" in which the Task class object named "Design" belongs to the Activity class object named "AnalysisDesign" and the Activity class object named "Implementation." This invalidates the rule, within the class model, that a task may only belong to one activity. We either must change the class model to support this possibility or determine that the object diagram is invalid. In this case, the object diagram is ill formed, and the rule is valid.

Object diagrams are described in greater detail in Chapter 7.

Sequence Diagrams

Sequence diagrams describe interactions among classes. These interactions are modeled as exchanges of messages. These diagrams focus on classes and the messages they exchange to accomplish some desired behavior. Sequence diagrams are a type of interaction diagram. Sequence diagrams contain the following elements:

- *Class roles*, which represent roles that objects may play within the interaction.

- *Lifelines*, which represent the existence of an object over a period of time.

- *Activations*, which represent the time during which an object is performing an operation.

- *Messages*, which represent communication between objects.

Figure 4-14 elaborates the Assign Skill to Resource use case. It shows how a resource manager uses the system to assign a skill to a resource, and how the classes within the system work together to provide this functionality. The objects at the top of the diagram represent class roles. They are named just like objects since they represent the objects that participate in the interaction. The dashed lines that extend from each object represent lifelines. The thin rectangles placed on lifelines represent activations. The horizontal arrows between lifelines indicate the messages exchanged between objects. The horizontal arrows are labeled with the message that is sent between the class roles. A message triggers an operation in the receiving object.

A resource manager will use the resource manager window, which is a user interface, to find a resource, find a skill, and assign the skill to the resource. The resource manager window will find a resource using a Resource class object, and a skill using a Skill class object. The window will assign a skill to a resource if the skill is not already assigned to the resource. This condition is called a *guard condition*

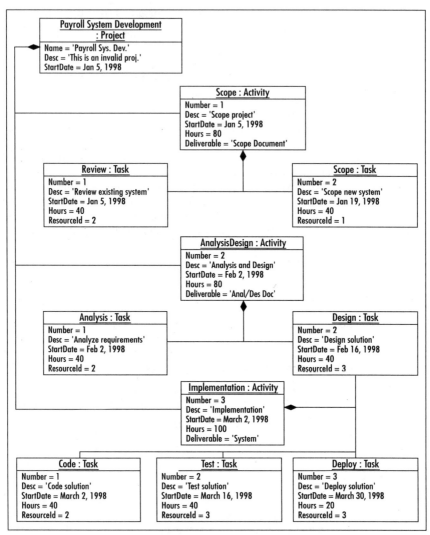

Figure 4-13: Invalid Project Object Diagram

and is indicated within square brackets on the message originating from the window lifeline to the Resource-Skill class role.

Figure 4-15 shows how a resource manger assigns the "A/D" skill to Nora. The class roles represent actual objects, which are anonymous in this case. The messages are replaced with actual messages sent between the objects. Notice that the condition on the message originating from the window lifeline to the Resource-Skill class role is satisfied and the message is sent. This diagram is called a *scenario* since it shows one possible use of the sequence diagram in Figure 4-14.

Figure 4-16 shows a scenario in which a resource manager assigns the "Impl" skill to Andy. The message originating from the window lifeline to the Resource-Skill

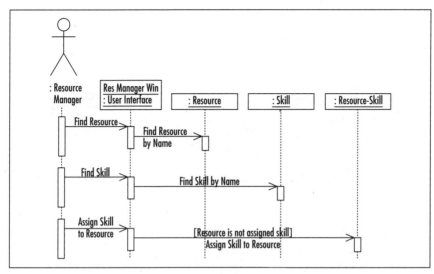

Figure 4-14: Assign Skill to Resource Sequence Diagram

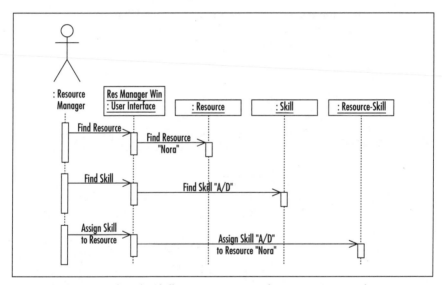

Figure 4-15: Assign the A/D Skill to Nora Scenario (Sequence Diagram)

class role is not shown since this skill is already assigned to Andy and the guard condition is not satisfied. This scenario and the scenario of Figure 4-15 are both satisfied by the sequence diagram of Figure 4-14. Just as object diagrams may be used to validate class models, scenarios validate sequence diagrams.

Figure 4-17 elaborates the Remove Project use case. It shows how a project manager uses the system to remove a project from the database, and how the classes within the system work together to provide this functionality. The rectangles enclosing a

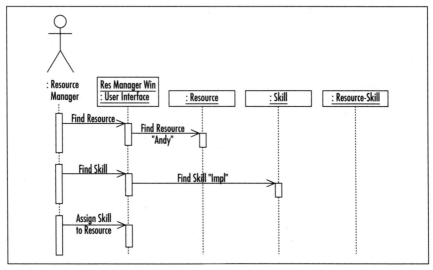

Figure 4-16: Assign the Impl Skill to Andy Scenario (Sequence Diagram)

set of messages represent *repetition,* or a loop. The condition for exiting a loop is shown at the bottom of the rectangle ("No More Tasks" or "No More Activities").

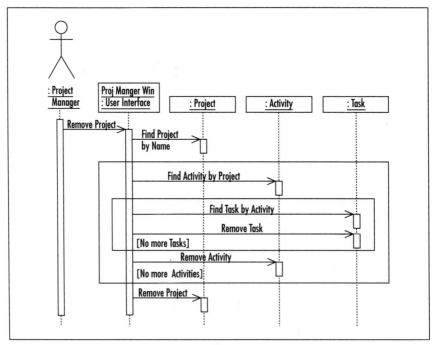

Figure 4-17: Remove Project Sequence Diagram (Version 1)

A project manager will use the project manager window, which is a user interface, to specify a project to remove. Then the project manager window will find the project using a Project class object. Once the project is found, the project manager window will repeatedly find the activities within the project, remove their tasks, and remove the activities. The window uses an Activity class object to find and remove activities, and a Task class object to find and remove tasks. The repetition continues until all the tasks and activities are removed. The window completes processing by removing the project entry from the database.

Figure 4-18 is equivalent to Figure 4-17. The only difference is in how the repetition is depicted. In this case, the loops are not represented using rectangles but using a dashed line with an attached constraint string. The constraint string specifies the extent of the loop, and the dashed line specifies those messages that are sent within the loop. The two diagrams are simply two alternative conventions for representing the same loops.

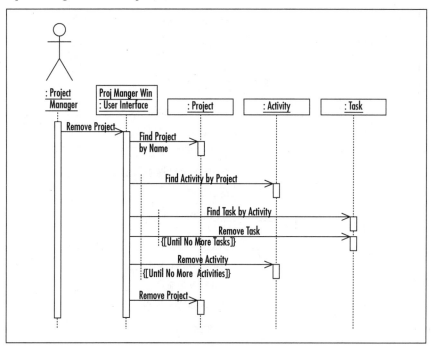

Figure 4-18: Remove Project Sequence Diagram (Version 2)

Figure 4-19 shows a scenario in which a project manager removes the "Human Resource System Development" project, modeled by Figure 4-11, from the system. Notice that all the loops within the diagram are removed, and the messages sent within the loops are shown. Again, this scenario is used to validate the sequence diagrams of Figures 4-17 and 4-18.

Figure 4-20 elaborates the Backup System use case. It shows how a system administrator uses the system to back up the database, and how the Backup System actor is used within this interaction. Because the Backup System actor is actually another system and not part of the original system, the two are concurrently active and

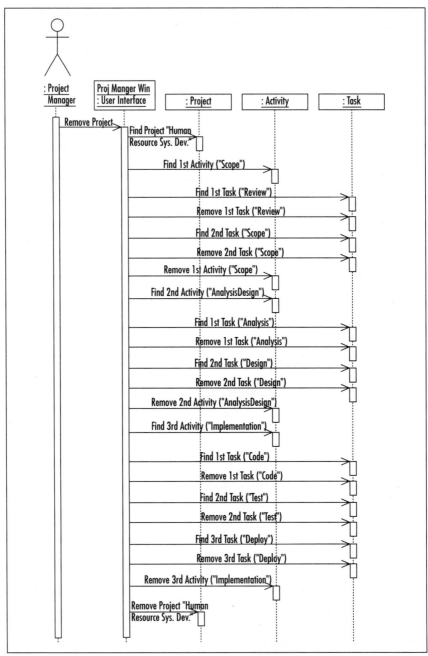

Figure 4-19: Remove Project Scenario (Sequence Diagram)

communicate in an asynchronous manner. Both systems are active, as indicated by the "active" constraint attached to their names. An active object or system may request services from other objects. Furthermore, two active objects may communicate asynchronously. The half-arrowhead messages represent *asynchronous messages* sent between objects. An asynchronous message indicates that the sender does not wait for the receiver to return control before continuing. *Synchronous messages* (represented by full arrowheads) indicate that the sender actually passes control to the receiver and waits until control is returned before continuing. The diagram shows how the systems will send messages back and forth asynchronously to coordinate the backing up of all the projects, their activities, and their tasks.

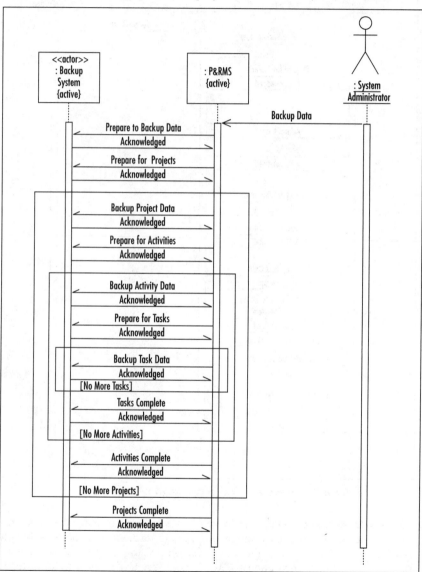

Figure 4-20: Back Up Project Data Sequence Diagram (Version 1)

UML Tutorial

Figure 4-21 is equivalent to Figure 4-20. The only difference is in how the repetition is depicted, using dashed lines rather than rectangles.

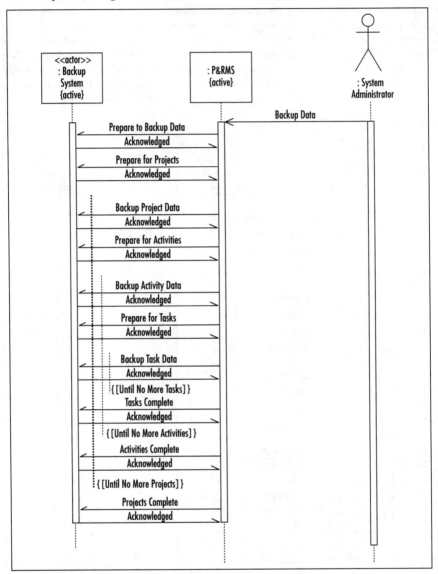

Figure 4-21: Back Up Project Data Sequence Diagram (Version 2)

Figure 4-22 shows a scenario in which a system administrator backs up the "Human Resource System Development" project data. All the loops within the diagram are removed, and the messages sent within the loops are shown. Messages are sent asynchronously. Again, this scenario is used to validate the sequence diagrams of Figures 4-20 and 4-21.

Figure 4-22: Back Up Project Data Scenario (Sequence Diagram)

UML Tutorial

Sequence diagrams are used to understand the messages (and operations) that classes within a system must support in order to perform some desired behavior or functionality. Scenarios are used to validate sequence diagrams, and a collection of sequence diagrams is part of the *dynamic model* of a system. Sequence diagrams are said to *specify* use cases because they specify the messages exchanged between class roles to realize use cases. Sequence diagrams are described in greater detail in Chapter 9.

Collaboration Diagrams

Collaboration diagrams describe interactions among classes and associations. These interactions are modeled as exchanges of messages between classes through their associations. Collaboration diagrams are a type of interaction diagram. Collaboration diagrams contain the following elements:

- *Class roles*, which represent roles that objects may play within the interaction.

- *Association roles*, which represent roles that links may play within the interaction.

- *Message flows*, which represent messages sent between objects via links. Links transport or implement the delivery of the messages.

Figure 4-23 elaborates the Assign Skill to Resource use case. It shows how a resource manager uses the system to assign a skill to a resource, and how the classes and their associations within the system work together to provide this functionality. The objects in rectangles represent class roles. The links (lines or paths) represent association roles. Class roles are named just like objects since they represent the objects that participate in the interaction. The arrows between class roles indicate message flows exchanged between objects. The message flows are labeled with both the sequence number of the message and the message that is sent between the class roles. A message triggers an operation in the receiving object.

The sequence numbers indicate the sequence of messages within the next higher level of nesting or passing of control. Each collaboration diagram starts with message 1. Messages that differ in one integer form a sequence at the same level of nesting. Within nesting level 1, message 1.1 precedes message 1.2, and message 1.2 precedes message 1.3, etc. Among nesting levels (or when messages originate from different class roles), messages are concurrent; that is, message 1 and message 2 are concurrent when originating from different class roles. Other numbering schemes may also be used, but they must be defined in the context in which they are used. Figure 4-23 is equivalent to Figure 4-14.

A resource manager will use the resource manager window, which is a user interface, to find a resource, find a skill, and assign the skill to the resource. The resource manager window will find a resource using a Resource class object, and a skill using a Skill class object. The window will assign a skill to a resource if the resource is not already assigned the skill. This condition is called a *guard condition* and is indicated within square brackets on the message flow originating from the window class role to the Resource-Skill class role.

Figure 4-24 shows how a resource manger assigns the "A/D" skill to Nora. The class roles represent actual objects, which are anonymous in this case. The

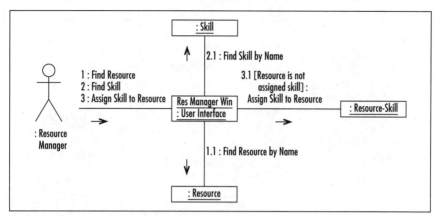

Figure 4-23: Assign Skill to Resource Collaboration Diagram

message flows are replaced with actual messages sent between the objects. Notice that the condition on the message originating from the window class role to the Resource-Skill class role is satisfied and the message is sent. This diagram is called a *scenario* since it shows one possible use of the collaboration diagram.

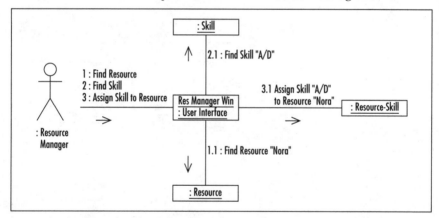

Figure 4-24: Assign the A/D Skill to Nora Scenario (Collaboration Diagram)

Figure 4-25 shows a scenario in which a resource manager assigns the "Impl" skill to Andy. The message flow originating from the window class role to the Resource-Skill class role is not shown since this skill is already assigned to Andy and the guard condition is not satisfied. This scenario and the scenario of Figure 4-24 are both satisfied by the collaboration diagram of Figure 4-23. Just as object diagrams may be used to validate class models, scenarios may be used to validate collaboration diagrams as well as sequence diagrams. The validation involves both the class roles used within the collaboration and the association roles that exist between the class roles.

Figure 4-26 elaborates the Remove Project use case. It shows how a project manager uses the system to remove a project from the database, and how the

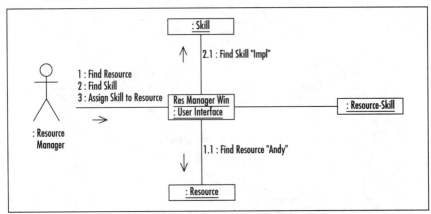

Figure 4-25: Assign the Impl Skill to Andy Scenario (Collaboration Diagram)

classes and their associations within the system work together to provide this functionality. The constraint strings enclosing an asterisk represent repetition, or a loop. The specification of the loop is enclosed in square brackets.

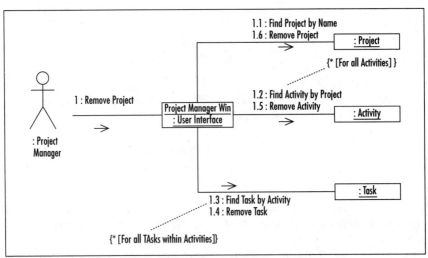

Figure 4-26: Remove Project Collaboration Diagram

A project manager will use the project manager window, which is a user interface, to specify a project to remove. Then the project manager window will find the project using a Project class object. Once the project is found, the project manager window will repeatedly find the activities within the project, remove their tasks, and remove the activities. The window uses an Activity class object to find and remove activities, and a Task class object to find and remove tasks. The repetition continues until all the tasks and activities are removed. The window completes processing by removing the project entry from the database.

Figure 4-27 shows a scenario in which a project manager removes the "Human Resource System Development" project from the system. Notice that all of the loops are removed, and the messages sent between class roles are shown. Again, this scenario is used to validate the collaboration diagram of Figure 4-26.

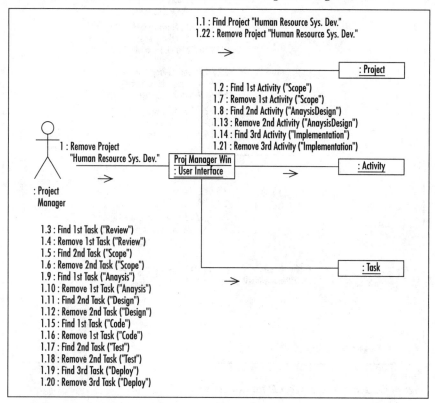

Figure 4-27: Remove Project Scenario (Collaboration Diagram)

Figure 4-28 elaborates the Backup System use case. It shows how a system administrator uses the system to back up the database, and how the Backup System actor is used within this interaction. Because the Backup System actor is actually another system and not part of the original system, the two are concurrently active and communicate in an asynchronous manner. Both systems are active, as indicated by the "active" constraint attached to their names. The diagram shows how the systems will send messages back and fourth asynchronously to coordinate the backing up of all the projects, their activities, and their tasks.

Some of the sequence numbers are preceded by other sequence numbers and a forward slash. The sequence numbers before the forward slash specify the messages that must have occurred to enable the message flow. This is used to synchronize concurrent active objects. All messages originating from the Backup System actor are synchronized with the messages from the other system, and all messages originating from the other system are synchronized with the messages from the Backup System actor.

Figure 4-29 shows a scenario in which a system administrator backs up the "Human Resource System Development" project data. All the loops within the diagram are

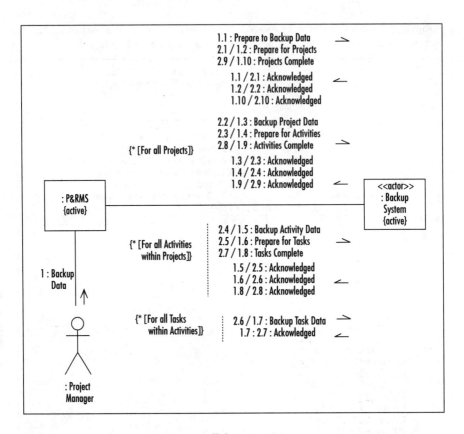

Figure 4-28: Back Up Project Data Collaboration Diagram

removed, and the message flows are shown with their synchronization. Again, this scenario is used to validate the collaboration diagram of Figure 4-28.

Collaboration diagrams are used to understand the messages (and operations) that classes within a system must support in order to perform some desired behavior or functionality, and the associations that must exist between classes to enable the messages to flow among them. Scenarios are used to validate collaboration diagrams, and a collection of collaboration diagrams are part of the dynamic model of a system. Collaboration diagrams are said to *realize* use cases because they specify the messages exchanged between class roles and their association roles. A collaboration diagram is really the result of overlaying the messages from a sequence diagram onto a class diagram. Collaboration diagrams are described in greater detail in Chapter 10.

Statechart Diagrams

Statechart (or state) diagrams describe the states and responses of a class. Statechart diagrams describe the behavior of a class in response to external stimuli. These diagrams contain the following elements:

- *States*, which represent the situations during the life of an object in which it satisfies some condition, performs some activity, or waits for some occurrence.

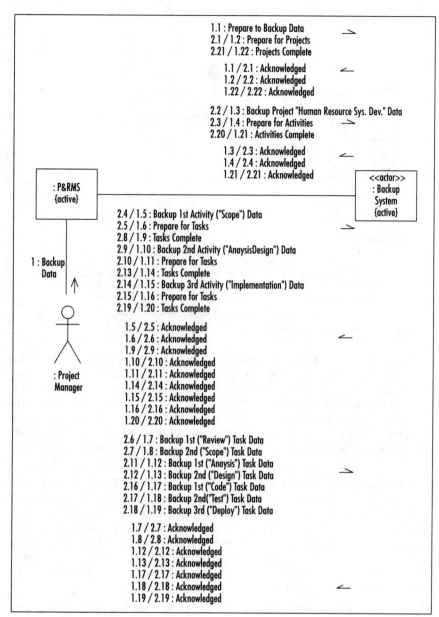

Figure 4-29: Back Up Project Data Scenario (Collaboration Diagram)

- *Transitions*, which represent relationships between the different states of an object.

Figure 4-30, a statechart diagram that might be associated with our sample project, shows that a resource may be assigned no tasks or may be assigned some tasks. The rectangles with rounded corners represent states. Each state has a name. The figure also shows that a resource is initially not assigned to any tasks. The small filled circle with an arrow points to the *initial state*.

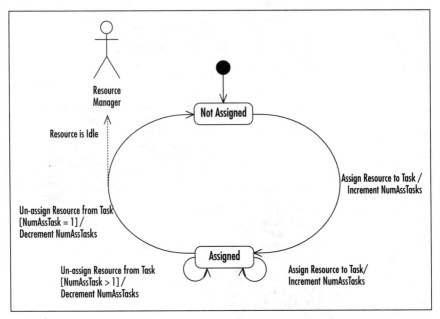

Figure 4-30: Resource Statechart Diagram

Assigning a task to a resource changes it from the Not Assigned state to the Assigned state. The solid arrow between these two states represents a transition. The transition is labeled with an event that triggers the transition, and an action that results from the transition. In this case, the NumAssTasks is incremented to keep track of the number of tasks assigned to the resource. When a resource is assigned, the resource may be assigned more tasks, in which case the resource remains in the Assigned state and the NumAssTasks attribute is incremented.

When a resource is unassigned from a task, the NumAssTasks attribute is decremented. An old value greater than 1 leaves the resource in the Assigned state, whereas an old value of exactly 1 causes a state transition so that the resource is in the Not Assigned state. The effect of unassigning a resource thus depends on a condition, which is specified in square brackets following the event that triggers the transition. When the resource returns to the Not Assigned state, a message is sent to inform the resource manager that the resource is idle. The dashed arrow from the transition to the Resource Manager actor represents a message sent to the object when the transition fires.

Figure 4-31 shows that when the overall system to which all the models belong (P&RMS) and the Backup System are deployed, they will both be inactive, and the P&RMS's state will depend on the state of the Backup System. The short heavy bar with two transitions leaving it represents a *splitting of control*. That is, when the incoming transition to "Deploy Systems" fires, two resulting transitions fire and multiple states become active.

When both systems are inactive, we may retire the systems concurrently. The short heavy bar with two transitions entering it represents a *synchronization of control.*

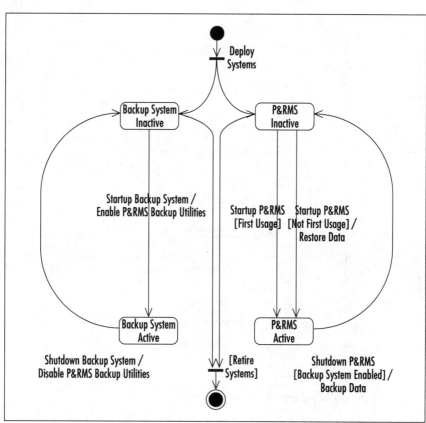

Figure 4-31: System Statechart Diagram

That is, when all the incoming transitions fire, the resulting transition fires. Once the two systems are retired, nothing else occurs. The circle surrounding a smaller filled circle represents the *final state*. Once the final state is reached, the objects whose states are depicted in the diagram are destroyed.

The left side shows that when the Backup System is started, the P&RMS backup utility is enabled. When the Backup System is shut down, the P&RMS backup utility is disabled. The right side of Figure 4-31 shows that when the P&RMS is started for the first time, the system simply becomes active. However, when the P&RMS is shut down and the Backup System is enabled, the Back Up Data action occurs and the system enters the P&RMS Inactive state. Then, when the P&RMS system is restarted (not the first use), the system becomes active and data is restored from the Backup System.

Figure 4-32 elaborates the P&RMS Active state by detailing the states of the different parts of the system.

When the P&RMS becomes active, the resource manager functionality, project manager functionality, and system administrator functionality are all inactive. The P&RMS Active state is called a *superstate* and has its name displayed at the top of

UML Tutorial

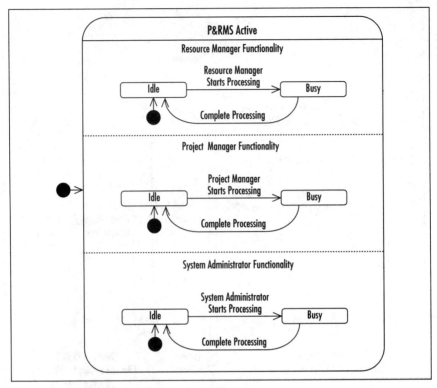

Figure 4-32: System Substate Statechart Diagram

the state. The superstate is divided into three concurrent *substates* for each part of the system. When a resource manager starts processing, the parts of the system that provide the resource manager functionality become busy until the processing is complete. Similar effects take place when a project manager starts processing or a system administrator starts processing.

Statechart diagrams are used to understand the messages (and operations) and attributes that classes within a system must support in order to perform some desired behavior or functionality. These diagrams are part of the dynamic model of a system. Statechart diagrams are described in greater detail in Chapter 11.

Activity Diagrams

Activity diagrams describe the activities of a class. These diagrams are similar to statechart diagrams and use similar conventions, but activity diagrams describe the behavior of a class in response to internal processing rather than external events as in statechart diagrams. These diagrams contain the following elements:

- *Swimlanes,* which represent responsibilities of one or more objects for actions within an overall activity; that is, they divide the activity states into groups and assign these groups to objects that must perform the activities.

- *Action states*, which represent atomic, or noninterruptible, actions of entities or steps in the execution of an algorithm.

- *Action flows*, which represent relationships between the different action states of an entity.

- *Object flows*, which represent the utilization of objects by action states and the influence of action states on objects.

Figure 4-33 shows how the Assign Skill to Resource use case is performed. The figure shows how the classes within the system work together and perform actions to provide this functionality: A Resource class object will find the resource by name, a Skill class object will find the skill by name, and a Resource-Skill class object will assign the skill to the resource. The regions denoted by vertical solid lines are swimlanes, and the objects at the top of the swimlanes are responsible for the action states within the swimlane. The shapes with straight top and bottom lines and convex arcs on the sides are action states.

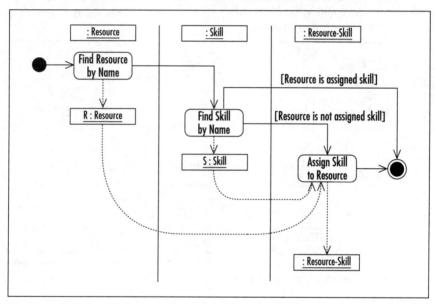

Figure 4-33: Assign Skill to Resource Activity Diagram

After a resource is found by name, the skill is found by name and is assigned to the resource. The solid arrows represent action flows that are automatically triggered at the completion of the action states. Notice that an initial and a final state are used, as in statechart diagrams.

Once a resource is found by name, a resource object is created. Once a skill is found by name, a skill object is created. Assigning a skill to a resource uses the two objects created by the previous steps. The dashed arrows represent object flows. Object flows originating from an action state indicate that the action creates or influences the object. Object flows from an object to an action state indicate that the action state uses the object.

Activity diagrams are similar to statechart diagrams. These diagrams are used to understand the operations that classes within a system must support in order to perform some desired behavior or functionality, and to understand how these objects interact with other objects in the system. These diagrams are part of the dynamic model of a system. Activity diagrams are described in greater detail in Chapter 12.

Component Diagrams

Component diagrams describe the organization of and dependencies among software implementation components. These diagrams contain *components,* which represent distributable physical units, including source code, object code, and executable code.

Figure 4-34 shows the development-time and run-time physical objects implementing the system. The rectangles with two small rectangles projected from the side represent components. The small labeled circle attached via a line to a component represents an interface.

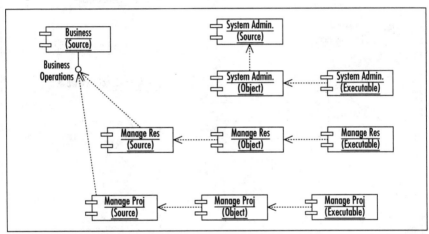

Figure 4-34: System Component Diagram

The object code components are dependent on their associated source code components. The dashed arrows represent *dependencies* between components. Thus, in Figure 4-34, the System Administrator executable program is dependent on the System Administrator object code component, and the System Administrator object code component is dependent on the System Administrator source code file. Similar dependencies are shown for the Manage Resource and Manage Project executable programs. Their source code files use the business operations provided by the Business component.

Component diagrams are described in greater detail in Chapter 13.

Deployment Diagrams

Deployment diagrams describe the configuration of processing resource elements and the mapping of software implementation components onto them. These diagrams contain components and *nodes,* which represent processing or computational resources, including computers, printers, and so forth.

Figure 4-35 shows that the resource manager application will execute on a resource manager desktop client computer. The three-dimensional cubes represent nodes. This figure also shows that the project manager application will execute on a project manager desktop client computer. Both types of computers have access to printers and an application server. The solid paths represent lines of communication between nodes.

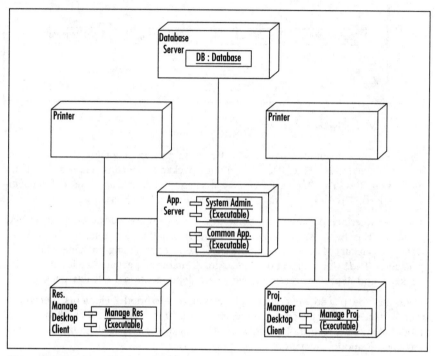

Figure 4-35: System Deployment Diagram

The system administrator application and other common application components will execute on the server and access a database server containing the database object named "DB."

Deployment diagrams are described in greater detail in Chapter 14.

Other Notation and Information

Figure 4-36 shows how model elements may be grouped into packages and related. The large rectangles with a small rectangle attached on one corner represent packages. *Packages* are general-purpose grouping mechanisms used to organize model elements. They are used within the other diagrams.

In Figure 4-36, the User Interface package contains classes that implement the user interface of a system. The Business package contains classes that represent business objects. The Communication package contains classes that are used to

---

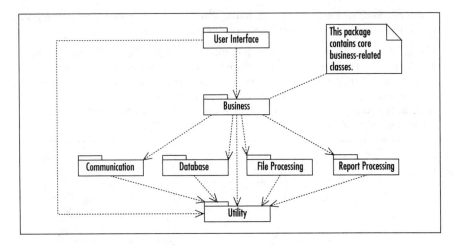

Figure 4-36: Packages

communicate with other systems. The Database package contains classes used to access a database. The File Processing package contains classes used for processing files. The Report Processing package contains classes used for generating reports. The Utility package contains general utility classes.

The User Interface package is dependent on the Business package and the Utility package. The Business package is dependent on the Communication package, Database package, File Processing package, Report Processing package, and Utility package. The Communication package, Database package, File Processing package, and Report Processing package are dependent on the Utility package.

Notes may be placed on diagrams to attach text to model elements. Rectangles with a bent upper right corner represent notes. They may be attached to specific model elements using dashed lines or attached to the whole diagram rather than any specific model element.

Packages, notes, and general diagramming are described in greater detail in Chapter 6.

Figure 4-37 shows a class diagram with rules or constraints attached to different elements. All projects in this diagram must start before January 1, 1999. The *constraint* string attached to the Project class represents this rule, to which all objects of the class must adhere.

All activities must belong to projects that start after January 1, 1998. The constraint string attached to the Activity class represents this rule. The term "project" references the Project class object of or linked with an Activity object, and the StartDate references the StartDate attribute of the Project class object. Note that there may only be one Project class object for any Activity class object (as specified by the multiplicity).

All resources must have less than 15 tasks assigned to them. The constraint string attached to the Resource class represents this rule. The term "task" references the collection of Task class objects of the Resource object, and the "size" is a predefined attribute of a collection (as explained in Chapter 16). Note that there

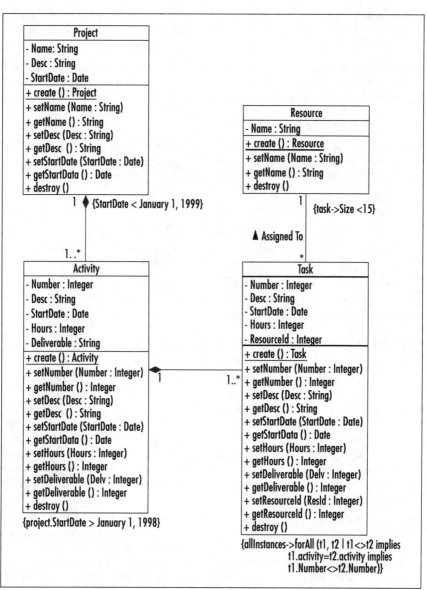

Figure 4-37: Detailed Project Class Diagram with OCL Expressions

may be any number of Task class objects associated with any Resource class objects (as specified by the multiplicity); this is why the arrow operator is used.

No two tasks within the same activity may have the same number. The constraint string attached to the Task class represents this rule. The "forAll" specifies that all objects of the class are iterated over. The "t1" variable references one object, and the "t2" variable references another object. "t1<>t2" dictates that we have two different tasks. If we do, "t1.activity=t2.activity" dictates that the tasks belong to the same activity, and, if so, the task numbers should be different. If this rule fails for any objects, the object model is ill formed.

The Object Constraint Language (OCL) is a language for expressing conditions attached to model elements. When attached to a class, these expressions specify rules to which objects of the class must adhere. The OCL is described in greater detail in Chapter 16. Some expressions can be very complex, and a natural language may be used in place of the OCL.

Figure 4-38 shows four different ways to represent an actor. An actor is a stereo-type of a class. The string "actor" enclosed in guillemets (<< >>), or double angle brackets, preceding the name of the element indicates the type of the element.

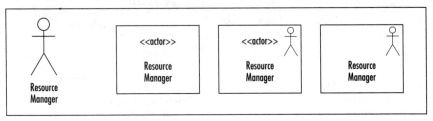

Figure 4-38: Stereotypes

The UML allows new types of elements to be established using a stereotype. Once a new type of element is established, there are four ways to depict an instance of the element: an icon, a stereotype string, both an icon and a stereotype string, or an icon with a class rectangle.

Figure 4-39 shows a project manager who is removing a project. Stereotype icons are used within the diagram to emphasize the types of objects involved. The Project Manager Window is an interface class. The Remove Project is a control class that is responsible for controlling interactions among a collection of objects. The Project, Activity, and Task classes are entity stereotypes representing database information. These stereotypes are predefined in the UML, and are explained in Chapter 15.

Figure 4-40 shows a Skill class with two properties or characteristics. The first property is a constraint specifying that an object of the class is created, and the second property is called a *keyword-value pair* or *tagged value*. The second prop-erty indicates that objects of the class have a keyword "documentation" and a value associated with this keyword. *Properties* of model elements are used by modeling tools and enable us to associate information with model elements.

The UML stereotypes enable the UML to be extended with new types of modeling elements, and properties enable the UML to be customized to support specialized characteristics of model elements. These are called *extension mechanisms*. They are described in greater detail in Chapter 15, including the standard stereotypes, constraints, and tagged values.

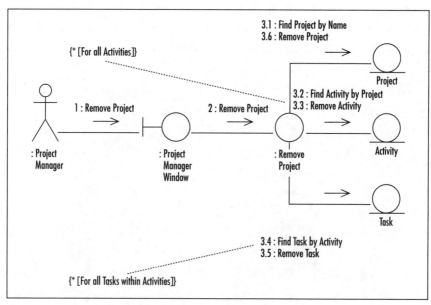

Figure 4-39: Remove Project Collaboration Diagram

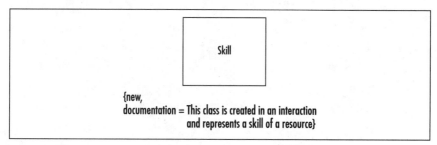

Figure 4-40: Constraints and Tagged Values

CHAPTER 5

UML Overview

This chapter presents an overview of the constituent parts of the UML, how they relate to one another, and how they contribute to a method or process utilizing the UML. The chapter provides a framework for understanding:

- An overall view of the constituent parts of the UML.

- How the UML renders knowledge about a problem or solution.

- How the UML facilitates problem solving and the application of knowledge.

I start with the architecture of the UML and the metamodel that defines the UML. I then introduce the details of how the UML provides a set of diagrams organized around architectural views for viewing problems and solutions. I also discuss how the UML relates to problem solving and how the diagrams may be used. The complete details of each diagram type are found in the reference chapters.

Architecture

Models are complete abstractions of systems, and diagrams are graphical projections of models or subsets of models. The UML is defined in a circular manner, in which a subset of the language notation and semantics is used to specify the language itself. The UML is defined within a conceptual framework for modeling that consists of four distinct layers or levels of abstraction (Chapter 3). This framework is based on the most fundamental UML notation that concepts are depicted as symbols, and relationships among concepts are depicted as paths (lines) connecting symbols. Both of these types of elements may be named. The concepts introduced by the UML are organized around architectural views (Chapter 2) to define the various diagrams. The UML diagrams are used to understand or conceptualize a problem, solve the problem, and implement or realize the solution.

To understand the UML architecture, consider how computer programs and programming languages are related. We develop programs in many different programming languages (C, C++, Java, etc.), and each particular program is

111

developed using a specific programming language. All programming languages support declarative constructs for declaring data, and procedural constructs for sequential, conditional, and repetitive logic. A model is an abstraction (Chapter 2). Therefore, these programming language concepts may be defined in a model called a *metamodel*. Each particular programming language may be defined in a model that utilizes and specializes the concepts within the metamodel. Each program implemented in a programming language may be defined in a model called a *user model* that utilizes and instantiates the concepts within the model of the appropriate language. This scheme of a metamodel representing computer programming constructs, models representing computer programming languages, and user models representing computer programs exemplifies the architecture of the UML.

The first level, within the conceptual framework for modeling, consists of the most basic element on which the UML is based, as depicted in Figure 5-1. The concept of a "Thing" represents anything that may be defined. Since this is the basis for all models, it is called the *meta-metamodel* and is used to formalize the notion of a concept.

The next level consists of those elements that constitute the UML, as depicted in Figure 5-2. This level introduces the concepts within the object-oriented paradigm. The Class concept is an instance of the meta-metamodel Thing concept. *Classes* are descriptions of a set of objects with common structural features, behavioral features, relationships, and semantics. They are used to model a set of entities with common characteristics. The Object concept is an instance of the meta-metamodel Thing concept. *Objects* are instances of classes. They are used to model particular entities. The Association concept is an instance of the meta-metamodel Thing concept. *Associations* are descriptions of a set of links with common structural features, behavioral features, relationships, and semantics. They are used to model a set of relationships that relate two or more other entities where the relationships have common characteristics. The Link concept is an instance of the meta-metamodel Thing concept. *Links* are instances of associations. They are used to model instances of relationships that relate two or more other objects. Associations relate classes, and links relate objects, as depicted in Figure 5-1 using the Relate relationship. Links are instances of associations, and objects are instances of classes, as depicted in Figure 5-1 using the "Instance of" relationship. These concepts are classes, and the paths connecting them are associations. This layer is called the *metamodel layer* and is used to formalize concepts within a paradigm.

Figure 5-3 completes the metamodel by introducing the multiplicity between the classes. The *multiplicity* specifies how many objects of a class are associated with a single object of the other class in the association. Any number (zero or more) of links may relate the same object, as depicted by a "*" string near the Link class and the Relate association leading to the Object class. A link may relate one or more objects, as depicted by a "1..*" string near the Object class and the Relate association leading to the Link class. The association between the Association class and the Class class specifies that each association must involve one or more classes, and each class may participate in zero or more associations. The association between the Link class and the Association class specifies that each link must be an instance of one association, and each association may have zero or more links.

The association between the Object class and the Class class specifies that each object must be an instance of one or more classes, and each class may have zero or more objects.

The next level consists of UML models. This is the level at which modeling of problems and solutions is done. Figure 5-4 shows that a person can be a member of only one team, and a team will have zero or more members. This layer is called the *model layer* and is used to formalize the concepts for a given subject, in this case, how people are related to teams. This layer corresponds to class diagrams, sequence diagrams, or collaboration diagrams.

The next level consists of those elements that exemplify UML models. Figure 5-5 shows that Si, Andy, Phillip, and Nora are all people. Si and Andy are members of the Requirements team, and Nora and Phillip are members of an unnamed team. Each object is depicted by specifying and underlining the name of the object followed by a colon and the class of the object. Each link is depicted by specifying the name of the association on the path connecting the objects. Figure 5-6 shows an ill-formed user model since Si belongs to both teams, whereas our model of Figure 5-4 shows that a person can only belong to one team. This layer is called the *user model layer* and is used to formalize specific expressions about a given subject, in this case, that Si and Andy belong to the Requirements team and Nora and Phillip belong to the unnamed team. This layer corresponds to object diagrams or to scenario diagrams of sequence diagrams or collaboration diagrams.

This brief example demonstrates that a metamodel is capable of defining concepts and relationships among concepts. However, it is not used to describe the notation used to render the concepts. Furthermore, because the concepts are defined using natural language, they may have various ambiguous interpretations. Thus, a formal constraint language similar to the Object Constraint Language (OCL) is used to specify constraints or rules for the concepts within the metamodel, and a notation guide is used to depict how concepts are rendered. The metamodel used in this example is not the actual UML metamodel. The UML metamodel is significantly more involved and is briefly discussed in the next section.

Figure 5-1: Meta-metamodel Example

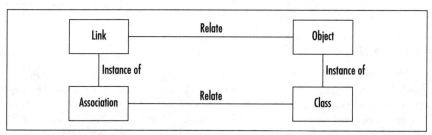

Figure 5-2: Incomplete Metamodel Example

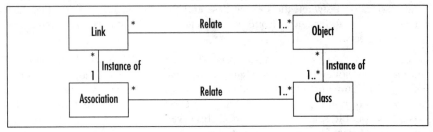

Figure 5-3: Complete Metamodel Example

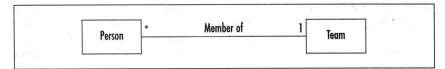

Figure 5-4: Model Example

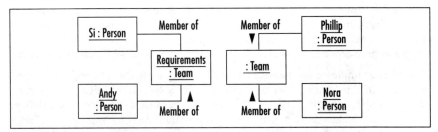

Figure 5-5: User Model Example

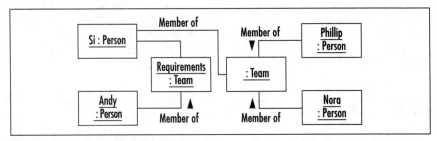

Figure 5-6: Ill-formed User Model Example

Metamodel

The UML metamodel is organized into a collection of logical packages (Figure 5-7). Packages are general-purpose grouping mechanisms used to organize semantically related model elements. The metamodel organizes metamodel elements within packages. Elements within the same package have strong cohesion with each other and loose coupling with elements in other packages. Dashed arrows between two packages or model elements indicate that a relationship exists between the elements, where the source of the dashed arrow is dependent on the

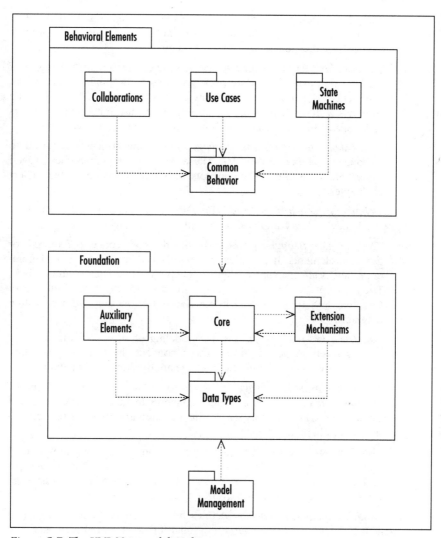

Figure 5-7: The UML Metamodel Architecture

presence or existence of the target of the dashed arrow. The UML is defined within the following packages.

- The *Foundation package* defines the concepts required for structural modeling and the mechanisms for extending the language. These modeling elements let you model the structure of a system. Other modeling elements enable the language to be extended. The Foundation package is composed of the following packages:

  - The *Data Types package* defines different data types used within the UML metamodel.

  - The *Core package* defines the most fundamental concepts of the UML. It actually contains sufficient semantics to define the remainder of the UML, but other packages extend these modeling elements to meet that purpose. Core concepts include classes and associations. The concepts within this package are the subject of Chapter 7.

- The *Auxiliary Elements package* defines other fundamental concepts of the UML that extend the Core package. These concepts include notes or comments, dependencies, templates, components, and nodes. The concepts within this package are appropriately distributed over Chapters 6, 7, 13, and 14 in correlation to how they are used within diagrams.

- The *Extension Mechanisms package* defines the concepts required to customize and extend the UML. These concepts are stereotypes, tagged values, and constraints. The concepts within this package are the subject of Chapter 15.

• The *Behavioral Elements package* defines the concepts required to model a system's behavior. It is composed of the following packages:

- The *Common Behavior package* defines the core concepts required for dynamic elements. It provides the foundation for use cases, collaborations, and state machines. These concepts include signals and actions. The concepts within this package are appropriately distributed over Chapters 8, 9, 10, 11, and 12 in correlation to how they are used within diagrams.

- The *Use Cases package* defines the modeling of an entity's functions, or what it offers to outside users. These concepts include use cases and actors. The concepts within this package are the subject of Chapter 8.

- The *Collaborations package* defines how different elements of a model interact to realize use cases. These concepts include collaborations and interactions. The concepts within this package are appropriately distributed over Chapters 9 and 10.

- The *State Machines package* defines how control and data flow among elements of a model interacting to realize use cases. These concepts include events, states, and transitions. The concepts within this package are appropriately distributed over Chapters 11 and 12.

• The *Model Management package* defines how modeling elements are organized. It defines packages as grouping units for other model elements. The concepts within this package are the subject of Chapter 6.

Architectural Views and Diagrams

The UML metamodel elements are organized into diagrams. Different diagrams are used for different purposes depending on the angle from which you are viewing the system. The different views are called *architectural views* (Figure 5-8). Architectural views facilitate the organization of knowledge, and diagrams enable the communication of knowledge. The knowledge itself is within the model or set of models that focuses on the problem and solution. The architectural views and their diagrams are summarized below.

• The *user model view* encompasses a problem and solution from the perspective of those individuals whose problem the solution addresses. This view pre-

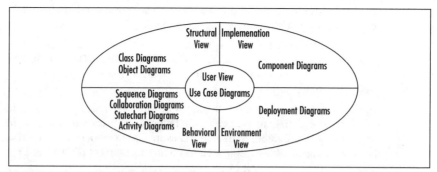

Figure 5-8: Model View and Diagrams

sents the goals and objectives of the problem owners and their requirements of the solution. This view is composed of *use case diagrams*. These diagrams describe the functionality provided by a system to external interactors. These diagrams contain actors, use cases, and their relationships. Use case diagrams are the subject of Chapter 8.

- The *structural model view* encompasses the static, or structural, aspects of a problem and solution. This view is also known as the static or logical view. This view is composed of the following diagrams:

  - *Class diagrams* describe the static structure of a system, or how it is declared rather than how it behaves. These diagrams contain classes and associations.

  - *Object diagrams* describe the static structure of a system at a particular time during its life. These diagrams contain objects and links.

  Class and object diagrams are the subject of Chapter 7.

- The *behavioral model view* encompasses the dynamic, or behavioral, aspects of a problem and solution. This view is also known as the dynamic, process, concurrent, or collaborative view. This view is composed of the following diagrams:

  - *Sequence diagrams* render the specification of behavior. These diagrams describe the behavior provided by a system to interactors. These diagrams contain classes that exchange messages within an interaction arranged in time sequence. In generic form, these diagrams describe a set of message exchange sequences among a set of classes. In instance form (scenarios), these diagrams describe one actual message exchange sequence among objects of those classes. Sequence diagrams are the subject of Chapter 9.

  - *Collaboration diagrams* render how behavior is realized by components within a system. These diagrams contain classes, associations, and their message exchanges within a collaboration to accomplish a purpose. In generic form, these diagrams describe a set of classes and associations involved in message exchange sequences. In instance form (scenarios), these diagrams describe a set of objects of those classes, links conforming to the associations, and one actual message exchange sequence that is consistent with the generic form and uses those objects and links. Collaboration diagrams are the subject of Chapter 10.

- *Statechart diagrams* render the states and responses of a class participating in behavior, and the life cycle of an object. These diagrams describe the behavior of a class in response to external stimuli. State diagrams are the subject of Chapter 11.

- *Activity diagrams* render the activities or actions of a class participating in behavior. These diagrams describe the behavior of a class in response to internal processing rather than external events. Activity diagrams describe the processing activities within a class and are the subject of Chapter 12.

- The *implementation model view* encompasses the structural and behavioral aspects of the solution's realization. This view is also known as the component or development view and is composed of *component diagrams*. These diagrams describe the organization of and dependencies among software implementation components. These diagrams contain components and their relationships. Component diagrams are the subject of Chapter 13.

- The *environment model view* encompasses the structural and behavioral aspects of the domain in which a solution must be realized. This view is also known as the deployment or physical view. This view is composed of *deployment diagrams*. These diagrams describe the configuration of processing resource elements and the mapping of software implementation components onto them. These diagrams contain nodes, components, and their relationships. Deployment diagrams are the subject of Chapter 14.

Mechanisms

When solving a problem, diagrams are used to communicate information about the problem and solution. When modeling and diagramming, there are a number of fundamental mechanisms that enable us to create better or more precise and communicable models. Thus, *mechanisms* are means or tools for approaching modeling and diagramming.

Fundamental to all mechanisms is the idea that information is being communicated for a purpose. When deciding what diagram to use, consider the reason for the communication. That is, what is the question or questions that the communication is addressing? Next, consider what diagram or set of diagrams may be used to most effectively communicate the response. The mechanisms discussed below may be utilized best if this notion of communication is kept in mind.

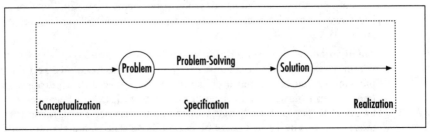

Figure 5-9: Perspectives

The first mechanism involves the perspective through which a diagram is rendered or interpreted. A *perspective* (Figure 5-9) defines a particular point of view from which to draw or read a diagram. The perspective must clearly identify the diagram's subject and goal. One of the following three perspectives should be selected:

- The *conceptualization* perspective is concerned with the problem and is directed at representing the problem in some malleable and communicable form. This is also known as the conceptual perspective of problem solving. This perspective addresses the following questions: What is the problem? What are the requirements of the problem that its solution must satisfy?

- The *specification* perspective is concerned with the problem and solution and is directed at specifying the solution that satisfies the requirements imposed by the problem. This is also known as the logical perspective of problem solving. This perspective addresses the following questions: What is the solution? What are the specifications of the solution that satisfies the requirements imposed by the problem?

- The *realization* perspective is concerned with implementing the solution and is directed at realizing the representation of the solution in some concrete and usable form. This is also known as the physical perspective of problem solving. This perspective addresses the following question: What tools, programs, or activities will realize the solution?

Once a perspective is selected, it should be made evident on the diagram, perhaps using a note (Chapter 6) attached to the diagram. When the diagram is interpreted, the reader will have a clear viewpoint from which to read it. This makes communication using the diagram much more effective, and the reader need not be left guessing as to what perspective was used to render the diagram.

The second mechanism involves the use of various dichotomies. A *dichotomy* defines how something may be viewed from two different perspectives. The following dichotomies are clearly evident:

- The *type-instance* dichotomy allows a generic descriptor to describe many individual items. This is the relationship that exists between a class and its objects, an association and its links, and an interaction and its scenarios. This dichotomy lets you create object diagrams that are combined into class diagrams, or class diagrams that are validated by considering their instantiated object diagrams. This dichotomy also enables scenario diagrams to validate sequence and collaboration diagrams.

- The *specification-realization* dichotomy specifies that knowledge gathered using the specification perspective is elaborated or translated into the realization perspective. This dichotomy allows for the capturing of a specification before a realization: for example, an operation specification before a method realization, a type specification before a class realization, or a sequence diagram specification of a use case before a collaboration diagram realization of the use case.

- The *static-dynamic,* or *structural-behavioral,* dichotomy specifies that knowledge gathered via the structural model view and the behavioral model view are complementary. This dichotomy enables the use of class diagrams to determine the participants of behavioral view diagrams, and the use of behavioral view diagrams to highlight the messages, events, and operations that participants from the structural model view must support. This dichotomy enables the structural model view and the behavioral model view to evolve concurrently and cooperatively from conceptualizing a problem, solving the problem, and realizing the solution.

The use of these dichotomies allows us to collect and represent knowledge using UML diagrams as we progress in problem solving. The dichotomies allow us to relate different diagrams from different perspectives through a problem-solving process.

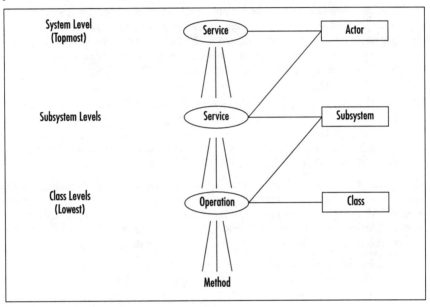

Figure 5-10: Levels of Abstraction

The third mechanism involves the use of *layers* or *levels of abstraction* through which a diagram is rendered or interpreted. A layer defines a particular level of abstraction (Figure 5-10) and establishes a level of detail at which attention and concentration are focused regarding the subject (problem or solution). The level of abstraction at which a diagram is drawn or interpreted must be clearly identified. One of the following layers should be selected:

- The *system level* specifies the complete services offered by a system to actors.

- *Subsystem levels* realize the next higher level of services by specifying the complete services offered by a system or subsystem. Any number of subsystem levels may be used.

- *Class levels* realize the next higher level of services by specifying functional fragments or operations offered by a class. Any number of class levels may be used.

- The *method level* realizes the next higher level of services.

This mechanism is crucial for consolidating all the UML diagrams into a coherent body of knowledge. This mechanism is the key for appropriately using use cases and is the subject of Chapters 6 and 8.

The final mechanism involves the means for customizing and extending the UML. These *extension mechanisms* include the following:

- *Stereotypes* are used for classifying or marking model elements and introducing new types of modeling elements.

- *Tagged values* are used for specifying properties or characteristics of model elements.

- *Constraints* are used for specifying semantics or conditions that must be maintained as true for model elements.

These extensibility mechanisms are fundamental to ensuring that the UML will evolve rather than be redefined to meet the changing needs and demands of its users. They are discussed in Chapter 15.

Problems, Solutions, and Problem Solving

The UML enables and promotes (but does not require or mandate) a process that is

- *Use case driven*, which means that use cases are utilized to
    - Capture requirements and define the behavior or services required of a system by actors, services required of a subsystem by other subsystems, and operations required of a class by other classes.
    - Analyze a problem to address the following questions: What is the problem? What are the requirements of the problem that its solution must satisfy?
    - Design a solution to address the following question: What are the specifications of the solution that satisfies the requirements imposed by the problem?
    - Validate the realization of the solution. Use cases that capture the requirements of the problem are used to validate the solution against the problem.
    - Manage and provide focus for a problem-solving effort. Use cases are work units that may be distributed over a complete project development cycle.

- *Architecture-centric*, which means that architecture is used to
    - Methodically and systematically specify, realize, and validate a solution to a problem.
    - Capture (acquire), enable the communication of (share), and enable the leveraging (utilizing) of knowledge. The knowledge that transpires within a problem-solving effort is organized around architectural views. This organization also emphasizes reuse within the effort and across multiple efforts.
    - Manage complexity and maintain integrity and focus as a solution to a problem evolves and is realized.

- *Iterative and incremental.* An iterative process is repetitive, and an incremental process is evolutionary. A problem-solving effort repeatedly applies a process to evolve a solution to a problem. An iterative and incremental process enables

  - A problem to change as required by those who own the problem. This allows the requirements imposed by a problem on its solution to evolve as a problem evolves.

  - Progressive integration of the different parts of a complex solution rather than a single point of integration.

  - The management of risks within each iteration rather than at a single or few points over the life of a problem-solving effort.

  - A focus on an architecture that evolves over time.

  - A focus on reuse since reusable elements may be identified at the end of each iteration and may be used within the following iterations.

  - A focus on self-improvement and refinement. Each iteration improves on previous iterations and provides lessons for future iterations.

Problems and Solutions

Problems and solutions occur within a context. The problem must be understood in order to be solved. The solution to a problem must be understood in order to be constructed and utilized. The solution must be organized in order to facilitate its realization and adhere to the various constraints of the context (available computer systems, development time, etc.) in which it will be realized. To solve the problem, appropriate knowledge about the problem and solution must be captured, organized around decisions regarding the problem and solution, and depicted using some language so that it can be communicated and leveraged in the problem-solving process.

When deciding what diagram to use for communication, consider the reason for the communication. That is, what is the question or questions the communication is addressing? Then consider what diagram or set of diagrams may be used to most effectively communicate the response. This decision centers on what aspect of a system or society of objects is to be emphasized in the response.

Each diagram emphasizes a particular aspect of the society of objects that constitute a system (Figure 5-11):

- The user model view and use case diagrams emphasize the functionality provided by a society. Use these diagrams to emphasize services and operations that a society offers to entities outside the society.

  Use case diagrams emphasize *functionality*, the services offered by a system to its users.

- The structural model view is composed of the following diagrams:

  - Class diagrams emphasize the static structure of a society.

    Class diagrams emphasize *structure*.

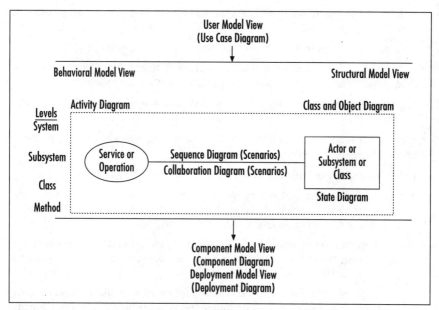

Figure 5-11: Model Views and Diagrams with Levels of Abstraction

- Object diagrams emphasize the static structure of a society at a particular time during its life. Use these diagrams to exemplify and validate the static structure of a society.

    Object diagrams emphasize *examples of structure.*

- The behavioral model view is composed of the following diagrams:

    - Sequence diagrams emphasize the messages exchanged over time among the objects within a society. Use scenarios to exemplify and validate sequence diagrams.

        Sequence diagrams emphasize *classes and messages.*

        Scenario sequence diagrams emphasize *objects and messages.*

    - Collaboration diagrams emphasize the messages exchanged over time among the objects and their links within a society. Use scenarios to exemplify and validate collaboration diagrams.

        Collaboration diagrams emphasize *classes, messages, and associations for propagating messages.*

        Scenario collaboration diagrams emphasize *objects, messages, and links for propagating messages.*

    - Statechart diagrams emphasize how an object changes or responds to external stimuli within a society.

        Statechart diagrams emphasize *changes of state due to messages.*

    - Activity diagrams emphasize how an object changes or responds to internal processing within a society.

        Activity diagrams emphasize the *flow of control and information.*

- The implementation model view and component diagrams emphasize the packaging of an object within a society as a solution.

  Component diagrams emphasize the *packaging of a solution.*

- The behavioral model view and deployment diagrams emphasize the deployment of objects within a society as a solution within an environment.

  Deployment diagrams emphasize the *deployment of a solution in an environment.*

A method must specify the order in which these diagrams are created; however, the following generic order is common:

1. Use case diagrams are used to drive the problem-solving process.

2. Structural diagrams and behavioral diagrams are concurrently used to elaborate a problem or solution. Focus should shift between these two types of diagrams until a solution is derived from a problem.

   - Structural (class and object) diagrams are used to initiate this concurrent process if the structural features of the problem and solution are more easily comprehensible or understood.

   - Sequence diagrams (with scenarios) followed by collaboration diagrams (with scenarios) are used to initiate this concurrent process if the dynamic features of the problem and solution are more easily comprehensible or understood.

   - State diagrams and activity diagrams are used to support the other diagrams.

3. Component diagrams are used to package the solution to a problem.

4. Deployment diagrams are used to determine how a solution is deployed in a specific environment.

Problem Solving

Problems and solutions are societies of objects. Methods specify how problem-solving efforts may be executed. They specify how knowledge is captured and communicated regarding a problem and solution, and the approach used to solve the problem and derive a solution.

Knowledge regarding problems and solutions is communicated using diagrams. While each diagram emphasizes a particular aspect of the society of objects that constitute a system (problem or solution), a method specifies which diagrams to use and the perspective and the level of abstraction used to render and interpret these diagrams. A method also specifies how this knowledge will be utilized to realize a solution to the problem, and must address the following questions:

- What activities are done?
- When are activities done?
- Who does the activities?
- Why are activities done?
- How are activities done?
- Where (and in what situations) ought the activities be done?

Development Cycles and Phases

	Inception	Elaboration	Construction	Transition
Perpective	Conceptualization	All	All	Realization
Level of Abstraction	System	System	All	System

Figure 5-12: Development Phases with Perspectives and Levels of Abstraction

Each phase of a development cycle (Chapter 2) focuses on a particular perspective and one or more levels of abstraction (Figure 5-12):

- The inception (initiating) development phase is primarily concerned with the conceptualization perspective and focuses on the system level of abstraction. This phase is used for understanding or forming a notion of the problem and the rationale for solving it (scoping and business case).

- The elaboration (planning) development phase is concerned with all perspectives and focuses on the system level of abstraction. This phase is used for

  - Understanding or forming a notion of the problem to determine the requirements the problem imposes on its solution.

  - Establishing and verifying the foundation for the overall solution.

  - Distributing the requirements among the iteration cycles of the construction phase.

- The construction (executing) development phase is concerned with all perspectives and focuses on all levels of abstraction. This phase is used for

  - Understanding or evolving the requirements the problem imposes on its solution so that the problem can be elaborated and the solution can be specified.

  - Elaborating the solution specification.

  - Updating the foundation for the overall solution and the foundation required to support the specific solution for the iteration cycle requirements.

  - Producing the solution for the iteration cycle requirements.

  - Verifying the solution for the iteration cycle requirements.

  - Providing or integrating the solution or a subset thereof.

- The transition (closing) development phase is primarily concerned with the realization perspective and focuses on the system level of abstraction. This phase is used for providing and integrating or delivering the solution.

Iteration Cycles and Phases

Each phase of an iteration cycle (Chapter 2) focuses on a particular perspective and one or more levels of abstraction (Figure 5-13):

- The management and support (controlling) phases are concerned with all perspectives and focus on all levels of abstraction as required by the development components.

UML Overview

	Req.	Analysis	Design	Implement.	Validation	Deployment
Perpective	Concept.	Specific.	Realization	Realization	Realization	Realization
Level of Abstraction	Subsystem, Class	Subsystem, Class	Subsystem, Class, Method	All	All	All

Figure 5-13: Iteration Phases with Perspectives and Levels of Abstraction

- Within the elaboration (planning) development phase, the following iteration phases apply:

  - The requirements phase and analysis phase are primarily concerned with the conceptualization perspective and focus on the system level of abstraction. These phases are for understanding or forming a notion of the problem to determine the requirements of the solution and distribute the requirements among iteration cycles of the construction phase.

  - The design phase is primarily concerned with the specification perspective and focuses on the system level of abstraction. This phase is for establishing and verifying the foundation for the overall solution.

- Within the construction (executing) development phase, the following iteration phases apply:

  - The requirements phase is primarily concerned with the conceptualization perspective and focuses on the subsystem and class levels of abstraction. This phase is for understanding or elaborating the requirements the problem imposes on its solution so that the problem can be elaborated and the solution can be specified.

  - The analysis phase is primarily concerned with the specification perspective and focuses on the subsystem and class levels of abstraction. This phase is for elaborating the solution specification.

  - The design phase is primarily concerned with the realization perspective and focuses on the subsystem, class, and method levels of abstraction. This phase is for updating the foundation for the overall solution and the foundation required to support the specific solution for the iteration cycle requirements.

  - The implementation phase is primarily concerned with the realization perspective and focuses on all levels of abstraction. This phase is for producing the solution for the iteration cycle requirements.

  - The validation (and integration) phase is primarily concerned with the realization perspective and focuses on all levels of abstraction. This phase is for verifying the solution for the iteration cycle requirements.

  - The deployment phase is primarily concerned with the realization perspective and focuses on all levels of abstraction. This phase is for providing and integrating or delivering the solution or a subset thereof.

PART III

The Unified Modeling Language Quick Reference

This section presents a detailed view of the UML constituents in a quick reference format.

Chapter 6, *Diagramming and Model Organization,* presents information on diagramming and model organization.

Chapter 7, *Class and Object Diagrams,* presents information on class and object diagrams.

Chapter 8, *Use Case Diagrams,* presents information on use case diagrams.

Chapter 9, *Sequence Diagrams,* presents information on sequence diagrams.

Chapter 10, *Collaboration Diagrams,* presents information on collaboration diagrams.

Chapter 11, *Statechart Diagrams,* presents information on statechart diagrams.

Chapter 12, *Activity Diagrams,* presents information on activity diagrams.

Chapter 13, *Component Diagrams,* presents information on component diagrams.

Chapter 14, *Deployment Diagrams,* presents information on deployment diagrams.

Chapter 15, *Extension Mechanisms,* presents information on extension mechanisms.

Chapter 16, *The Object Constraint Language,* presents information on the Object Constraint Language.

CHAPTER 6

Diagramming and Model Organization

Diagramming involves the use of diagrams to pictorially or graphically render a model.

Model organization involves the use of packages to organize the various elements of a model.

Diagrams

Diagrams render views of a model pictorially or graphically. Diagrams

- Are drawn at a level of abstraction or detail and from a viewpoint or perspective.

- Are graphical representations of a set of model elements. These model elements include classes, objects, associations, and links.

- Contain graphical constructs or symbols, which

    - Are model elements, relationships among model elements, and information associated with model elements.

    - May be nodes (vertices), paths (arcs), or strings.

    - May be suppressed on a diagram when they are not relevant or of interest.

    - May have adornments or attached graphical constructs that provide information.

- Contain visual relationships among graphical symbols, which

    - Are connection relationships, where paths are drawn to nodes.

    - Are containment relationships, where graphical constructs are within nodes.

    - Are attachment relationships, where strings are near paths or nodes.

- May be defined as required. There are nine predefined types of diagrams: class, object, use case, sequence, collaboration, statechart, activity, component, and deployment diagrams. New types of diagrams (models) may be defined as required.

- May have stereotypes and properties that apply to every element in the diagram (Chapter 15).

Nodes

Nodes (Figure 6-1) are graphical constructs that render model elements.

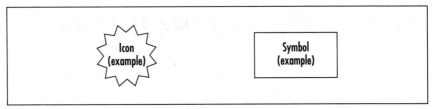

Figure 6-1: Nodes

Nodes

- May be icons, that is, graphical figures of fixed size and shape that do not expand to hold content.

- May be two-dimensional symbols, that is, figures of variable height and width that expand to hold content within their boundaries. These symbols may expand to hold lists of strings or other symbols, and they may also be divided into compartments in which to hold their contents.

- May reside in containers.

- May have names and associated information contained in, below, or above their symbols or icons.

- May have stereotypes and properties (Chapter 15).

Paths

Paths (Figure 6-2) are graphical constructs that render model element relationships between other model elements.

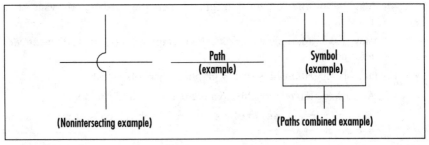

Figure 6-2: Paths

Paths

- Are sequences of line segments whose endpoints connect or attach to nodes.

- May consist of orthogonal, oblique or diagonal, and curved line segments.

- May cross one another without intersecting, as depicted by a small semi-circular jog by one of the paths.

- May be part of a set of paths that individually connect to a single node. These paths may be combined into a single path that branches into several paths in a treelike manner provided that the original paths of the set are of the same kind and that the modeling information on those paths is identical.

- May reside in containers.

- May have names and associated information contained below or above their line segments.

- May have stereotypes and properties.

Strings

Strings are sequences of text characters. Strings

- Are used to present information in an unparsed form.

- May present underlying model information.

- May exist as standalone elements on diagrams.

- May be a single line or a paragraph.

- May exist as singular elements of symbols or within compartments of symbols.

- May exist as elements in lists or as labels attached to symbols or paths. The position of a string in a list may also convey information.

- May express information in a particular language (pseudocode, computer language, natural language, or the OCL). This applies to the various types of strings used in diagrams.

Names

Names (Figure 6-3) are strings that are attached to other graphical constructs.

<<Stereotype>> Visibility ... / Name ... {Properties}

Container-Name :: Sub-Container-Name :: ... :: Element-Name

Figure 6-3: Names

Names

- Are also known as selectors or qualifiers.

- Are used to uniquely identify model elements within some container or context. They must be unique within their container or the context in which they are used. Furthermore, OCL expressions may be used to resolve ambiguities in referencing elements within a given context or among a collection of related model elements (Chapter 16).

- May have a stereotype keyword enclosed in guillemets (<< >>), or double angle brackets, preceding the name (Chapter 15).
- May have properties enclosed in curly braces following the name (Chapter 15).
- May have a visibility symbol or character indicating the visibility of an element outside of its container. The visibility symbol is specified for an element when it is declared on a structural diagram.

  - "+" indicates public visibility. Elements are available to importing containers (packages using the import dependency) and specialized or subtype containers. Public elements within classes are accessible from outside their container.

  - "#" indicates protected visibility. Elements are available to specialized or subtype containers. Protected elements within classes are accessible from descendants of the container.

  - "-" indicates private visibility. Elements are not available outside their container. Private elements within classes are not accessible from outside their container.

  - The visibility of an element when exported to an importing container is the most restrictive of the element's visibility and its container's visibility. Elements of imported containers may be referenced by pathname or an alias if visibility permits. Elements of inherited containers may be referenced by name if visibility permits.

  The absence of a visibility marker indicates that visibility is not shown. This does not mean that it is undefined or has a default value.

- May have other information around the name. This is determined by the particular use of the name and the type of modeling element to which it is attached.
- May be alias names. When a container receives an element from another container, the received element may have the same name as an already existing element in the receiving container. To avoid a name conflict, where two elements have the same name, the received element is given a pseudo or alias name. The original name is attributed to the element originally in the container, and the alias name is attributed to the element received from another container.
- May be pathnames that identify model elements from some starting point, such as the root of the system. This is a sequence of names concatenated by a delimiter (two colons). Each name references an inner container, and the last name in the sequence references the actual element.

  - When a pathname is used to reference an element, the element is defined elsewhere.

  - When an element is explicitly named, the element is defined within the context.

- May be attached to derived elements, that is, elements that can be computed from other elements. A slash (/) in front of the name is used to specify a derived element. The details of computing the elements may be attached in a constraint string (Chapter 15).

Labels

Labels are strings that are attached to other graphical constructs. They are used to represent information or adornments attached to graphical constructs on a diagram.

Expressions

Expressions are strings consisting of linguistic formulas that yield values of a particular type when evaluated. Expressions

- Must be expressed in a particular language (pseudocode, computer language, natural language, or the OCL). This applies to the various types of expressions used in diagrams.

- May be run through a linguistic analyzer to yield values of the appropriate type and express their meaning.

- May yield results of a given type. The OCL specifies a set of predefined types (Chapter 16).

Keywords

Keywords are text strings that represent a variation on a common theme. Keywords

- Must be enclosed in guillemets (<< >>). Double greater-than and double less-than characters may be used.

- That are predefined are treated as reserved words and may not be redefined by a user.

- May be added by users as stereotype names.

Compartments

Compartments (Figure 6-4) are divisions of two-dimensional symbols.

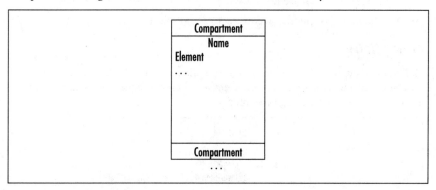

Figure 6-4: Compartments

Compartments

- Are used to partition a two-dimensional symbol so that specific semantics may be associated with a compartment.

- Are indicated by dividing a symbol using horizontal separator lines.
- May be suppressed, in which case no separator line is shown.
- May have a compartment name. Compartment names are typically centered, in plain type, and located at the top of the compartment.
- May contain a list of names or strings denoting elements of the compartment.
- May contain a subdiagram of the elements within the compartment.

Lists

Lists (Figure 6-5) are a sequence of names or strings.

<<Stereotype>> Visibility ... / Name ... {Properties}
. . .

Figure 6-5: Lists

Lists

- Are rendered one element per line.
- May be contained within compartments.
- May contain stereotype keywords. Such keywords apply to all succeeding elements of the list until another stereotype keyword list element appears, an empty stereotype keyword nullifies it, or the end of the list is reached.
- May contain property strings, which apply to all succeeding elements of the list until another property string list element appears or the end of the list is reached. Property strings applied to a list of elements are not superseded by property strings attached to individual elements, but may be augmented or modified by them.
- May have an ellipsis (...) as the final element to indicate that there exist additional elements that are not shown.
- May be sorted or filtered according to some selection rule.

Multiplicity

Multiplicity (Figure 6-6) is a string that specifies a range of allowable cardinalities for a set. Cardinality is explicitly the number of elements in a set, which can be an infinite subset of the nonnegative integers.

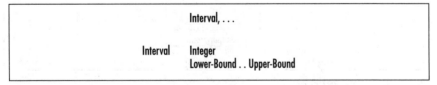

Figure 6-6: Multiplicity

Multiplicity

- Is a comma-separated sequence of integer intervals.

- May have literal integer values.

- May have closed ranges of integers. Ranges are inclusive; that is, they include their boundaries.

- May use the asterisk character (*) for the lower bound or upper bound to denote an unlimited bound.

- May use a single asterisk (*) to denote the unlimited nonnegative integer range; it is equivalent to *..* and 0..* (zero or more).

- Must not be 0..0 since this would not allow an element to exist at all.

- Must have monotonically increasing (or decreasing) intervals; that is, it must be ordered by increasing (or decreasing) intervals.

- Must have contiguous intervals combined into a single interval; that is, when one interval ends where the next interval begins, they are combined into one interval.

- May explicitly show the lower bound and upper bound. That is, "1" may be shown as "1..1," and "*" shown as "0..*". This notation explicitly indicates that both bounds have been considered.

Type-Instance Correspondence

A type-instance dichotomy (Figure 6-7) allows a generic descriptor to describe many individual items (nodes, paths). This correspondence between a generic descriptor and its individual items adheres to the following properties:

- The generic descriptor is known as a typelike element and is a class of elements.

- The individual items are known as instancelike elements and are objects of a class of elements.

- Generic descriptors

    - Are rendered using a geometric symbol.

    - Must have a name or identifier string that represents the name of the generic descriptor.

    - Contain a description of the content of the descriptor.

- Individual items

    - Use the same geometric symbol employed by their generic descriptor.

    - May have a name or identifier string that represents the name of the item. The name must be underlined. When omitted, the colon remains and the item is considered an anonymous item.

    - May have a colon followed by a name or identifier string that represents the name of the item's generic descriptor. The name must be underlined.

    - Contain values for their contents

- The stereotype of an instancelike element must match the stereotype of its typelike element (Chapter 15).

Notes

Notes (Figure 6-8) are graphical constructs or notational items containing and rendering textual information.

Diagramming

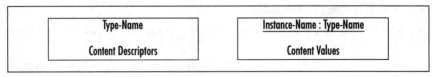

Figure 6-7: Type-Instance Correspondence

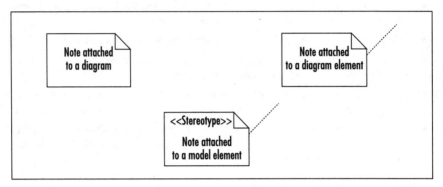

Figure 6-8: Notes

Notes

- Are denoted as rectangles with a bent upper right corner.

- Are used to render comments, constraints, properties, method bodies, and so forth.

- May be attached to zero or more model elements or graphical constructs by dashed lines.

- May be comments that do not have any underlying model elements and are attached to the diagram itself or to a diagram element.

- May be stereotyped to designate that it is part of the model and not just part of the diagram or view.

Packages

Packages (Figure 6-9) are general-purpose grouping mechanisms used to organize semantically related model elements.

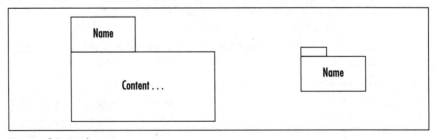

Figure 6-9: Packages

Packages

- Are denoted as large rectangles with a small rectangle attached on one corner (usually the left upper side of the large rectangle).

- Are used to define a namespace or context (container) wherein each name must be unique.

- May contain subordinate or nested packages and ordinary model elements.

- May be used at the highest level to denote a system.

- Must not be instantiated. Packages only serve as containers for elements that may be instantiated; however, packages are not instantiated.

- Own their contents. Each element may only be owned by a single package, so that an ownership hierarchy or tree results.

- May have their contents visually suppressed.

- May contain elements that have relationships within the same package.

- May contain elements that use other elements from other packages, so that a usage network results.

- May have relationships to other packages, indicating that the relationships exist between at least some elements they contain. Such relationships are transitive; that is, if package *A* imports package *B,* and package *B* imports package *C,* package *A* also imports package *C.*

- Must use element pathnames to reference elements outside the current scope or context.

- May be nested. This establishes an implied import relationship. That is, each nested package imports the contents of its parent package.

- May have an import dependency (association) to other packages. This association must use the "import" stereotype keyword. The importing package may reference all public elements of the imported package. This represents a has-a relationship in which the importing package has the elements of the imported package.

- May have generalization relationships to other packages. The more specific package may reference all public and protected elements of the more general package. This represents an is-a-kind-of relationship in which the subpackage is a kind of superpackage.

- May be stereotyped using the "system" keyword (Figure 6-10). System packages

  - Contain the entire set of models for a complete system; this includes a specification model containing specification elements and a realization model containing realization elements.

  - Must have the requirements specified by the specification model fulfilled by the realization model.

  - Must contain a specification model consisting of a package stereotyped using the "use case model" keyword. This package contains specification elements; they specify the behavior of the containing system and establish the boundary of the containing system. This package consists of use

Diagramming

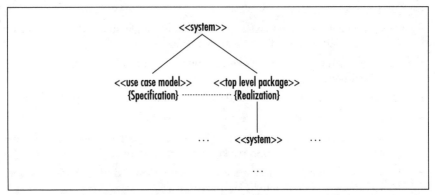

Figure 6-10: Systems, Use Case Models, Top-Level Packages, and Subsystems

cases (Chapter 8) that define the operations and interfaces of the system. The specification model is at a high level of abstraction relative to the realization model.

– Must contain a realization model consisting of a set of packages. The topmost package is stereotyped using the "top level package" keyword. Other subordinate packages are stereotyped using the "system" keyword. Subsystem packages contain realization elements; they realize or offer the behavior of the containing system. Instances of realization elements collaborate to perform the specified behavior of use cases or operations and interfaces within the containing system. Because each subsystem package is a system, it may have its own specification and realization models and elements.

– May be used as classes. That is, they may be instantiated and may have associations. The package itself is not literally instantiated; rather, its contents are instantiated.

The Role of Tools

Diagramming tools play a key role in creating and maintaining diagrams. When working with diagramming tools, the following aspects should be considered:

- Diagrams on a piece of paper are static and do not have any invisible hyperlinks.

- Diagrams on a computer screen viewed using a tool are dynamic and may contain additional invisible hyperlinks that can be invoked dynamically to access other information.

- Each graphical construct, including a diagram itself, may have its own presentation style (style sheet).

- Information may also be presented in textual or tabular format rather than only graphical format.

- Tools should maintain consistency across diagram types.

CHAPTER 7

Class and Object Diagrams

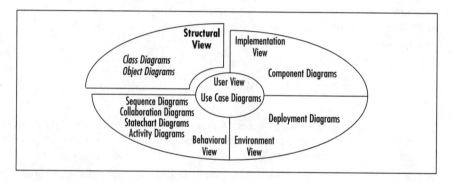

Figure 7-1: Structural Model View—Class Diagrams and Object Diagrams

Class diagrams (Figure 7-1) render the structural view of a system. These diagrams describe the static structure of a system, or how it is structured rather than how it behaves. These diagrams contain classes and associations. They may be constructed using the following technique:

1. Model classes.

2. Model associations between classes.

3. Refine and elaborate as required.

Class diagrams

- May be constructed in conjunction with object diagrams. Object diagrams may be used to explore different configurations of objects, and then combined or generalized into class diagrams. This results in a single class diagram that describes many possible object diagrams.

- May also be called *static structural diagrams* to distinguish them from behavioral diagrams.

139

- Contain classifiers. Classifiers

  - Are constructs that describe structural features and behavioral features. Structural features include attributes, whereas behavioral features include operations and methods.

  - May participate in associations.

  - Have many specific forms that are designated using stereotype keywords.

  Classes are the most common classifiers. The discussion of classes applies to the other element kinds as semantically appropriate. A type-instance correspondence exists between classifiers and instances, classes and objects, associations and links, and data types and values.

- May contain objects. A class diagram with objects and no classes is an object diagram.

- May have the various expressions (attributes, operations, etc.) they utilize be expressed using pseudocode or another language.

Object diagrams (Figure 7-1) render the structural view of a system at a particular time during its life. These diagrams describe a particular instantiation of a class diagram. These diagrams contain object and links. They may be constructed using the following technique:

1. Model objects.

2. Model links between objects.

3. Refine and elaborate as required.

Object diagrams

- May be considered special cases of class diagrams. That is, class diagrams with only objects and links are object diagrams; such diagrams do not have classes or associations.

- May be constructed in conjunction with class diagrams. Object diagrams may be used to explore different configurations of objects, and then combined or generalized into class diagrams. This results in a single class diagram that describes many possible object diagrams.

- May have the various expressions (attributes, operations, etc.) they utilize be expressed using pseudocode or another language.

Classes

Classes (Figure 7-2) are descriptions of a set of objects with common structural features, behavioral features, relationships, and semantics. They are used to model a set of concepts or entities with common characteristics. Classes

- Are denoted as solid-outline rectangles with compartments.

- Must have a name compartment. This contains a class's name. Class names are typically centered, in boldface, and begin with an uppercase letter. If they are abstract classes, they are in italics.

- May have an attribute compartment named "attributes" (Chapter 6). This contains a class's attributes.

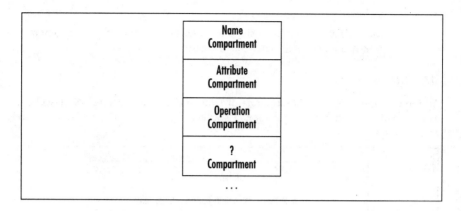

Figure 7-2: A Class

- May have an operation compartment named "operations" (Chapter 6). This contains a class's operations and methods.

- May have other compartments, which may be used for other model properties (business rules, responsibilities, variations, events, exceptions, etc.).

- May be referenced by using pathnames. This indicates that the class is referenced or used in this context rather than being defined.

- May have interfaces to specify collections of operations provided to its environment. All operations must have associated methods.

- May have generalization relationships with other classes.

- May be active. Active classes

  - Own a thread of control. A *thread* is a path of execution or control. A *process* is the physical construct that houses one or more threads. A thread executes through a process. Multiprocessing involves multiple processes. Multithreading involves multiple threads per process.

  - Are denoted by a heavy border.

  - May initiate control activity. That is, they may request services from other objects and classes.

- May be passive. Passive classes

  - React to the requests of other classes. They primarily hold data and provide services to other classes.

  - Are denoted by a normal border.

  - May not initiate control activity unless they are passed control from an active object requesting service.

- May represent signals used in statechart diagrams (Chapter 11) and activity diagrams (Chapter 12). Signals

  - Must be stereotyped using the "signal" keyword.

  - Must have their parameters shown in the attribute compartment.

- Must not have any operations.
- Must not have any relationships to other classes, but may have generalization relationships to other signal classes.

Attributes

Attributes (Figure 7-3) are descriptions of structural or static features of classifiers. They are used to model information associated with an entity; this is what an entity knows.

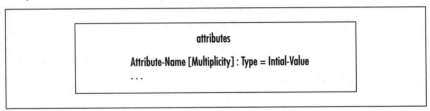

attributes

Attribute-Name [Multiplicity] : Type = Intial-Value

. . .

Figure 7-3: Attribute Compartment of a Class

Attributes

- Are denoted as text strings within an attribute compartment.
- Are named slots that describe the types of values that an instance of a classifier may hold.
- May be shown by composition. A class is composed of its attributes.
- Are typically left justified, in plain type, and begin with a lowercase letter.
- Must have a name or identifier string that represents the name of the attribute. Names must be unique within the containing class.
- May have square brackets containing a multiplicity expression that indicates the number of attributes per instance of the class. An attribute without this expression must hold exactly one value.
- May have a colon followed by a type expression that indicates the types of values an attribute may have.
- May have an equal sign followed by an initial value that is used to initialize attributes of newly created objects.
- May have class scope, as denoted by underlining.

Operations

Operations (Figure 7-4) are descriptions of behavioral or dynamic features of classifiers. They are used to model services or operations associated with an entity; this is what an entity may do. Operations

- Are denoted as text strings within an operation compartment.
- Are named services that may be requested of instances of a classifier.
- Are implemented by methods.

```
                    operations

        Operations-Name (Parameter-List) : Return-List

        . . .


  Parameter-List    Kind Parameter-Name : Type = Default-Value, . . .

  Return-List       Return-Type
                    Return-Name : Type, ...
```

Figure 7-4: Operation Compartment of a Class

- Are typically left justified, in plain type, and begin with a lowercase letter. If they are abstract operations, they are in italics.

- Must have a name or identifier string that represents the name of the operation. Names must be unique within the containing class.

- May have parentheses containing a comma-separated parameter list that indicates the formal parameters passed to a method. When the parameter list is suppressed, the colon and return list must also be suppressed. Parameters

  - May have a kind specified. This value may be "in," indicating that the parameter is only passed into the operation; "out," indicating that the parameter is only returned from the operation; or "inout," indicating that the parameter may be passed into and returned from the operation. The default is "in."

  - Must have a name or identifier string that represents the name of the parameter. Names must be unique within the parameter list.

  - May have a colon followed by a type expression that indicates the types of values a parameter may have.

  - May have an equal sign followed by a default value that is used to set the value for unspecified parameters when the method is invoked.

- May have a return list consisting of a single return type expression.

- May have a return list consisting of a comma-separated list of formal parameters passed back from a method. This indicates that an operation returns multiple values. Return parameters

  - Must have a name or identifier string that represents the name of the parameter. Names must be unique within the parameter list.

  - May have a colon followed by a type expression that indicates the types of values a parameter may have.

- May have class scope, as denoted by underlining.

- May be specified or elaborated (implemented) in notes (using plain text) or other behavioral view diagrams attached to operations.

- May have extension points specifying where additional behavior may be inserted by subclasses.
- May be stereotyped using the "signal" keyword to indicate that objects of a class accept and respond to a given signal that triggers the operation. The response of an object to a signal is shown with a state machine (Chapter 11).

Types

Types (Figure 7-5) are classes that define a collection of operations without methods. They are used to model a collection of operations applicable to different classes of objects. Types

- Are denoted as stereotyped class rectangles.
- Are equivalent to abstract classes with no methods and only abstract operations.
- Must be stereotyped using the "type" keyword.
- Must not contain any methods.
- Are implemented by implementation classes.
- May have generalization relationships to other types.

Implementation Classes

Implementation classes (Figure 7-5) are classes that define the realization or implementation of other classes.

Figure 7-5: Type and Implementation Classes

Implementation classes

- Are denoted as stereotyped class rectangles.
- Must be stereotyped using the "implementation class" keyword.
- May implement other classes via a realizes generalization relationship from the implementation class to the implemented class. The implementation class inherits operations but not structure (attributes or associations).
- May have generalization relationships to other implementation classes. These are generalization relationships between implementation classes rather than generalization relationships between an implementation class and a nonimplementation class.

Interfaces

Interfaces (Figure 7-6) are classes that define a set of externally accessible operations without methods. They are used to model a collection of operations defining a service that may be offered by different classes.

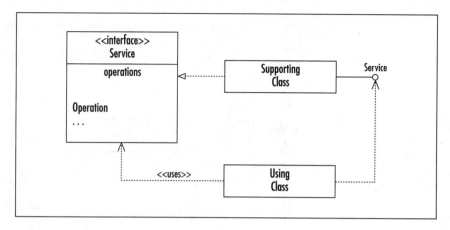

Figure 7-6: Interfaces

Interfaces

- Are denoted as stereotyped class rectangles, or as small circles with the name of the interface attached.

- Are equivalent to abstract classes with no attributes and no methods and only abstract public operations.

- Must be stereotyped using the "interface" keyword.

- Must not have an attribute compartment. The attribute compartment is omitted because it is always empty.

- Must not have associations.

- Must have an operation compartment named "operations." This contains an interface's operations.

- Must have only public operations.

- May have generalization relationships with other interfaces.

- May be supported by other classes via a realizes generalization relationship from the supporting class to the interface class. The supporting class must offer all the operations defined in the interface class, and may offer new operations, but does not have to support any of the data structures of the interface class.

- May be used by other classes via a dependency stereotyped using the "uses" keyword.

Templates

Templates (Figure 7-7) are constructs defining a family of classes having a common form. The differences between classes in the family are represented by parameters, allowing a single template to instantiate many classes. Specific classes within this family are defined by specifying actual values that are bound to formal parameters. In the template, the formal parameters are unbound or unspecified.

Class/Object
Diagrams

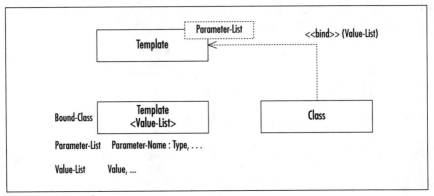

Figure 7-7: Template

Templates

- Are denoted as class rectangles with a dashed rectangle superimposed on the upper right corner.

- Must not be instantiated.

- Must not be superclasses within generalization relationships.

- May be subclasses of ordinary classes within generalization relationships.

- Must have a name or identifier string that represents the template name.

- May use their formal parameters in their definition.

- Must have a comma-separated parameter list that indicates the formal parameters used to create a class. Formal parameters

    - Must have a name or identifier string that represents the name of the parameter. Names must be unique within the parameter list.

    - May have a colon followed by a type expression that indicates the types of values a parameter may have. If a type expression is not specified, the argument for the parameter must resolve to a classifier.

- Must be bound to actual values using a comma-separated value list in order to be used. Values must match the order, number, and types specified in the parameter list of the template.

- May have bound classes. Bound classes

    - Are bound by referencing their template and specifying a value list.

    - Must not extend the template; that is, they cannot add attributes or operation.

    - May be extended via generalization relationships.

    - May be bound via a dependency association stereotyped using the "bind" keyword and specifying a value list.

Binding a template involves duplicating the model fragment or template, replacing formal parameters with argument values, and making the result part of the effective model.

- May be applied to packages and any class of modeling elements.

Data Types

Data types are classes that define data values. They are used to model simple values. Data types

- Are represented as strings on diagrams.

- Have unique values that do not have identity. That is, occurrence of the same value cannot be differentiated. For example, the value "1" stored in a variable *X* is no different than the value "1" stored in a variable *Y*.

- Must have operations only.

Objects

Objects (Figure 7-8) are instances of classes. They are used to model particular entities.

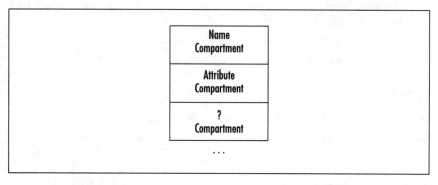

Figure 7-8: Object

Objects

- Are denoted as solid-outline rectangles with compartments.

- Are unique and have identity. That is, every object may be differentiated from every other object, even if the objects have the same attribute values.

- Are defined by their classes.

- Must have a name compartment (Figure 7-9).

- May have a name or identifier string that represents the name of the object. The name must be underlined. When omitted, the colon remains and the object is considered an anonymous object.

- May have a colon followed by a comma-separated class list that indicates the types and class of an object. Objects

  - May have multiple types (roles), which may change dynamically.

  - May have only one implementation class, which may not change.

- May have a comma-separated state list within square brackets that indicates the concurrent states of the object.

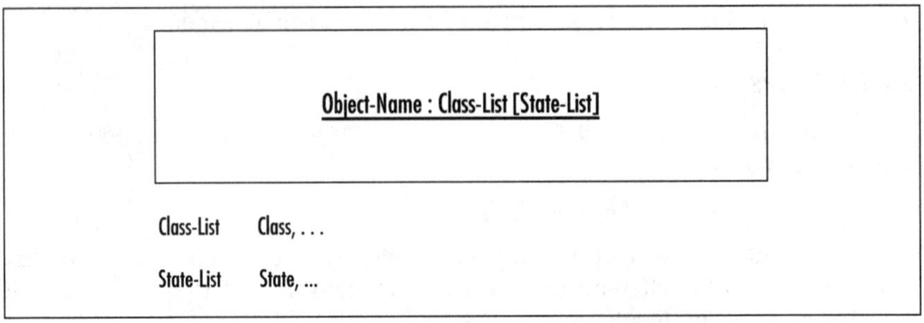

```
┌─────────────────────────────────────────────────────┐
│   ┌─────────────────────────────────────────────┐   │
│   │                                             │   │
│   │      Object-Name : Class-List [State-List]  │   │
│   │                                             │   │
│   └─────────────────────────────────────────────┘   │
│                                                     │
│      Class-List    Class, . . .                     │
│                                                     │
│      State-List    State, ...                       │
│                                                     │
└─────────────────────────────────────────────────────┘
```

Figure 7-9: Name Compartment of an Object

- May have an attribute compartment named "attributes." This compartment consists of an object's attribute values. Only attributes of interest in the current context (or the current diagram) need be shown.
- May have other compartments as defined by their classes, but may not have an "operations" compartment.
- May be active, that is, instances of active classes.
- May be passive, that is, instances of passive classes.

Attributes

Attributes (Figure 7-10) are an object's attribute values.

```
┌─────────────────────────────────────────────────────┐
│   ┌─────────────────────────────────────────────┐   │
│   │                   attributes                │   │
│   │  Attribute-Name [Index] : Type = Value, . . .│   │
│   │  . . .                                       │   │
│   └─────────────────────────────────────────────┘   │
└─────────────────────────────────────────────────────┘
```

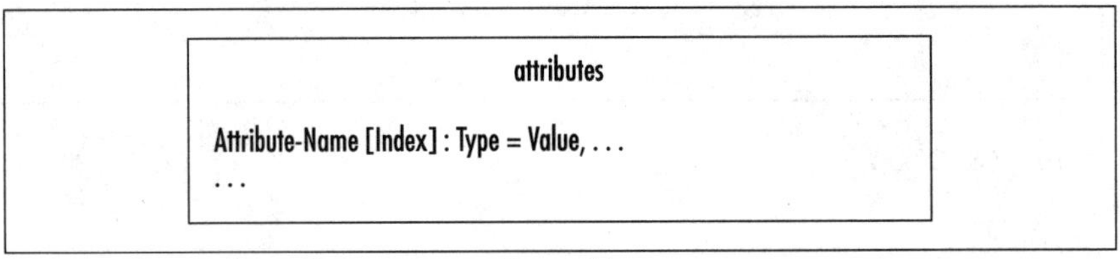

Figure 7-10: Attribute Compartment of an Object

Attributes

- Are denoted as text strings within an attribute compartment.
- May be suppressed if their values are not of interest in a diagram.
- May be shown by composition. An object is composed of its attributes.
- Must have a name or identifier string that represents the name of the attribute.
- May have an index within square brackets that indicates the specific attribute if the multiplicity of the attribute (as defined in its class) is more than one.
- May have a colon followed by a type expression that indicates the types of values an attribute may have. This type expression must match the type expression specified in the object's class.
- May have an equal sign followed by a literal value that represents the value of the attribute for the object. This may be represented as a comma-separated

list of values that indicates the different values that the attribute has had over a period of time.

- May have class scope, as denoted by underlining.

Associations

Associations (Figure 7-11) are descriptions of a set of links with common structural features, behavioral features, relationships, and semantics. They are used to model a set of relationships that relate two or more other concepts or entities where the relationships have common characteristics.

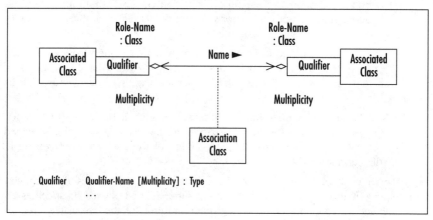

Figure 7-11: Binary Association

Associations

- Are denoted as lines or paths connecting two or more class symbols.

- Have association ends that connect association paths to two or more other classes. Association ends may have properties (Chapter 15) enclosed in curly brackets near the associated class.

- Must relate other classes, not themselves.

- May be reflexive (or recursive). That is, they may associate the same class to itself or associate two objects of the same class.

- May have a name or identifier string that represents the name of the association.

- May have a name-direction arrow. This is a small solid triangle attached to the name, where the point of the triangle indicates the direction in which to read the name of the association. When the small solid triangle is omitted, associations are read from left to right and top to bottom.

- May be association classes. Association classes

    - Are denoted as class symbols attached by dashed lines to associations.

    - Are associations with class properties or classes with association properties.

- Define a set of characteristics that belong to the relationship. The characteristics are not owned by any of the classes they relate.
- Are attached to their association paths by a dashed line.
- May be suppressed, but the association path may not be suppressed.

Association class names

- May be placed on association paths and in association class symbols. They must be the same when placed in both places.
- May be placed on association paths and omitted from association class symbols. This is often used for association classes with attributes and no operations or other associations. This emphasizes an association's "associative nature," or its role in relating other classes.
- May be placed in association class symbols and omitted from association paths. This is often used for association classes that have operations or other associations. This emphasizes an association's "class nature," or its role as a class.

- May have a role name that indicates the role or specific behavior of an associated class as it participates in the association. If a visibility symbol is specified for the role name, it represents the visibility of the association traversing in the direction toward the role name.

- May have a class name (near the role name) that indicates the behavior expected of an associated class by the other related classes. It specifies an interface or type indicating the behavior required of the associated class in order to enable the association. The associated class must support the interface, and the interface is required for the class to participate in the association. When omitted, the association allows full access to the associated class.

The use of role names and interface or type names may be used in creating collaborations (Chapter 10). These collaborations include the association as an association role, and include the role name as the class role name and the class name of the interface or type as the class of the class role within the collaboration.

- May have a multiplicity expression that indicates the number of potential instances involved in the association when the other associated classes are fixed, that is, the number of instances of a given class associated with the other classes involved in the association. If the multiplicity is omitted, the model is incomplete.

- May have a navigation arrow that indicates that navigability is supported toward an associated class attached to the arrow. This is indicated by placing an arrow on the association path. One of the following presentation options is possible:

- All arrows are shown. The absence of an arrow indicates navigability is not supported.

- No arrows are shown. No inferences can be drawn about navigability. This is similar to any situation where information is suppressed in a diagram.

- Arrows for navigability in both directions are suppressed, and only arrows for one-way navigability are shown.

- May have an aggregation indicator, represented as a diamond. Diamonds

  - May be hollow to indicate the weak, or shared, form of aggregation. Associated class objects may belong to multiple aggregates and change owners over time. They are not deleted if one of their owners is deleted.

  - May be filled to indicate composition, or the strong form of aggregation. Associated class objects must belong to only one component, and are deleted if the composite is deleted.

  - Must not be attached to both ends of an association.

- May have a qualifier, that is, an attribute or list of attributes of an association whose values partition or divide a set of objects (called the *targets*) associated with a given object (called the *source*). The qualifier is attached to the source class of an association and determines how objects on the target side of an association are partitioned and identified. Qualifiers

  - Are denoted as small rectangles attached to the end of an association path between the final path segment and the symbol of the class to which they connect.

  - Must have a name or identifier string that represents the name of the attributes of the association.

  - May have a multiplicity expression within square brackets that indicates the number of attributes per instance of the association. The default multiplicity is one.

  - May have a colon followed by a type expression that indicates the types of values an attribute may have.

  - Reduce the effective multiplicity of an association. That is, if the multiplicity of a class involved in an association is more than one, a qualifier specifies a set of values or attributes that will return a subset of the objects of the class.

An object of a source class together with a qualifier value uniquely selects a partition of the target class. Every object of the target class may be a constituent of exactly one partition.

Multiplicity attached to the target class in an association denotes the possible cardinalities of the set of target objects selected by pairing a source object and a qualifier value. The following multiplicity values are common:

- "0..1" indicates that a unique qualifier value may or may not select a target object; that is, not every possible qualifier value has to select a target object.

- "1" indicates that a unique qualifier value selects a unique target object; that is, every possible qualifier value has to select a target object.

- "*" indicates that a unique qualifier value selects a set of target objects; that is, every possible qualifier value is an index or key that partitions the target objects into subsets. The qualifier is similar to a key that may be used to index a subset of the target objects.

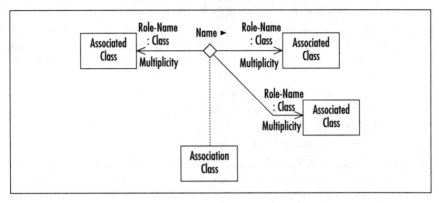

Figure 7-12: N-*ary Association*

• Among three or more classes, are shown as a diamond with paths from each corner or side (Figure 7-12). Such an association

  – Must not involve aggregation or qualifiers.

  – May have a single class appear more than once or on multiple paths.

Generalizations

Generalizations (Figure 7-13) are associations between more general elements and more specific elements in which the more specific elements are fully consistent with the more general elements and inherit and may add information to the characteristics provided by the more general elements. Two elements are fully consistent if they are the same type of elements. For example, two implementation classes are consistent since they both are classes of implementation constructs, and two actor classes are consistent since they both model actors. Generalizations are used to model taxonomic relationships between concepts.

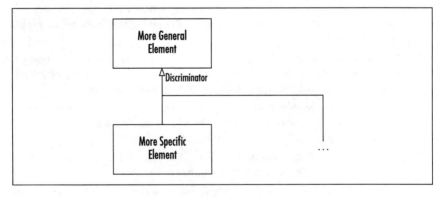

Figure 7-13: Generalization

Generalizations

- Are denoted as solid paths with a large hollow triangle pointing at the more general element.
- More specific elements
  - Specialize more general elements.
  - Receive all the characteristics (attributes, operations, methods, and associations) of the more general elements via the mechanism of inheritance.
  - May add their own characteristics (attributes, operations, methods, and associations).
  - May override inherited methods.
  - May be substituted for their more general elements.
- Must not be circular; that is, an element cannot have a generalization relationship to itself.
- May have discriminators. Discriminators
  - Specify the basis for the specialization. They define a named dimension of specialization through which more general elements are partitioned into groups of more specific elements.
  - Must be role names or attributes of more general elements whose values enumerate the partitions. The actual type of the attribute or role name that is used as a discriminator is known as the *powertype*.
- May have an ellipsis (...) in place of a more specific element to indicate that additional more specific elements exist in the model but are not shown on the diagram.

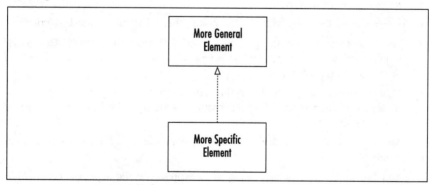

Figure 7-14: Realizes Relationship (Generalization)

- May be realizes relationships (Figure 7-14).
  - If the more general element is an implementation class, it implies inheritance of operations but not of structure (attributes and associations).
  - If the more general element is an interface, the more specific element supports the operations of the interface.

Dependencies

Dependencies (Figure 7-15) are associations between a collection of dependent client elements and another collection of independent supplier elements. The client elements require knowledge of and the presence of the supplier elements. Dependencies are used to model dependencies among model elements where changes in the independent supplier elements may require changes to the dependent client elements.

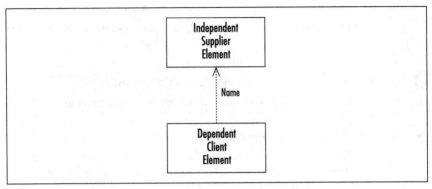

Figure 7-15: Dependency

Dependencies

- Are denoted as dashed arrows with the arrowhead pointing at the independent element.

- Relate elements of a model.

- Don't require instances to associate; rather, they exist among model elements.

- Have elements that exist at the same level of abstraction or detail. That is, the dependent client element and the independent supplier element are described at the same level of detail.

- May be stereotyped using the "refinement" keyword to depict different semantic levels of abstraction. The refinement may be described in a note attached to the dependency.

- May serve as a container for a group of dependencies from parts of a client element to parts of a supplier element.

- May be stereotyped using a keyword to express specific dependencies.

- May have a name.

- May have the arrowhead suppressed when used to attach notes or constraint strings to model elements. The direction is clear: the note or constraint string is the source of the arrow and the model element is the target of the arrow.

Links

Links (Figure 7-16) are instances of associations. They are used to model relationships that relate two or more other instances of concepts or entities.

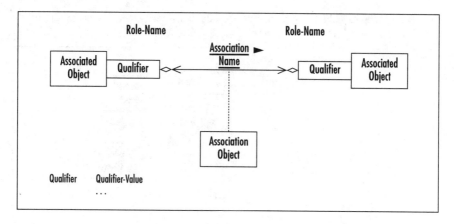

Figure 7-16: Binary Link

Links

- Are denoted as paths between objects.

- Have link ends that connect link paths to two or more other objects. Link ends may have properties (Chapter 15) enclosed in curly brackets near the objects they link.

- Are unique and have identity. That is, every link may be differentiated from every other link, even if the links are between the same objects.

- Are defined by their associations.

- Establish relationships between instances and are similar to objects. They are lists of references to related objects.

- May be reflexive. That is, they can associate two objects of the same class.

- Must not have a name or identifier string. They take their identity from the objects they relate.

- May have their association name rendered. The name must be underlined.

- May have a name-direction arrow. This must match the link's association name-direction arrow.

- May be instances or objects of association classes.

- May have a role name that indicates the role of an associated class. This must match the link's association role name.

- Must not have a class name following the role name, like associations have. Instead, the link's association indicates the behavior of the associated object.

- Must not have a multiplicity expression because they relate instances.

- May have a navigation arrow that indicates navigability is supported toward the associated objects attached to the arrow. This must match the link's association navigation arrow.

- May have an aggregation or composition indicator.

Class/Object Diagrams

- May have a qualifier value or list of qualifier values, as expressed by the link's association.

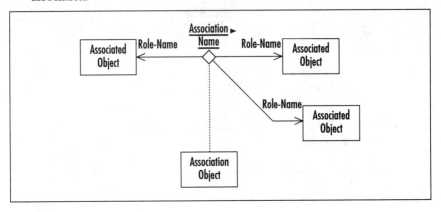

Figure 7-17: N-*ary Link*

- Among three or more classes are shown as a diamond with paths from each corner or side (Figure 7-17). Such an association

  - Must not involve aggregation or qualifiers.

  - May have a single object appear more than once or on multiple paths.

Compositions

Compositions (Figure 7-18) involve composite classes or classes involved in composite aggregations. Compositions are used to model parts that exist or live and die with their associated owner.

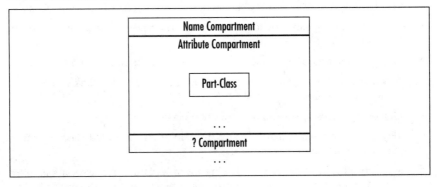

Figure 7-18: Composite Class

Compositions

- May be depicted in generic form using classes and associations.

- May be depicted in instance form using objects and links.

- Must have composite classes. Composite classes

- Must have a name compartment.
- Must have an attribute compartment depicting the parts of the composite. Attributes are effectively composition relationships between a class and the classes of its attributes.

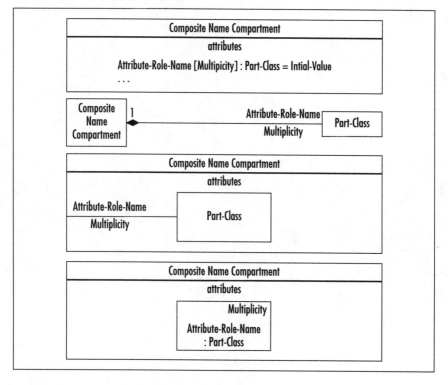

Figure 7-19: Composite Aggregation Association

- May have composite aggregation associations (Figure 7-19). Composite aggregation associations
  - Must only link objects belonging to the same container object or composite.
  - May be shown as a line ending in a filled diamond (as a composition association) or by using one of two different graphically nested forms.
  - Have parts that may have a multiplicity; it defaults to many.
  - Have Role names of the parts, which correspond to attributes of the composite.
- May have other associations.
  - If an association is drawn entirely within the border of a composite, the association is considered to be part of the composite; any objects on such a link must be from the same composite.

—   If an association is drawn such that its path crosses the border of the composite, the association is not considered to be part of the composite; any objects on such a link may be from the same or a different composite.

CHAPTER 8

Use Case Diagrams

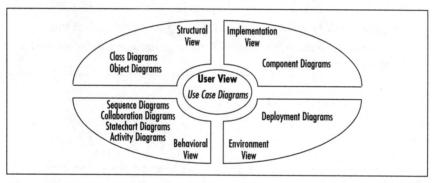

Figure 8-1: User Model View—Use Case Diagrams

Use case diagrams (Figure 8-1) render the user view of a system. These diagrams describe the functionality provided by a system or class to external interactors. These diagrams contain actors, use cases, and their relationships. They may be constructed using the following technique:

1. Model actors.

2. Model use cases. This is the normal behavior of an entity.

3. Model communicates relationships between actors and use cases.

4. Model extends relationships between use cases. This is exceptional or variant behavior of an entity.

5. Model uses relationships between use cases. This is behavior of an entity that is reused by the services it offers.

6. Refine and elaborate as required.

Use case diagrams

- May be contained in a package stereotyped using the "use case model" keyword. This package represents the specification of requirements of a system.

- May correlate to a package stereotyped using the "top level package" keyword. This package represents the specification of the implementation of a system that satisfies the requirements.

- May be part of a package stereotyped using the "system" keyword that contains a "use case model" package, "top level package" package, and a set of classes organized around analysis and design models in a package hierarchy.

- May have the various expressions (conditions, etc.) they utilize be expressed using pseudocode or another language.

Actors

Actors (Figure 8-2) are classes that define roles that objects external to a system may play. They are used to model users outside of a system that interact directly with the system as part of coherent work units. This includes human users and other systems. Actors

- Are characterized by their external view rather than their internal structure.

- Participate in interactions involving message exchanges and actions with systems.

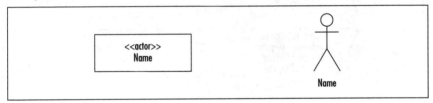

Figure 8-2: Actors

- Are denoted as stereotyped class rectangles or as stick person icons.

- Have goals to be achieved by interacting with systems.

- Have instances that are objects playing the role of an actor.

- Have one role for each use case with which they interact, that is, one role per communicates relationship.

- Must be stereotyped using the "actor" keyword. This is usually used for system interactors and nonhuman systems.

- Must have a name or identifier string that represents the name of the actor.

- May be denoted using the standard stereotype icon (stick person). This is usually used for human interactors.

- May be played by a single object; that is, an object may play several roles simultaneously.

- May have generalization relationships with other actors. That is, an actor may inherit the characteristics of a more general actor.

- May not have aggregation relationships with other classifiers. That is, an actor may not contain any other classes.

- May have operations.

- May have interfaces that define how other actors may interact with them.

Use Cases

Use cases (Figure 8-3) are classes that define units of functionality or behavior provided by a system. They specify the external requirements of the system and the functionality offered by the system. The set of use cases may be enclosed by a system boundary or rectangle labeled with the system name. The system container is an actor. Use cases are used to model work units that the enclosing system provides as services to outside interactors. The system is enclosed by a boundary and performs the functionality for actors. Use cases

- Are *specified* by sequence diagrams (Chapter 9) representing the external interaction sequences among the system and its actors. These interaction sequences represent how a system provides functionality or services to its interactors.

- Are *realized,* or implemented, by collaboration diagrams (Chapter 10) representing the internal refinement of the services provided by a system to its actors.

Figure 8-3: Use Cases

- Are denoted as ellipses or ovals.

- Yield results of value to at least one of their actors; however, there may be other actors who simply participate and gain no value from their participation. When use cases are not complete specifications and are just fragments of functionality, they may be at the incorrect level of abstraction.

- Have instances that are scenarios or single paths of activity through use cases. Use cases are reified through scenarios that may be depicted as sequence diagrams (Chapter 9) or collaboration diagrams (Chapter 10).

- Must have a name or identifier string that represents the name of the use case.

- May not have aggregation relationships with other classifiers.

- May have operations and attributes.

- May have interfaces that define and describe how actors may interact with them.

- May be described in plain text or using behavioral view diagrams.

- May have extension points, which

    - Are strings representing points within a use case at which variations in the action sequence may be inserted.

    - Must have unique names in a use case.

- May be abstract. Abstract use cases are never used by themselves; that is, they do not have any communicates relationships with actors, but they may have uses or extends relationships with other use cases.

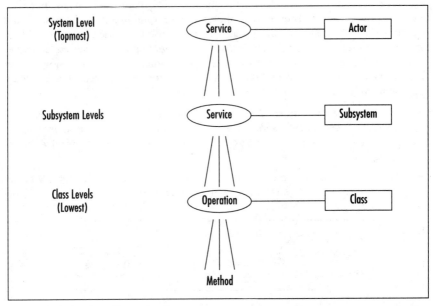

Figure 8-4: Use Case Organization

- Are organized hierarchically (Figure 8-4). The hierarchy organizes the overall functionality provided by a system. Within such a hierarchy, use cases have the following characteristics:

    - Use cases specify the services offered by their containers.

    - Use cases are refined into a set of smaller use cases. The use cases of a container are superordinate to refining use cases; the refining use cases are subordinate to the use cases of the whole.

    - Subordinate use cases collaborate to perform superordinate use cases.

    - Actors of superordinate use cases may appear as actors of subordinate use cases.

    - Interfaces of superordinate use cases may appear as interfaces of subordinate use cases.

    - Cooperating use cases are actors of one another.

    - The functionality of superordinate use cases is traceable to their subordinate use cases. That is, the functionality provided by a superordinate use case is a composite of the functionality provided by each of its subordinate use cases.

- Interfaces of superordinate use cases are traceable to interfaces of subordinate use cases that communicate with the same actors of the superordinate use cases. That is, the interfaces of a superordinate use case are the summation of the interfaces provided by its subordinate use cases.

• May be used by a system. These use cases

- Specify the complete services offered by the system. This is the topmost level in a use case diagram and is known as the *system level*.

- Are realized by interaction sequences or collaborations among multiple elements contained within the system.

- Have external interactors that are actors or other systems.

- Use signals to interact with their external interactors.

• May be used by a subsystem within a hierarchy. These use cases

- Specify the complete services offered by the subsystem. Any number of levels involving subsystems may be utilized. These are known as *subsystem levels*.

- Are realized by a single element or by interaction sequences or collaborations among multiple elements contained within the subsystem.

- Have external interactors that are other subsystems and higher-level interactors.

- Use signals or other communication mechanisms to interact with their external interactors.

- Realize the next higher level of use cases.

- Specify the next lower level of use cases.

• May be used by a class within a hierarchy. These use cases

- Specify functional fragments or operations offered by the class. Any number of levels involving classes may be utilized. These are known as *class levels*.

- Are realized by a single element or by interaction sequences or collaborations among multiple elements contained within the class.

- Have external interactors that are other classes and higher-level interactors.

- Use signals or other communication mechanisms to interact with their external interactors.

- Realize the next higher level of use cases.

- Specify the next lower level of use cases.

• May be used at the lowest level of a hierarchy. These use cases

- Are methods.

- Realize the next higher level of use cases.

Communicates Relationships

Communicates relationships (Figure 8-5) are associations between actors and use cases. They are used to model communications between actors and use cases in which an actor participates, communicates with, or takes part in a use case.

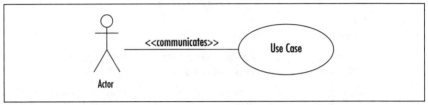

Figure 8-5: Communicates Relationship

Communicates relationships

- Are denoted as solid associations.

- Are the only relationships permissible between actors and use cases.

- May be stereotyped using the "communicates" keyword.

- May have an arrow to indicate the actor's behavior within the use case.

  - If the actor initiates the use case, the communication association has an arrow pointing to the use case.

  - If the actor utilizes the services provided by the use case, the communication association has an arrow pointing to the actor.

  - An association may have arrows in both directions.

- At the topmost level within a use case hierarchy, involve signals or uninterruptible atomic transactions.

- At lower levels within a use case hierarchy, involve various communication mechanisms.

- Allow a single actor to participate in any number of use cases.

- Allow a single use case to have any number of participating actors.

Extends Relationships

Extends relationships (Figure 8-6) are generalizations between use cases. They are used to model relationships between use cases in which a base use case instance may include the behavior specified by an extending use case, subject to conditions specified in the extension. Extends relationships

- Are used to capture exceptional behavior (or variations of normal behavior).

- Allow an extending use case to continue the activity sequence of a base use case when the extension point is reached in the base use case and the extension condition is fulfilled. Upon completion of the extension activity sequence, the original use case continues.

- Are denoted as generalization arrows.

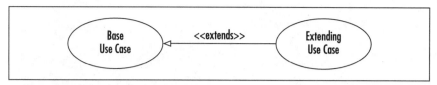

Figure 8-6: Extends Relationship

- Must be stereotyped using the "extends" keyword.

- May exist between use cases within multiple systems, but only if the system containing the extending use case specializes, via a generalization relationship, a system containing the base use case.

- Must have a condition determining when the extending use case will be inserted.

- May reference an extension point in the base use case determining where the extending use case may be inserted.

   Extending use cases may insert their parts (subordinate use cases) at different extension points within the base use case. Each part may have its own condition; however, if only one condition is used for the overall extending use case, all parts are inserted in the base use case if the condition is satisfied.

Uses Relationships

Uses relationships (Figure 8-7) are generalizations between use cases. They are used to model relationships between use cases in which a base use case instance will also include the behavior specified by a common use case.

Figure 8-7: Uses Relationship

Uses relationships

- Are used to share common behavior among use cases.

- Are denoted as generalization arrows.

- Must be stereotyped using the "uses" keyword.

- May exist between use cases within multiple systems, but only if the system containing the base use case specializes, via a generalization relationship, a system containing the common use case.

   Base use cases may interleave all their associated common use cases together with new pieces of behavior.

CHAPTER 9

Sequence Diagrams

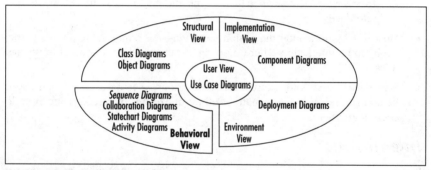

Figure 9-1: Behavioral Model View—Sequence Diagrams

Sequence diagrams (Figure 9-1) lie within the behavioral view of a system and render the specification of behavior. These diagrams describe the behavior provided by a system to interactors. These diagrams contain classes that exchange messages within an interaction arranged in a time sequence. They may be constructed using the following technique:

1. Identify behavior to be specified.

2. Model class roles.

3. Model lifelines.

4. Model activations.

5. Model messages.

6. Refine and elaborate as required.

Sequence diagrams

- May exist in generic form. These describe a set of message exchange sequences among a set of classes, that is, interactions among class roles.

167

- May exist in instance form. These describe one actual message exchange sequence consistent with the generic form, that is, a scenario among objects conforming to class roles. This form does not include repetition sequences (loops) or conditional sequence (branches).

- Are types of interaction diagrams that focus on one message exchange sequence or a set of such sequences involved in specifying behavior. This is depicted as a set of class roles involved in an interaction arranged in a time sequence.

- Show sequences of messages exchanged by class roles (horizontal dimension) within a time sequence (vertical dimension). The axes may be interchanged.

- Are particularly valuable for real-time specifications and for complex scenarios.

- Must have a vertical dimension representing the time over which an interaction occurs.

  - Time proceeds down the page. This may be reversed.

  - Only sequences are important, not the absolute span of time, but this dimension may have an actual metric.

  - Labels may be shown either in the margin or near the elements they reference.

- Must have a horizontal dimension specifying the different class roles participating in an interaction. There is no significance to the ordering of these class roles.

- May have the various expressions (activations, messages, guard conditions, iterations, and message signatures) they utilize be expressed using pseudo-code or another language.

Interactions

Interactions are classes that define message exchange sequences or patterns of message exchanges among other classes participating to accomplish a specific purpose. Interactions are used to model communications between entities. Interactions

- Are defined in the context of collaborations (Chapter 10).

- May be associated with use cases (Chapter 8) or operations. They *specify* the behavior provided.

- Are illustrated by scenarios. Scenarios are specific sequences of message exchanges and actions.

Class Roles

Class roles (Figure 9-2) are classes that define roles or specific parts played by class participants in interactions or collaborations. They are used to model roles that entities may play within interactions or collaborations.

Class roles

- Are denoted as class rectangles.

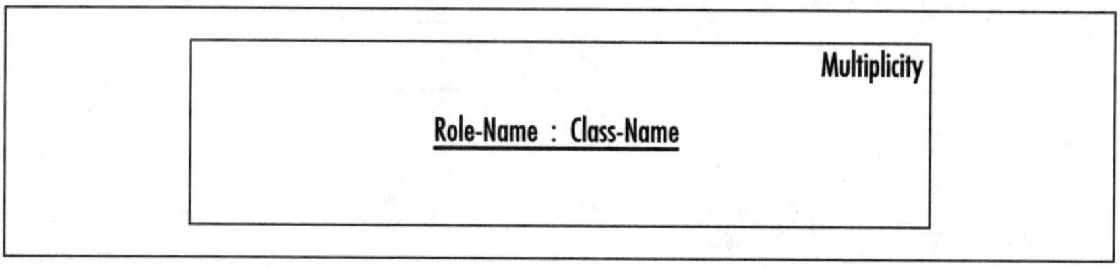

Figure 9-2: Class Role

- Specify the types of objects that may participate within interactions and collaborations.

- Specify a restricted view of classes. That is, they define what is required of a class for its participation in the interaction or collaboration.

- May use other notation of classes and objects.

- Represent roles that bind to actual objects when interactions or collaborations are used.

- Must have a name compartment.

- May have a role name or identifier string that represents the name of the role. The name must be underlined. When omitted, the colon remains and the role is played by an anonymous object.

- May have a colon followed by a class name or identifier string that represents the class of the role. The name must be underlined.

- May have a multiplicity expression that indicates that a set of objects participates within a role. When suppressed, it indicates a role for a single object.

- May have other compartments, which may be used for other model properties (business rules, responsibilities, variations, events, exceptions, etc.). These are not normally shown.

Lifelines

Lifelines (Figure 9-3) are graphical constructs that represent the existence of class roles over a period of time. They are used to model the existence of entities over time. Lifelines

- Are denoted as dashed lines.

- Must have their class roles identified.

- Must start at the top of the diagram, above the first message, if they exist when the interaction starts.

- Must end at the bottom of the diagram, below the last message, if they exist when the interaction ends.

- Must start when the class role object is created if it is created during the interaction. The message that creates it must be drawn with its arrowhead to the class role.

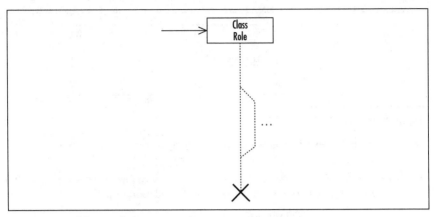

Figure 9-3: Lifeline

- Must end when the class role object is destroyed if it is destroyed during the interaction. The destruction is marked with a large "X" at the message that causes the destruction or at the final return message from the class role.

- May split into two or more concurrent lifelines to show conditionality. Each track corresponds to a conditional branch. They may merge together at some subsequent point in the class role's lifeline.

- May subsume an entire set of objects on a diagram representing a high-level view.

Activations

Activations (Figure 9-4) are graphical constructs that represent the time during which a class role is performing an action or when it is active and has focus of control (thread). They are used to model the time during which entities are active or performing some operation and to model control relationships among entities. Activations

- Are denoted as thin rectangles.

- Must have an initiation time. This coincides and is aligned with a rectangle's top. It may have an incoming message.

- Must have a completion time. This coincides and is aligned with a rectangle's bottom. It may be the tail of a return message.

- May be labeled to indicate their actions or operations. Labels

    - May be placed next to activation symbols.

    - May be placed in the margins of the diagram. Other information regarding the activation may also be placed in the margins of the diagram.

    - May be attached to incoming messages (and omitted from the activation symbol itself).

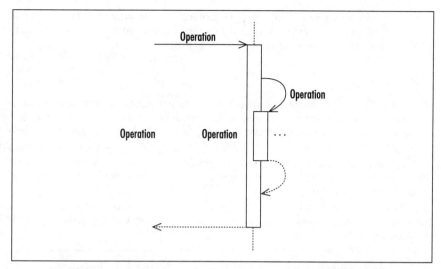

Figure 9-4: Activation

- May be used with concurrent objects or multiple active objects.

    - Direct computation involves a thread owner performing an operation.

    - Indirect computation involves a non–thread owner performing an operation via a nested thread.

    - An activation shows the time during which each object is performing an operation. Operations of other objects or other threads are not relevant.

    - If the distinction between direct and indirect computation is unimportant, the entire lifeline may be shown as an activation, or all activations may be omitted and only lifelines shown.

- May be used with nonconcurrent objects.

    - All objects share one thread of control. The thread may be nested or passed among objects as they request services from one another and perform operations to fulfill their responsibilities.

    - An activation shows the time when an object is performing an operation or another object is performing an operation via the thread being nested. That is, all of the active nested activations may be summarized by an object at a given time.

- May be recursive (self-delegating); that is, an operation may invoke itself. This is depicted using an activation symbol slightly to the right of the first activation symbol. Nesting may occur to an arbitrary depth.

- May be distinguished as actually computing or being live.

    - *Computing* activations are actually performing an operation. They are involved in direct computation. This may be indicated by shading the activation region.

- *Live* activations call or pass control to another object for actual processing. They are involved in indirect computation. This may be indicated by not shading the activation region.

Messages

Messages (Figure 9-5) are classes that define information that is exchanged in interactions and collaborations. They are used to model the content of communication between entities. They are used to convey information between entities and enable entities to request services of other entities. Class roles communicate by sending and receiving messages. A request is a specification of a communication, and a message shows a request in an interaction. When two instances communicate, an instance of a message class is passed between the two instances. The message instance has a sender, a receiver, and possibly other information according to the characteristics of the request. An event within the receiver will signal the receipt of the message from the sender.

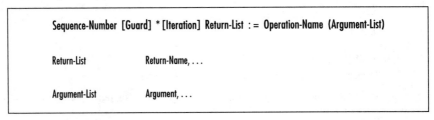

Figure 9-5: Message

Messages

- Are denoted as labeled horizontal arrows between lifelines. The sender will send the message and the receiver will receive the message.

- May have a sequence number. This is an integer that indicates the sequence of the message in the overall interaction. It starts at 1 and increments by 1. They are often omitted in sequence diagrams since the physical location of arrows shows the relative sequence of messages, but are necessary for collaboration diagrams (Chapter 10).

- May have square brackets containing a guard condition. This is a Boolean condition that must be satisfied to enable the message to be sent.

- May have an asterisk followed by square brackets containing an iteration specification. This specifies the number of times the message is sent. An asterisk without a specified iteration (and without square brackets) indicates that the message is repeatedly sent an unspecified number of times.

- May have a return list consisting of a comma-separated list of names that designate the values returned by the operation. These values may be used as actual parameters in subsequent messages. The return names must match the order, number, and types specified in the formal return list of the operation. When the return list is omitted, the assignment operator (:=) is omitted.

- Must have a name or identifier string that represents the name of the operation. The operation must be in the class role receiving the message.

- May have parentheses containing an argument list consisting of a comma-separated list of actual parameters passed to a method. The actual parameters must match the order, number, and types specified in the formal parameter list of the operation.

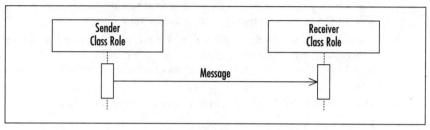

Figure 9-6: Simple Message

- May be simple (Figure 9-6).
  - This represents a flat flow of control.
  - This type of message is depicted using a stick arrowhead.
  - Control is passed from the sender to the receiver.
  - No other details about the communication are provided, either because they are not known or are not relevant.

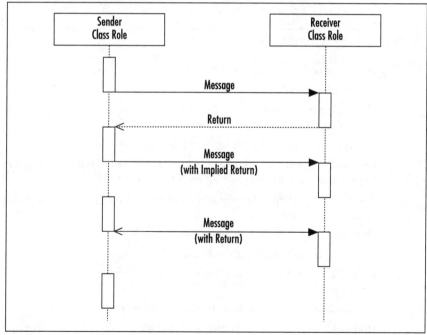

Figure 9-7: Synchronous Messages

- May be synchronous (Figure 9-7).
    - Are denoted as filled solid arrowheads.
    - This represents a nested flow of control via an operation call. The operation call invokes an operation synchronously.
    - This type of message is depicted using a filled arrowhead.
    - The sender passes control to the receiver via the message and pauses to wait for the receiver to relinquish or return control.
    - The receiver performs the operation, may pass control to other class roles if necessary, and returns control to the caller once the operation is completed. The receiver may also return or send information back to the sender.
    - Nested sequences complete before their outer sequences resume.
    - The receiver must be a passive object.
    - The return message may be omitted since it is implicit at the end of an activation, or it may be shown on the message line as a dashed arrow with a stick arrowhead.

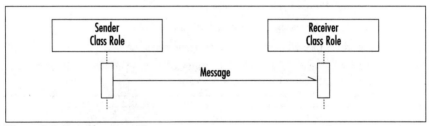

Figure 9-8: Asynchronous Message

- May be asynchronous (Figure 9-8).
    - Are denoted as half stick arrowheads.
    - This represents a nonnested flow of control via a signal. The signal invokes an operation asynchronously.
    - This type of message is depicted using a half-arrowhead.
    - The sender signals the receiver via the message and continues with the sequence without pausing to wait for the receiver.
    - The receiver performs the operation and may return or send information back to the sender.
    - The sender and receiver sequences are concurrent.
    - The receiver must be an active object.
    - If the receiver returns information to the sender, the information must be shown explicitly.
- May require time to travel between the sender and receiver (Figure 9-9).
    - Horizontal messages indicate that the time required to send the message is atomic, or brief compared with the activation. That is, the message transmission is negligible.

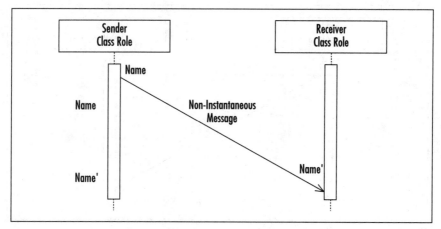

Figure 9-9: Noninstantaneous Message

- Slanted messages indicate that the time required to send the message is nonatomic, or requires some time. That is, the message transmission requires some time and other occurrences may take place, including messages in the opposite direction.

- May have sending times and receiving times (Figure 9-9). These are formal names that may be used in constraint expressions.

  - These formal names are useful for real-time applications.

  - The transition is given a name that represents the time the message is sent.

  - The transition name with a prime sign appended to it represents the time the message is received.

  - Transition times may be shown in the margin or attached to the message.

- May be part of branching (Figure 9-10). Branching involves multiple messages originating at the same time from a single class role.

  - The branch represents conditionality if the guard conditions on all the messages are mutually exclusive. Thus, only one message is sent.

  - The branch represents concurrency if the guard conditions on the messages are mutually inclusive. Thus, multiple messages are sent.

- May be part of iterations (Figure 9-11). Iterations involve a set of messages being sent multiple times.

  - Iterations may have square brackets containing a continuation condition specifying the condition that must be satisfied in order to exit the iteration and continue with the sequence.

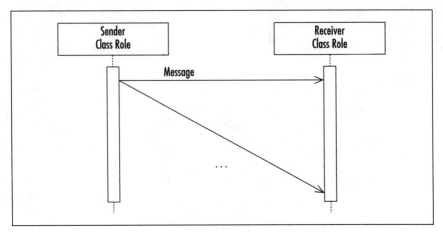

Figure 9-10: Branching and Concurrency

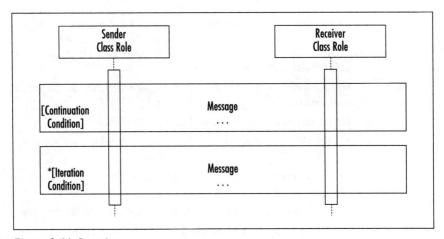

Figure 9-11: Iteration

- Iterations may have an asterisk followed by square brackets containing an iteration expression specifying the number of iterations.

- Iterations may be specified by placing square brackets containing a continuation condition or an asterisk followed by square brackets containing an iteration expression in a constraint expression (Chapter 15) that is attached to the messages within the iteration. This notation does not use the surrounding rectangle to enclose the messages.

CHAPTER 10

Collaboration Diagrams

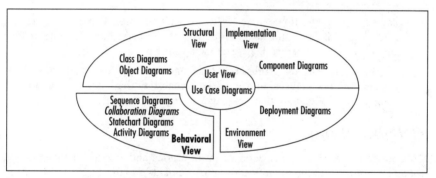

Figure 10-1: Behavioral Model View—Collaboration Diagrams

Collaboration diagrams (Figure 10-1) lie within the behavioral view of a system and render the realization and implementation of behavior. This is a definition of how behavior is realized by components within a system. These diagrams contain classes, associations, and their message exchanges within a collaboration to accomplish a purpose. They may be constructed using the following technique:

1. Identify behavior whose realization and implementation is to be specified.

2. Model class roles.

3. Model association roles.

4. Model message flows.

5. Refine and elaborate as required.

Collaboration diagrams

- May exist in generic form. They describe a set of classes and associations involved in message exchange sequences, that is, a collaboration among class roles and association roles, and their interactions.

- May exist in instance form. They describe a set of objects, links, and one actual message exchange sequence consistent with the generic form, that is, a scenario among objects conforming to class roles and links conforming to association roles.

- Are types of interaction diagrams that focus on a set of classes and associations involved in realizing and implementing behavior. This is depicted as a set of interactions arranged around the involved class roles and association roles.

- Show relationships among objects within an interaction.

- Are valuable for exploring all the effects of one object upon another and for exploring detailed procedural behavior.

- Must have class roles that are relevant to realizing the behavior. This includes indirectly affected or accessed transient classes (including method arguments and local variables).

- Must have association roles that are relevant to realizing the behavior. This includes transient associations among classes (including links to method arguments and local variables).

- May have message flows attached to association roles. If messages are not used on the diagram, the diagram depicts the context in which interactions can occur, but no interactions are explicitly shown.

- May have the various expressions (message flows, guard conditions, iterations, recurrence clauses, and message signatures) they utilize be expressed using pseudocode or another language.

Collaborations

Collaborations are classes that define a set of classes and associations meaningful for a set of purposes. The identification of participants and their relationships need not have global meaning; that is, the participants may be related only for the purpose of the collaboration. Collaborations are used to model a set of entities and relationships that are capable of interacting for a given set of purposes. Collaborations

- Define a context for interactions. A *context* is a set of related class roles and association roles that are used for a particular purpose. Contexts are not fully shown in sequence diagrams, since they do not show association roles; however, they are fully shown in collaboration diagrams.

- May be associated with use cases (Chapter 8). They *realize* use cases by describing the context in which behavior occurs and the interactions that realize the behavior.

- May be associated with operations. They describe the context in which operations occur. Such collaborations

  - Must have refinement relationships to the behavior they implement.

  - Must include the target class role of the operation. This class role represents the object on which the operation is applied.

- Must include any other class roles that are called on to provide services within the execution of the behavior.

- Must include roles for objects and links that exist before the behavior and after the behavior.

- Must include roles for objects and links that exist only during the behavior.

- May include objects and links that are created during an interaction. These have the keyword "new" as a constraint.

- May include objects and links that are destroyed during an interaction. These have the keyword "destroyed" as a constraint.

- May include objects and links that persist throughout the interaction. These have the keywords "transient" or "new destroyed" as a constraint.

- May have message flows that are superimposed on association roles. These correspond to steps within the behavior.

- May be associated with classes to describe their static structure. The union of all the collaborations for all the operations of a class establishes an overall collaboration for the entire class. This union shows the context for the implementation of the class.

- May be used for different interactions and purposes using different sets of messages.

- May be organized hierarchically to realize a system. This is explicitly how use cases are organized.

- May have a set of constraining model elements. These are constraints expressed using classes and associations. They express extra constraints on the participating elements.

- Are anonymous when explicitly attached to named model elements.

- May be parameterized. Parameterized collaborations are also known as *template collaborations* or *patterns* (Figure 10-2). Patterns

  - Are denoted as dashed ellipses connected to classes and associations or to objects and links using dashed lines. The attached classes and associations or objects and links participate in the pattern as specified by their role names.

  - Are constructs defining a family of collaborations having a common form. The differences among collaborations in the family are represented by class and association roles, allowing a single template to instantiate many collaborations. Specific collaborations within this family of prototypes are defined by specifying actual objects and links that are bound to formal class and association roles.

  - May have a name or identifier string that represents the name of the pattern. When omitted, the collaboration is no longer freestanding and must be attached to a model element.

  - Must specify the role names to which model elements may bind. These must correspond to names of elements within the context of the

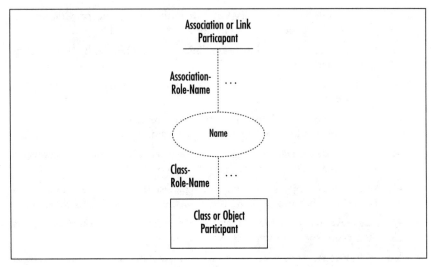

Figure 10-2: Pattern

collaboration. They are treated as parameters that are bound to specific elements on each occurrence or use of the pattern.

– Must be bound to particular model elements in order to be used. The model elements must be capable of supporting the requirements of the roles to which they bind in order to participate in the collaboration.

Association Roles

Association roles (Figure 10-3) are classes that define roles or specific parts played by association participants in collaborations. They are used to model roles that relationships may play within collaborations.

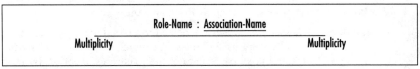

Figure 10-3: Association Role

Association roles

- Are denoted as association paths.
- Specify the types of links that may play particular roles or participate within collaborations.
- Specify a restricted view of associations. That is, they define what is required of an association for its participation in the collaboration.
- May use other notation of associations and links.
- Represent roles that bind to actual links when collaborations are used.

- Have association role ends that connect association role paths to two or more other class roles. Association role ends may have properties (Chapter 15) enclosed in curly brackets near the associated class roles.

- May have a role name or identifier string that represents the name of the role. The name must not be underlined. When omitted, the colon remains and the role is played by an anonymous link.

- May have a colon followed by an association name or identifier string that represents the association class of the role. The name must be underlined.

- Must have a multiplicity expression when connected to class roles representing sets of objects.

Multi-roles

Multi-roles (Figure 10-4) are class roles or association roles representing a set of objects or links that participate in interactions or collaborations. They are used to model roles that a set of entities plays within interactions or collaborations.

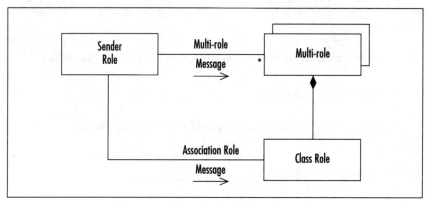

Figure 10-4: Multi-role

Multi-roles

- Are denoted as two rectangles in which the top rectangle is shifted slightly vertically and horizontally to suggest a stack of rectangles.

- May use other notation of classes, objects, associations, and links.

- Require two messages to perform an operation on each object in a set of instances. This includes one message to extract links to individual objects, and one message to each individual object using the extracted link. The two mentioned messages may be combined into a single message that includes an iteration and an application of an operation to each individual object.

- As class roles, they

  - Appear as two rectangles in which the top rectangle is shifted slightly vertically and horizontally to suggest a stack of rectangles.

- May receive messages. This indicates that a message is received by the set of instances and not each instance in the set. This use of multi-roles may include a selection operation to find an individual object. Such messages return a reference to an individual object with which the sender may interact. Messages to single class roles indicate a message to an individual object.
- May be attached to the multiclass role using a composition link.
- As association roles, they
    - Must use the many multiplicity indicator (*) attached to multiclass roles to show that many individual links are implied.
    - May propagate messages.

Message Flows

Message flows (Figure 10-5) involve the sending of messages between class roles via association roles, including a method call, a signal sent between active objects, or an explicit raising of an event. Message flows correspond to messages sent between class roles in sequence diagrams.

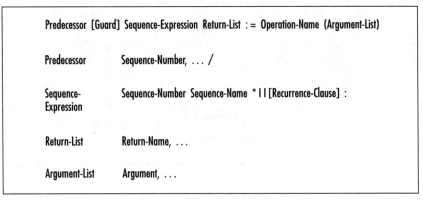

Predecessor [Guard] Sequence-Expression Return-List : = Operation-Name (Argument-List)	
Predecessor	Sequence-Number, ... /
Sequence-Expression	Sequence-Number Sequence-Name * I I [Recurrence-Clause] :
Return-List	Return-Name, ...
Argument-List	Argument, ...

Figure 10-5: Message Flow

Message flows

- Are denoted as labeled arrows attached to association roles between class roles. The sender will send the message, and the receiver will receive the message. The link is used to transport or otherwise implement the delivery of the message.
- May have multiple messages attached to the same arrow.
- May have a predecessor specification consisting of a comma-separated list of sequence numbers that must have occurred (and completed) in order to enable the message flow. Each sequence number must match the sequence number of another message. Numerically preceding sequence numbers are implicit predecessors and need not be explicitly listed. Predecessor specification is used for the synchronization of threads.

- May have square brackets containing a guard condition. This is a Boolean condition that must be satisfied in order to enable the message flow.

- May have a sequence expression. This is an expression involving nesting, concurrency, branching, and iteration control. Sequence expressions

  - Must have a sequence number. This is an integer that indicates the sequence of the messages within the next higher level of nesting. It starts at 1 and increments by 1. Messages that differ in one integer are sequentially related at the same level of nesting when associated with the same class role; that is, within activation 1, message 1.1 precedes message 1.2, message 1.2 precedes message 1.3, and so forth. This represents the nesting of control via the dot notation. If control is concurrent, nesting does not occur; that is, messages 1 and 2 are concurrent if these messages are associated with different class roles. Other numbering schemes may also be used, but they must be defined in the context in which they are used.

  - May have a sequence name. This is a string representing the thread of control. Messages that differ in the final name are concurrent at the same level of nesting. Within activation 1, message 1.1a and message 1.1b are concurrent via threads a and b. All threads of control are equal within a nesting level. This represents concurrency.

  - May have a recurrence clause.

    An asterisk indicates that the recurrence clause is an iteration specification in which messages are executed sequentially at the nesting depth. An asterisk followed by a double vertical line indicates that the recurrence clause is an iteration specification in which messages are executed concurrently. The clause specifies the number of times the message is sent. An asterisk (with or without a double vertical line) without a specified iteration (and without square brackets) indicates that the message is repeatedly sent an unspecified number of times. When the recurrence clause is omitted, the asterisk, double vertical lines, and square brackets are omitted.

    Square brackets alone indicate that the recurrence clause is a condition specification. This specifies that the execution of the message is contingent on the truth of the condition. When the clause is omitted, the square brackets are omitted.

    A loop involving multiple messages at the same level of nesting may be specified by placing an asterisk and a recurrence clause in a qualifier attached to the class role and attaching all messages within the loop as originating from the qualifier. Alternatively, the loop may be specified by placing an asterisk and a recurrence clause in a constraint expression (Chapter 15) that is attached to the messages within the iteration.

  - Are concatenated together in a dot-separated list at each level of nesting. Each nesting level may have sequence numbers and sequence names concatenated. However, recurrence clauses are not concatenated since each nesting level specifies its own recurrence clause within the enclosing context.

- May have a return list consisting of a comma-separated list of names that designate the values returned by the operation. These values may be used as actual parameters in subsequent messages. The return names must match the order, number, and types specified in the formal return list of the operation. When the list is omitted, the assignment operator (:=) is omitted.

- Must have a name or identifier string that represents the name of the operation. The operation must be in the class role receiving the message.

- May have parentheses containing an argument list consisting of a comma-separated list of actual parameters passed to a method. The actual parameters must match the order, number, and types specified in the formal parameter list of the operation.

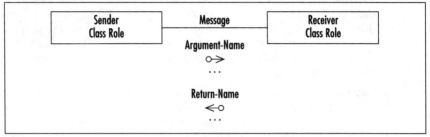

Figure 10-6: Data Tokens

- May express argument lists and return lists using data tokens (Figure 10-6). Data tokens

    - Represent argument names or values and return names.

    - Are small circles shown near messages.

    - Are labeled with argument names or return names.

    - Have a small arrow pointing in the direction of the movement of data. For argument names, they point in the direction of the message. For return names, they point in the opposite direction from the message.

Figure 10-7: Simple Message Flow

- May be simple messages (Figure 10-7).

    - Are denoted as stick arrowheads.

    - This type of message flow represents a flat flow of control.

    - This type of message flow is depicted using a stick arrowhead.

    - Control is passed from the sender to the receiver.

    - No other details about the communication are provided, either because they are not known or are not relevant.

- May be synchronous messages (Figure 10-8).

    - Are denoted as filled solid arrowheads.

Figure 10-8: Synchronous Message Flow

- This type of message flow represents a nested flow of control via an operation call. The operation call invokes an operation synchronously.
- This type of message flow is depicted using a filled arrowhead.
- The sender passes control to the receiver via the message and pauses to wait for the receiver to relinquish or return control.
- The receiver performs the operation, may pass control to other class roles if necessary, and returns control to the caller once the operation is completed. The receiver may also return or send information back to the sender.
- Nested sequences complete before their outer sequences resume.
- The receiver must be a passive object.

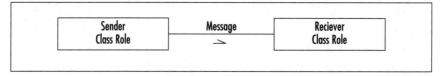

Figure 10-9: Asynchronous Message Flow

- May be asynchronous messages (Figure 10-9).
  - Are denoted as half stick arrowheads.
  - This type of message flow represents a nonnested flow of control via a signal. The signal invokes an operation asynchronously.
  - This type of message flow is depicted using a half-arrowhead.
  - The sender signals the receiver via the message and continues with the sequence without pausing to wait for the receiver.
  - The receiver performs the operation and may return or send information back to the sender.
  - The sender and receiver sequences are concurrent.
  - The receiver must be an active object.
  - If the receiver returns information to the sender, the information must be shown explicitly.

CHAPTER 11

Statechart Diagrams

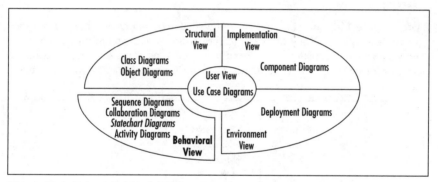

Figure 11-1: Behavioral Model View—Statechart Diagrams

Statechart (or state) diagrams (Figure 11-1) lie within the behavioral view of a system and render the states and responses of a class. These diagrams describe the behavior of a class in response to external stimuli. Statechart diagrams describe the life cycle of an object. These diagrams contain states and transitions. They may be constructed using the following technique:

1. Identify a class participating in behavior whose life cycle is to be specified.

2. Model states.

3. Model events.

4. Model transitions.

5. Refine and elaborate as required.

Statechart diagrams

- Are also known as state diagrams.

- Represent *state machines*, which are graphs of states and transitions that describe the responses of an object of a given class to outside stimuli. States represent the condition of an object. Transitions specify how these conditions are related. Objects

- Have one current state. The state of a composite object is the union of the states of all its parts.

- Have an initial state when they are created.

- May change states due to events.

- May perform actions or activities within states.

- May perform actions or activities when changing states.

- Have final states before they are destroyed.

• May be associated with classes or methods. They describe the response of an object of a given class to outside stimuli.

• May have the various expressions (guard conditions, transitions, events, action clauses, send clauses, and actions) they utilize be expressed using pseudocode or another language.

States

States (Figure 11-2) are classes that define status conditions an object may satisfy during its existence. They are used to model the situations during the life of an entity in which it satisfies some condition, performs some activity, or waits for some occurrence. An entity remains in a state for a finite and noninstantaneous time.

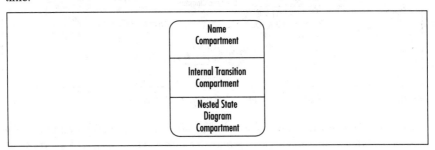

Figure 11-2: State

States

• Are denoted as rectangles with rounded corners.

• May be active or inactive. States become active when entered as a result of a transition firing. States become inactive when exited as a result of a transition firing.

• May be destinations of incoming transitions. These states function as a destination vertex for a transition.

• May be sources of outgoing transitions. These states function as a source vertex for a transition.

- May have a name compartment. This contains a state's name. States without names are distinct.

- May have an internal transition compartment named "internal transitions." These transitions specify actions or activities performed in response to events received while an object is in a particular state; however, they are performed without the object changing states. These transitions do not invoke the entry or exit actions of the state.

- May have one or more nested state machines. These are statechart diagrams within states, and can be shown as multiple statechart diagrams tiled in a single state. Each nested state machine corresponds to one ongoing activity within a state, and each state without nested state machines corresponds to one action. Actions are atomic executable statements that involve the invocation of an operation. Activities are nonatomic sequences of actions that have some duration. When nested state machines are used, the enclosing state is a composite state containing nested states. The nested states are substates of the composite state (or superstate). The nested states may be referenced by pathnames. The names are similar to class pathnames, but correspond to composite or containing state names.

- May have other compartments, which may be used for other model properties (business rules, responsibilities, variations, events, exceptions, etc.). These are not normally shown.

- May have their text compartments (name, internal transitions, and other compartments, not including the nested state diagram compartment) shrunk horizontally within the nested state compartment's graphic region (see Figures 11-3 and 11-4). This is only a convenience for appearance.

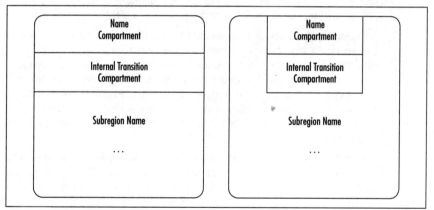

Figure 11-3: Disjoint Substates

- May be composite states having one nested state diagram (Figure 11-3). This corresponds to one activity within a state.

  - The subregion must include an initial state and a final state. A transition to the enclosing state represents a transition to the initial state. A transition to the final state within the subregion represents the completion of activity in the enclosing state. Completion of the outermost state of an object corresponds to its death. An object that transitions to its outermost final state ceases to exist.

- The state is decomposed using an OR relationship into mutually exclusive disjoint substates. That is, there is only one subregion and there may be only one current or active substate.

- The subregion may have an optional name and must contain a nested state diagram.

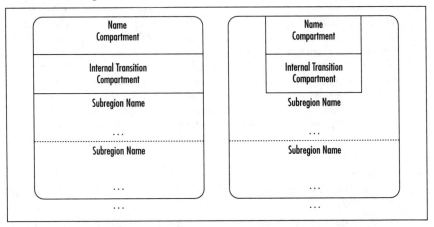

Figure 11-4: Concurrent Substates

- May be composite states having multiple state machines, each in a subregion (indicated by dashed lines) of the nested state diagram compartment (Figure 11-4). This corresponds to multiple activities within a state.

  - Each subregion must include an initial state and a final state. A transition to the enclosing state represents a transition to all initial states in all concurrent subregions. A transition to the final state within a subregion represents the completion of activity in the enclosing region. Completion of activity in all concurrent regions represents completion of activity by the enclosing state. Completion of the outermost state of an object corresponds to its death. An object that transitions to its outermost final state ceases to exist.

  - The state is decomposed using an AND relationship into mutually exclusive concurrent subregions with disjoint substates. That is, there are multiple subregions and each subregion may have its own current or active state. Each subregion has a current substate.

  - Subregions may have an optional name and must contain a nested state diagram with disjoint states. That is, subregions may not share states.

- May be simple states. These are states that do not have any substates.

- May be top-level states. These are the states owned by the state machine. Nested states are owned by their parent composite states. Top states

  - Are composite states. Each state machine has one composite state that contains all its states.

- – Must not be owned by any other state.

- – Must not be the source or target of a transition.

- May be pseudostates. Pseudostates

  - – Are states that are only used as notational devices.

  - – Represent transient points in transition paths between states.

  - – Must not be the current state. They implicitly transition to an actual or non-pseudostate.

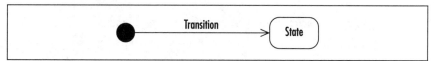

Figure 11-5: Initial (Pseudo) State

- May be initial pseudostates (Figure 11-5). Initial states

  - – Represent any transition to the enclosing state. That is, any transition to the enclosing state would make the nested initial state the current state.

  - – Are depicted as a small solid circle.

  - – Must not have any incoming transitions.

  - – Must have only one outgoing transition.

  - – May be labeled with a transition string. This is the event that creates the object.

  - – May be unlabeled. This represents any transition to the enclosing state.

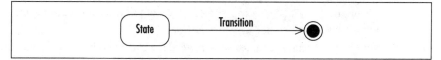

Figure 11-6: Final (Pseudo) State

- May be final pseudostates (Figure 11-6). Final states

  - – Represent the completion of activity in an enclosing state.

  - – Are depicted as a circle surrounding a small solid circle.

  - – May have any number of incoming transitions.

  - – Must not have any outgoing transitions.

  - – May be labeled with a transition string.

- May be history pseudostates (Figure 11-7). History states (or indicators)

  - – Represent the previous state within the state region that directly contains them. When a transition to the history indicator fires, the object resumes the state it last had within the region, and any entry actions are performed.

  - – Are depicted as a small circle containing an "H."

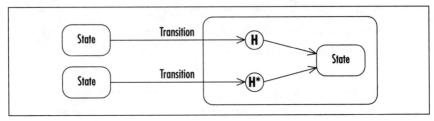

Figure 11-7: History (Pseudo) States

- Apply to the state region that directly contains them.
- Must not be used in the top state of a state machine.
- May have any number of incoming transitions from outside states.
- May have at most one outgoing unlabeled transition. This is the default "previous state" if the region has never been entered.
- May be deep history indicators, specified by a small circle containing an "H*." This indicates that the object reuses the state it last had at any depth within the complex state region rather than being restricted to a state at the same level as the history indicator.

- May have generalization relationships with other states. Generalization relationships between states may have one of the following interpretations:

  - Using subtyping, specialized states have the same outgoing transitions, may add outgoing transitions, have a different set of incoming transitions, and may add actions.
  - Using subclassing, specialized states have some of the same incoming transitions (may add or drop some), add outgoing transitions, and may add actions.
  - Generally, specialized states may have different outgoing and incoming transitions and different actions. They add and delete transitions and actions.

Transitions

Transitions (Figure 11-8) are associations between states. They are used to model relationships between the different states of an entity. An entity in one state will perform actions and possibly enter another state when an event occurs and a condition is satisfied (if specified); this occurrence is known as the *firing* of a transition. Transitions

- Are denoted as solid arrows between states and are labeled with a transition string.
- Relate source state vertices and target state vertices.
- May be internal state transitions. These are actions or activities performed in response to events received while an object is in a particular state; however, they are performed without the object changing states. Such transitions do not invoke the entry or exit actions of the state.

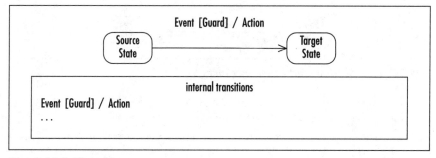

Figure 11-8: Transitions

- May be self-transitions. These are transitions in which the source state and target state are the same state. Such transitions do invoke the entry and exit actions of the state.

- May have an event expression that indicates the event that causes or triggers the transition to fire. The parameters of the event are available to the action on the transition and actions in the subsequent state.

> in State-Name, . . .
>
> not in State-Name, . . .

Figure 11-9: Guard Conditions

- May have square brackets containing a guard condition. Guard conditions
    - Are Boolean conditions that must be satisfied in order to enable the transition to fire.
    - May refer to the parameters of the triggering event and to attributes and links of the object that owns the state machine.
    - May involve tests of concurrent states of the current state machine. This includes expressions such as "in State-Name" to test whether the machine is in a state, and expressions such as "not in State-Name" to test whether the machine is not in a state (Figure 11-9).

- May have a forward slash followed by an action expression or action sequence that indicates the actions or effects that result when the transition fires.

- May be completion transitions (or automatic transitions). Every state may have one transition without an event trigger. The transition is automatically triggered upon the completion of the actions within the state.

- May conflict with one another. This occurs when multiple transitions are simultaneously enabled. Priorities are used to resolve the conflict. Transitions of substates have higher priority than transitions from any containing states. Otherwise, priorities must be explicitly specified. These priorities are useful for real-time applications.

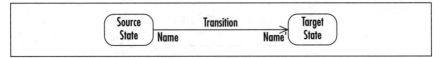

Figure 11-10: Sending and Receiving Names

- May have sending times and receiving times (Figure 11-10). These are formal names that may be used in constraint expressions.

  - The transition is given a name that represents the time at which it fires or is triggered.

  - The transition name with a prime sign appended to it represents the time at which the target state is reached via the transition.

  - These formal names are useful for real-time applications.

- May be compound transitions. These are transitions that consist of a cluster of simple transitions. The simple transitions are clustered using branching and complex transitions (fork and join transitions).

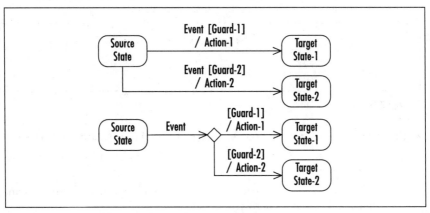

Figure 11-11: Branching (Decisions)

- May be part of a branching, or decision, construct (Figures 11-11 and 11-12). A decision utilizes guard conditions to indicate different possible transitions. Decisions

  - Are shown by labeling multiple outgoing transitions of a state with different guard conditions.

  - May use the diamond shape with one or more incoming transitions and two or more outgoing transitions. The incoming transitions to the diamond contain an event trigger. The outgoing transitions from the diamond must have distinct guard conditions with no event triggers. All possible outcomes of the decision should appear on one of the transitions, such that only one path may be selected as a result of the decision.

  - May be chained as part of complex transitions. However, only the first incoming transition may contain an event expression. All outgoing transitions may have guard conditions and action expressions.

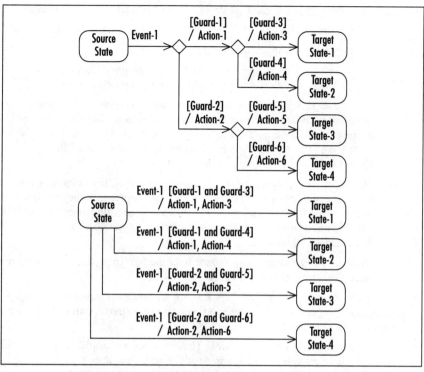

Figure 11-12: Chained and Unchained Branching (Decisions)

— May be unchained. This results in an individual transition for each path through the decision construct. The guard condition on the transition is the AND of all the conditions along the path.

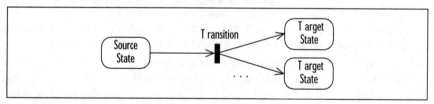

Figure 11-13: Splitting of Control

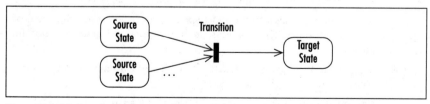

Figure 11-14: Synchronization of Control

- May be complex transitions (Figures 11-13 and 11-14). Complex transitions
    - Are transitions that involve multiple source states and multiple target states.
    - Are depicted as a short heavy bar.
    - Are enabled when all the source states are occupied. After the transition fires, all its destination states are occupied or activated concurrently.
    - May have multiple target states, indicating a splitting of control into concurrent threads without concurrent substates. The short heavy bar represents the forking of threads. This is a fork (pseudo) state. Fork states must have at least two outgoing transitions and one transition expression for the fork, and must originate from a state.
    - May have multiple source states, indicating a synchronization of control of concurrent threads. The short heavy bar represents the synchronization of threads. This is a join (pseudo) state. Join states must have at least two incoming transitions and one transition expression for the join, and must target a state.
    - May have a transition string shown near the bar. Individual arrows do not have their own transition strings.
- May point to complex states. This kind of transition is equivalent to transitions to a complex state's enclosed initial state or to initial states of each concurrent subregion.
- May originate from complex states. These transitions apply to each of the states within a complex state at any depth. That is, transitions are inherited by nested states. They may be masked or hidden (overridden) by the presence of nested transitions with the same trigger event. If a complex state's transition fires, any nested states are forcibly terminated and perform their exit actions before the transition action occurs and the new state is established.
- May be drawn directly to states within a complex state region at any nesting depth. All entry actions are performed for any states that are entered on such a transition. If a fork bar is used, the resulting concurrent states are established, and any other concurrent subregions start with their default initial states.
- May be drawn directly from states within a complex state region at any nesting depth to outside states. All exit actions are performed for any states that are exited on such a transition. If a join bar is used, specific states in other regions are irrelevant to triggering the transition.
- May be stubbed transitions (Figure 11-15). Stubbed transitions
    - Are transitions drawn to the most specific accessible enclosing state of a suppressed state. The contents of the suppressed state are not fully depicted.
    - Are depicted using stubs, which are small vertical lines drawn inside the boundary of the enclosing state.
    - May be drawn to stubs if they do not go to an unlabeled initial state. Stubs are not used for transitions to initial states.

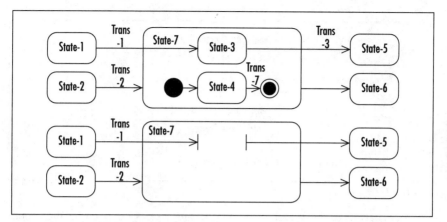

Figure 11-15: Stubbed Transitions

- May be drawn from stubs if they do not come from an unlabeled final state. Stubs are not used for transitions from final states.

- May have events depicted when leading into a state. These transitions lead either to a state or to an internal substate.

- Must not have events shown when leading from a suppressed state to an external state. The transition information belongs to its source state; if the source state is suppressed, so are the details of outgoing transitions. Final state transitions are depicted as unlabeled transitions from the border of a complex state. This represents the implicit event "action complete" (or "completion of activity" event) for the corresponding state.

• May have generalization relationships with other transitions. Generalization relationships between transitions may have one of the following interpretations:

- Using subtyping, specialized transitions may go to new target states and may add negative guard conditions. The guard conditions negate existing guard conditions.

- Using subclassing, specialized transitions may go to new target states. They must have the same source states, and may have different guard conditions.

- Generally, specialized transitions may have different source states and target states, and different guard conditions. They add and delete transitions and guard conditions.

Events

Events (Figure 11-16) are classes that define occurrences that may trigger an object to change states. They are used to model significant occurrences or stimuli that affect an entity. Events

• Are denoted as strings.

```
┌─────────────────────────────────────────────────────────────┐
│                                                               │
│                    Event-Name (Parameter-List)                │
│                            entry                              │
│                             exit                              │
│                              do                              │
│                   when (Boolean-Expression)                   │
│                   after (Time-Expression)                     │
│                                                               │
│        Parameter-List      Parameter-Name, ...                │
│                                                               │
└─────────────────────────────────────────────────────────────┘
```

Figure 11-16: Events

- Must have a name or identifier string that represents the name of the event. The event name must reference an operation or signal in the class receiving the event.

- May have parentheses containing a comma-separated parameter list that indicates the formal parameters passed to the event.

- May be used with internal state transitions. For internal state transitions, the following events are predefined and cannot be used for user-defined events:

  - Entry events indicate an entry action and are specified using the "entry" keyword. This is an action sequence that is executed when the state is entered. The action is atomic, may not be avoided, and precedes any internal activities or other transitions. Entry events may not have any parameters or guard conditions because they are implicitly rather than explicitly invoked. However, the entry event at the top level of a state machine for a class may have a parameter list that corresponds to the arguments an object of that class receives when it is created. This event does not occur for internal state transitions since there is no state change. This event does occur for self-transitions since there is a state change.

  - Exit events indicate an exit action and are specified using the "exit" keyword. This is an action sequence that is executed when the state is exited. The action is atomic, may not be avoided, and follows any internal activities, but precedes any outgoing transitions. Exit events may not have any arguments or guard conditions because they are implicitly rather than explicitly invoked. This event does not occur for internal state transitions since there is no state change. This event does occur for self-transitions since there is a state change.

  - Do events indicate an invocation of a nested state machine and are specified using the "do" keyword. The nested state machine must have an initial and final state. The nested state machine begins with its initial state after any entry action. When the nested state machine reaches its final state, any exit action occurs. The current state may then fire a transition based on the implicit completion of activity. Activities associated with do events must reference nested state machines rather than operations of the containing object.

- Must appear at most once in a single state.

- May be signal events. Signal events
  - Represent the reception of a request to invoke an operation. The request is issued using a signal action.
  - Are caused by the asynchronous invocation of an operation. The receiver class must declare the operation to be a signal using the "signal" stereotype keyword.
  - Have a name and a parameter list. They are declared as operations on class diagrams.
  - May have generalization relationships with other signal events. This indicates that an occurrence of the subevent triggers any transition dependent on the event or any of its ancestors.
  - May be declared on class diagrams as classes stereotyped using the "signal" keyword. These are signal names that may be used to trigger transitions. These classes must have their parameters shown in the attribute compartment. They must not have any operations. They must not have any relationships to other classes.

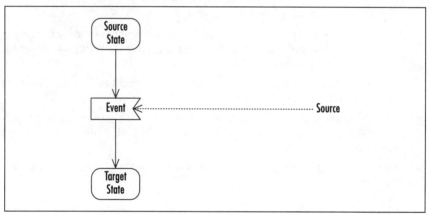

Figure 11-17: Signal Receipt Stereotype Icon

  - May use the signal receipt stereotype icon (Figure 11-17). This is a concave pentagon (or rectangle with a notch) representing the receipt of a signal. The event is indicated inside the symbol. An unlabeled transition is drawn from the previous state to the pentagon. An unlabeled transition is drawn from the pentagon to the next state. A dashed arrow may be drawn from the sender object to the notch on the pentagon. This symbol replaces the event label on a transition.
- May be call events. Call events
  - Occur when an operation is involved. The caller requests the operation using a call action.
  - Are caused by the synchronous or asynchronous invocation of an operation. The caller determines whether to wait for the operation to complete. If the caller waits for the operation to complete, the operation is invoked

synchronously. If the caller does not wait for the operation to complete, the operation is invoked asynchronously.

- Have a name and a parameter list. They are declared as operations on class diagrams.

- May be change events. Change events

  - Represent a notification that a condition has become true.

  - Are specified using the "when" keyword.

  - Must have a Boolean expression enclosed in parentheses designating the condition that must become true in order for the transition to fire.

  - Are different from guard conditions. Guard conditions are evaluated when the event fires. Change events fire when a condition becomes true; they are continuously checked when an object changes.

- May be time events. Time events

  - Represent a notification that a period of time has elapsed since entering a state or that a particular date/time has been reached.

  - Are specified using the "after" keyword.

  - Must have a time expression enclosed in parentheses designating the time that must elapse or the date/time that must be reached in order for the transition to fire.

- May occur without triggering any transition. The event is simply ignored or lost if it is not deferred (see the section entitled "Actions").

- May trigger more than one transition within the same region. Only one transition will fire, and the choice may be nondeterministic if a firing priority is not specified.

- May be applied to an initial transition if the event is stereotyped using the "create" keyword.

Actions

Actions (Figure 11-18) are classes that define executable statements or computational procedures. Actions are atomic (non-interruptible) computational procedures, typically involving invocation of an operation. Activities are nonatomic (interruptible) and consist of a sequence of steps or actions that have some duration. Activities may be expressed using nested statechart diagrams. Actions and activities are used to model the responses of an entity. Actions

- May be used to defer an event. This uses the "defer" keyword. Normally, an event that is ignored or not handled immediately is lost. Using the deferred action, a state may specify a set of events that are deferred or postponed if they occur while the state is active performing some activity. Deferred events are saved and recur when the object transitions to another state. All other events not included in the set of deferred events are lost. However, after the state completes its activity, the deferred events may trigger a transition or may remain deferred until the next state is reached. In the new state, the events

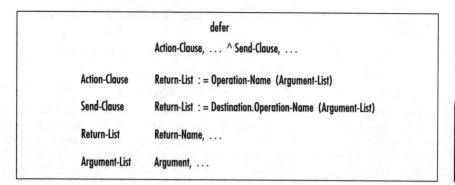

Figure 11-18: Action

may be accepted, deferred again, or lost. Events deferred within a composite state are also deferred for the nested states of the composite state.

- May have an action expression consisting of a comma-separated list of action clauses. Action clauses

  - Are call actions. They result in the invocation of an operation.

  - Are executed when the transition fires.

  - Are executed from right to left.

  - May have a return list consisting of a comma-separated list of names that designate the values returned by the operation. These values may be used as actual parameters in subsequent operations. The return names must match the order, number, and types specified in the formal return list of the operation. When the return list is omitted, the assignment operator (:=) is omitted.

  - Must have a name or identifier string that represents the name of the operation. The operation must be in the class receiving the message.

  - May have parentheses containing an argument list consisting of a comma-separated list of actual parameters passed to a method. The actual parameters must match the order, number, and types specified in the formal parameter list of the operation.

  - May refer to the parameters of the triggering event and to the operations, attributes, and links of the object that owns the state machine.

  - Must be atomic operations. That is, they may execute without interruption and must completely execute before any other actions or transitions are considered.

  - May be used with internal entry and exit state transitions. The action may refer to the attributes and links of the owning object, and to parameters of incoming transitions if the parameters appear on all incoming transitions.

  - May be used with internal do state transitions. In this case, the action must reference a nested state machine. The operation name corresponds to the name of the nested state machine.

- May have a "∧" symbol followed by a comma-separated list of send clauses. Send clauses

  - Are send actions. They result in the asynchronous sending of a signal.

  - Are executed when the transition fires.

  - Are executed from right to left after the action clauses.

  - May have a return list consisting of a comma-separated list of names that designate the values returned by the operation. These values may be used as actual parameters in subsequent operations. The return names must match the order, number, and types specified in the formal return list of the operation. When the return list is omitted, the assignment operator (:=) is omitted.

  - May have a destination string that indicates the object or class that will receive the message.

  - Must have a name or identifier string that represents the name of an operation or signal. The operation must be in the class receiving the message.

  - May have parentheses containing an argument list consisting of a comma-separated list of actual parameters passed to a method. The actual parameters must match the order, number, and types specified in the formal parameter list of the operation.

  - May refer to the parameters of the triggering event and to the attributes and links of the object that owns the state machine.

  - Must be atomic operations. That is, they may execute without interruption and must completely execute before any other actions or transitions are considered.

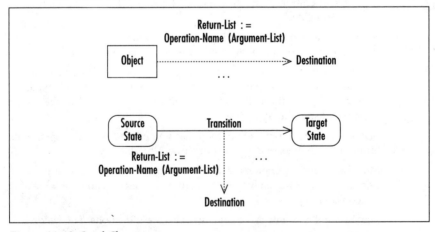

Figure 11-19: Send Clauses

  - May be depicted graphically (Figure 11-19). The sender may be a transition or an object, and the receiver may be a transition, an object, or a class. This requires each state diagram to be nested physically within an object symbol. There may be one object enclosing the main state diagram. This is the object that owns the diagram. The message is shown as a dashed arrow from the sender to the receiver labeled with the send clause, but the destination expression is omitted from the send clause since it is indicated by the dashed arrow. If the sender is a transition, the message is sent when the transition fires. If the sender is an object, the message is sent by the object at some point in its life. The actual point is unspecified. If the receiver is a transition, the transition must be the only transition in the object involving the event or be the only transition that would be triggered in response to the message. This notation may not be used if the transition triggered depends on the state of the receiving object and not just the state of the sender. If the receiver is an object, the message may trigger a transition on the corresponding event. There may be many transitions involving the event. This notation may not be used when the target object is computed dynamically. If the receiver is a class, the message may invoke a class scope operation. This notation may be used in other diagrams to show the sending of a message between objects and classes.

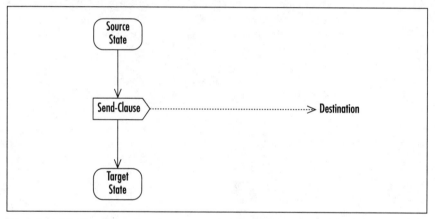

Figure 11-20: Signal-Sending Stereotype Icon

– May use the signal-sending stereotype icon (Figure 11-20). This is a convex pentagon (or rectangle with a point) representing the sending of a signal. The send clause is indicated inside the symbol, but the destination expression is omitted from the send clause since it is indicated by the dashed arrow. An unlabeled transition is drawn from the previous state to the pentagon. An unlabeled transition is drawn from the pentagon to the next state. A dashed arrow may be drawn from the point of the pentagon to the receiver of the signal. This symbol replaces the send clause on a transition.

• May be create actions. Create actions create an instance of a class. They must not have any target object.

• May be destroy actions. Destroy actions destroy an instance of a class. They must have a target object.

- May be return actions. Return actions return a value or set of values to the caller.

- May be terminate actions. Terminate actions cause the self-destruction of objects. They must not have any arguments.

- May be local invocation actions. Local invocation actions invoke a local operation without generating a call event or signal event.

- May be uninterpreted actions. Uninterpreted actions are actions that are not predefined.

- May be exception actions. Exception actions raise a signal in the case of an error during execution. The sender aborts execution, and execution resumes with the receiver of the exception. The receiver is determined implicitly by the interaction sequence during execution and is not explicitly specified.

CHAPTER 12

Activity Diagrams

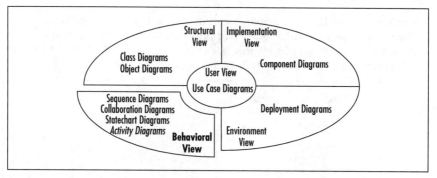

Figure 12-1: Behavioral Model View—Activity Diagrams

Activity diagrams (Figure 12-1) lie within the behavioral view of a system and render the activities or actions of a class participating in behavior. These diagrams describe the behavior of a class in response to internal processing rather than external events as in statechart diagrams (Chapter 11). Activity diagrams describe the processing activities within a class. These diagrams contain action states, action flows, and object flows. They may be constructed using the following technique:

1. Identify a class participating in behavior whose processing activities are to be specified.

2. Model swimlanes.

3. Model action states.

4. Model action flows.

5. Model object flows.

6. Refine and elaborate as required.

Activity diagrams

- Are variations of state machines or statechart diagrams (Chapter 11), in which states are activities representing operations, and transitions are triggered by the completion of actions within states.

- May be associated with classes, methods, or use cases (Chapter 8). They describe activities among a set of objects.

- May have the various expressions (guard conditions and actions) they utilize expressed using pseudocode or another language.

- Are types of interaction diagrams that focus on the flow of control and information within behavior.

- May have the various expressions (conditions, etc.) they utilize be expressed using pseudocode or another language.

- May be used to validate use cases.

- May be used for business modeling.

Swimlanes

Swimlanes (Figure 12-2) are graphical constructs that represent a partitioned set of actions. They are used to model the responsibilities of one or more objects for actions within an overall activity; that is, they divide the activity states into groups and assign these groups to objects that must perform the activities.

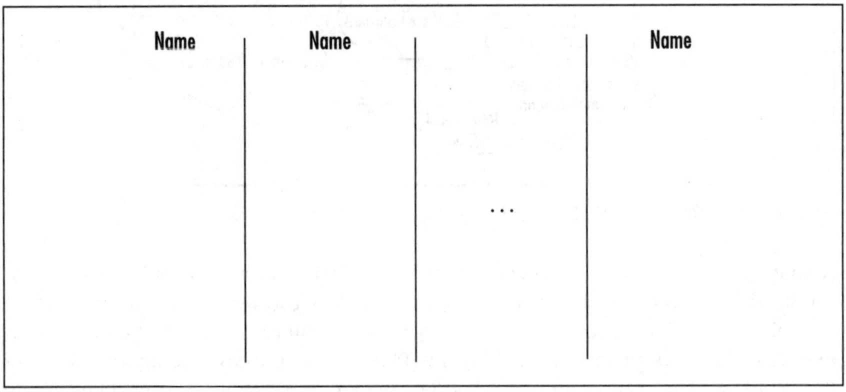

Figure 12-2: Swimlanes

Swimlanes

- Are denoted as regions separated from neighboring swimlanes by vertical solid lines.

- Have no significance to their order.

- May contain activities or action states.

- May have transitions that cross the lanes to get to their actions or target action states.

- Must have a name or identifier string that represents the name of the object responsible for the actions within the swimlane.

Action States

Action states (Figure 12-3) are states representing the execution of atomic actions or operations. They are used to model atomic actions of entities or steps in the execution of an algorithm.

Figure 12-3: Action State

Action states

- Are denoted as shapes with straight top and bottom lines and convex arcs on the sides.

- Are regular statechart diagram states with other constraints. That is, they may use other notation of statechart diagram states.

- Are shorthand for states with an internal action and at least one outgoing transition for the implicit event of completing the internal action.

- Must have an internal action expression that indicates the action within the state. These actions are equivalent to actions within statechart diagrams (Chapter 11).

- Must be assigned to a single swimlane. The object responsible for the swimlane's activities performs the action states in the swimlane.

- Must not have an entry action.

- Must not have an exit action.

- Must not have internal transitions.

- May have incoming transitions. These are action flows or object flows.

- May have outgoing transitions. These must not be based on explicit events. These are action flows or object flows.

- May use the links and attributes of the owning object to specify the action.

- Need not be unique within a diagram. That is, they may appear more than once within the same diagram. These are distinct states with the same action.

- May be activity states when representing nonatomic actions or operations. These activities require time to complete.

- Must defer all nonrelevant events so they are consumed when they become relevant. Relevant events are those events that appear on outgoing transitions from a state, and nonrelevant events are those that do not appear on outgoing transitions from the state.

Action Flows

Action flows (Figure 12-4) are associations between action states. They are used to model relationships between the action states of an entity. Action flows are activities performed by objects on objects. An entity in one action state will perform the specified action and enter another action state when the first action is completed.

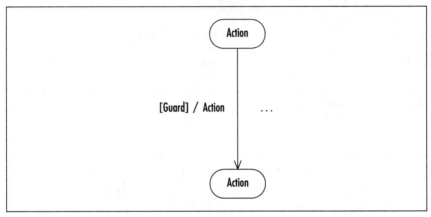

Figure 12-4: Action Flow

Action flows

- Are denoted as solid paths.

- Specify the flow of control between states.

- Are regular statechart diagram transitions with other constraints. That is, they may use other notation of statechart diagram transitions.

- May have square brackets containing a guard condition. Guard conditions

  - Are Boolean conditions that must be satisfied in order to enable the transition to fire.

  - May use the attributes and links of the object that owns the state machine.

- May have a forward slash followed by an action expression that indicates the resulting actions when the transition fires. These actions are equivalent to actions within statechart diagrams (Chapter 11).

- May be omitted between two action states when an object flow exists between the states. That is, when an action produces some output, and this output becomes the input of a subsequent action, the object flow relationship implies an action flow.

Object Flows

Object flows (Figure 12-5) are associations between action states and objects. They are used to model the utilization of objects by action states and the influence of action states on objects.

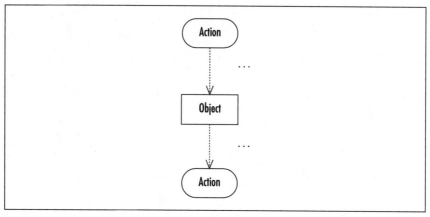

Figure 12-5: Object Flows

Object flows

- Are denoted as dashed paths.

- Specify the flow of objects between action states.

- May have object symbols (Chapter 7). Objects

    - May be the output of actions. This means that the action creates the object or modifies the object. This relationship is depicted as a dashed arrow from the action to the object symbol.

    - May be the input to actions. This means that the action uses the object. This relationship is depicted as a dashed arrow from the object symbol to the action.

    - May be manipulated by any number of activities. The output object of an action state may be input to one or more action states.

    - May appear multiple times on the same diagram. Each appearance denotes a different point in the life of the object. The object's state may be specified and placed in square brackets appended to the name of the object (Chapter 7).

CHAPTER 13

Component Diagrams

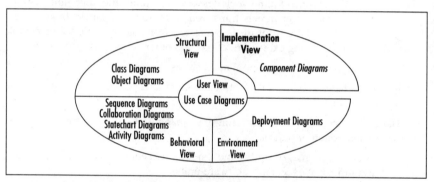

Figure 13-1: Implementation Model View—Component Diagrams

Component diagrams (Figure 13-1) render the implementation view of a system. These diagrams describe the organization of and dependencies among software implementation components. These diagrams only have a type form, not an instance form. These diagrams contain components and their relationships. They may be constructed using the following technique:

1. Model components.

2. Model development-time relationships between components.

3. Model calls relationships between components.

4. Refine and elaborate as required.

Component diagrams may have the various expressions (conditions, etc.) they utilize be expressed using pseudocode or another language.

Components

Components (Figure 13-2) are classes that define development-time and run-time physical objects. They are used to model distributable physical units containing model elements and having identity and a well-defined interface. Units in software systems include software code in source, binary, or executable form. Units in human systems include humans, business documents, and so forth.

Figure 13-2: Components

Components

- Are denoted as rectangles with two small rectangles projected from the side.

- Have types that represent different kinds of software modules. Component types

    - Exist at development time, or the time that compilation of software modules occurs, and represent software units of storage and manipulation. Development time includes compile time and link time. During compile time, software is translated from source code to binary code. During link time, software is translated from binary code to executable code by resolving external references to other code units.

    - Are represented on component diagrams.

    - Must have a name or identifier string that represents the type of the component.

- Have instances that represent run-time manifestations of software module types. Component instances

    - Exist at run time, or during the time that execution of the system occurs, and represent executable software units.

    - Are represented on deployment diagrams (Chapter 14) (or degenerate deployment diagrams without nodes).

    - Must have a name or identifier string that represents the name of the component. The name must be underlined.

    - May have a colon followed by a type expression that indicates the type of the component.

- May have aggregation relationships with other components, objects, and processes (or active objects). The "location" tagged value may be used to specify this relationship (Chapter 15).

- May use other notation of classes and objects.

- May have a property string to indicate the form of the component (source, binary, executable) (Chapter 15).

- May be located on nodes.

Development-Time Relationships

Development-time relationships (Figure 13-3) are associations between components. They are used to model compile-time and link-time dependencies, that is, the dependency of one component on another component during development time.

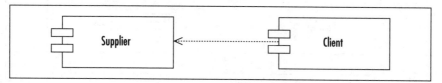

Figure 13-3: Development-Time Relationship

Development-time relationships

- Are denoted as dashed arrows.
- Have components with the following properties:
    - Client components are dependent on supplier components.
    - Supplier components exist at development time but need not exist at run time.
- May be stereotyped to depict an implementation-specific development-time dependency. When not stereotyped, the relationship represents a development-time communication or calls relationship.

Calls Relationships

Calls relationships (Figure 13-4) are associations between components. They are used to model calling or communication dependencies among components, that is, one component calling or using the services of another component. Calls relationships

- Are denoted as dashed arrows.
- Have components with the following properties:
    - Client components call or use the services (interfaces) of supplier components.
    - Supplier elements may be objects.
- May be stereotyped to depict an implementation-specific invocation.
- Exist at development time among development-time component types. They are represented on component diagrams.
- Exist at run time among run-time component instances. They are represented on deployment diagrams (Chapter 14) (or degenerate deployment diagrams without nodes).

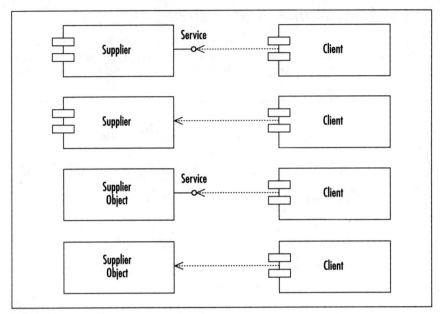

Figure 13-4: Calls Relationships

Deployment Diagrams

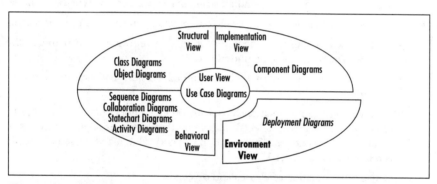

Figure 14-1: Environment Model View—Deployment Diagrams

Deployment diagrams (Figure 14-1) render the environment view of a system. These diagrams describe the configuration of processing resource elements and the mapping of software implementation components onto them. These diagrams contain nodes, components, and their relationships. They may be constructed using the following technique:

1. Model nodes.

2. Model communication relationships between nodes.

3. Model components (from component diagrams).

4. Model run-time relationships between components.

5. Model calls relationships between components (from component diagrams).

6. Model supports relationships between nodes and components.

7. Model becomes relationships between components.

8. Refine and elaborate as required.

Deployment diagrams may have the various expressions (conditions, etc.) they utilize be expressed using pseudocode or another language.

Nodes

Nodes (Figure 14-2) are classes that define run-time physical objects. They are used to model processing or computational resources. Nonhuman resources generally have at least a memory and often processing capability. Human resources are people.

Figure 14-2: Nodes

Nodes

- Are denoted as three-dimensional cubes.

- Have types that represent different kinds of computational resources. Node types must have a name or identifier string that represents the type of the node.

- Have instances that represent specific computational resources. Node instances

  - Must have a name or identifier string that represents the name of the node. The name must be underlined.

  - May have a colon followed by a type expression that indicates the type of the node.

- May have aggregation relationships with other components, nodes, objects, and processes (or active objects), indicating that instances reside on nodes or are deployed onto nodes. The "location" tagged value may be used to specify this relationship (Chapter 15).

- May use other notation of classes and objects.

Communication Relationships

Communication relationships (Figure 14-3) are associations between nodes. They are used to model communication paths or connections between nodes.

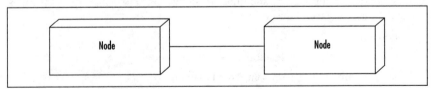

Figure 14-3: Communication Relationship

Communication relationships

- Are denoted as solid associations.

- May be stereotyped to indicate the nature of the communication path or connection.

- May use other notation of associations and links.

Run-Time Relationships

Run-time relationships (Figure 14-4) are associations between components. They are used to model execution dependencies, that is, the dependency of one component on another component during run time.

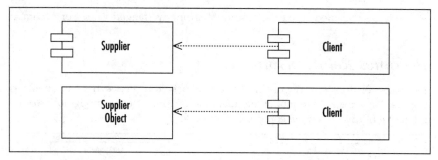

Figure 14-4: Run-Time Relationships

Run-time relationships

- Are denoted as dashed arrows.
- Have components with the following properties:
    - Client components are dependent on supplier components.
    - Supplier elements may be objects.
    - Supplier components exist at run time but need not exist at development time.
- May be stereotyped to depict an implementation-specific run-time dependency. When not stereotyped, the relationship represents a run-time communication or calls relationship.

Supports Relationships

Supports relationships (Figure 14-5) are associations between nodes and components or objects. They are used to model a component's or object's ability to execute on a node or a node's capability to host a component or object.

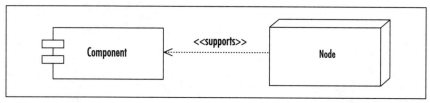

Figure 14-5: Supports Relationship

Supports relationships

- Are denoted as dashed arrows.

- May be stereotyped using the "supports" keyword. When no stereotype key-word is used, the "supports" keyword is assumed.

- May be more precisely stereotyped to depict an implementation-specific dependency.

- May be specified using the "location" property (tagged value) of a compo-nent or object.

Becomes Relationships

Becomes relationships (Figure 14-6) are associations between components or objects. They are used to model the migration of components among nodes or the migration of objects among components or nodes.

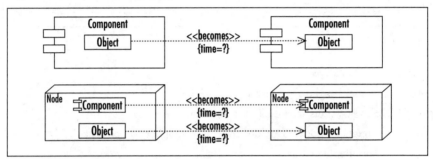

Figure 14-6: Becomes Relationships

Becomes relationships

- Are denoted as dashed arrows.

- Must be stereotyped using the "becomes" keyword.

- May have a time property attached to indicate the time at which the move-ment or migration occurs. Messages are directed to the correct occurrence of the component.

CHAPTER 15

Extension Mechanisms

Extension mechanisms are the means for customizing and extending the UML. The model elements described in Chapters 6 through 14 are instances of metamodel elements that can be considered the core of UML diagrams. (See Chapter 5 for a description of the metamodel.) The UML defines properties for each model element and a system of stereotypes and constraints that permit you to add new elements. This chapter describes the basic extension mechanisms and two particular extensions that have already proven useful: one for software engineering and one for business modeling.

Stereotypes

Stereotypes (Figure 15-1) are a mechanism for classifying or marking model elements and introducing new types of modeling elements.

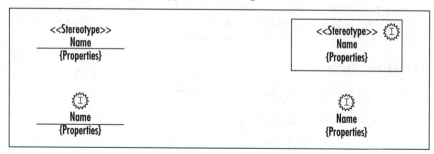

Figure 15-1: Stereotypes

Stereotypes

- Are strings enclosed in guillemets (<< >>), or double angle brackets, preceding the name of an element. A property may follow the name of the element.

- Are limited to one per model element.

- May be elements within a list of strings. The stereotype applies to all succeeding elements of the list until another stereotype keyword list element appears, an empty stereotype keyword nullifies it, or the end of the list is reached.

- May be used for classifying or marking model elements, in which case stereotypes are depicted when the element is rendered.

- May be used for introducing new types of modeling elements. New modeling elements

  - Must be subclasses of existing modeling elements.

  - Must have the same form or characteristics (attributes and operations) as their base metamodel classes. That is, they inherit the characteristics of their base classes via a generalization relationship.

  - Must have a different intent or semantics than their base classes. That is, they have a different meaning or purpose then their base classes.

  - May extend their base classes by adding properties (constraints and tagged values) to the characteristics they receive from their base classes. These properties are implicitly attached to model elements of the new stereotype. If tagged values are left unspecified in the new modeling element, they must be specified when the stereotype is attached to a model element.

  - May have an associated graphic icon or graphic marker.

  - May be rendered using the base model element symbol in addition to the stereotype keyword with or without the graphic icon, or rendered using the graphic icon and collapsing the base model element symbol.

  - May be described in a classification hierarchy that extends the metamodel hierarchy. This is a user-defined metamodel diagram that describes how stereotypes extend the UML metamodel. These classes must themselves be stereotyped using the "stereotype" keyword. The attributes of these classes may be referenced by model elements using the attribute names as keywords in tagged values. Properties and attributes must not conflict with those that a stereotype inherits.

Standard Stereotypes

Table 15-1 shows the standard stereotype elements predefined in the UML.

Table 15-1: Standard Stereotypes

Name	Application	Semantics
<<actor>>	Class	The class defines a set of external objects that interact with a system.
<<association>>	Association role end	The corresponding element is accessible via an association.

Table 15-1: Standard Stereotypes (continued)

Name	Application	Semantics
<<becomes>>	Dependency	The dependency is between a source instance and a target instance. The dependency specifies that the source and target represent the same instance at different points in time, but with different state and roles. That is, the source instance becomes the target instance with possibly different state and role.
<<bind>>	Dependency	The dependency is between a source class and a target template. The dependency specifies that the class is created by binding actual values to the formal parameters of the template.
<<call>>	Dependency	The dependency is between a source operation and a target operation. The dependency specifies that the source operation invokes the target operation. The target operation must be accessible or within the scope of the source operation.
<<constraint>>	Note	The note is a constraint.
<<constructor>>	Operation	The operation creates an instance of the classifier to which the operation is attached. This is equivalent to the "create" stereotype. See the "create" and "destructor" stereotypes.
<<classify>>	Dependency	The dependency is between a source instance and a target classifier. The dependency specifies that the source instance is an instance of the target classifier. See the "declassify" stereotype.
<<copy>>	Dependency	The dependency is between a source instance and a target instance. The dependency specifies that the source and target represent different instances with the same state and roles. The target instance is an exact copy of the source instance. The source and target are unrelated after the copy.

Table 15-1: Standard Stereotypes (continued)

Name	Application	Semantics
<<create>>	Operation	The operation creates an instance of the classifier to which the operation is attached. The operation is a constructor. This is equivalent to the "constructor" stereotype. See the "constructor" and "destroy" stereotypes.
	Event	The event denotes that an instance of the class enclosing the state machine is created. The event may be applied only to an initial transition at the topmost level of the state machine.
<<declassify>>	Dependency	The dependency is between a source instance and a target classifier. The dependency specifies that the source instance is no longer an instance of the target classifier. See the "classify" stereotype.
<<destroy>>	Operation	The operation destroys an instance of the classifier to which the operation is attached. This is equivalent to the "destructor" stereotype. See the "destructor" and "create" stereotypes.
	Event	The event denotes that an instance of the class enclosing the state machine is destroyed.
<<delete>>	Refinement	The refinement is between a source element and a target element. The refinement specifies that the source element can no longer be refined.
<<derived>>	Dependency	The dependency is between a source element and a target element. The dependency specifies that the source element is derived from the target element. That is, the source element is not an instance of the target element, but an instance of another element that is a subclass or subtype of the target element.
<<destructor>>	Operation	The operation destroys an instance of the classifier to which the operation is attached. This is equivalent to the "destroy" stereotype. See the "destroy" and "constructor" stereotypes.
<<document>>	Component	The component represents a document.

Table 15-1: Standard Stereotypes (continued)

Name	Application	Semantics
<<enumeration>>	Data type	The data type specifies a set of identifiers that are the possible values of an instance of the data type.
<<executable>>	Component	The component represents an executable program that may be run on a node.
<<extends>>	Generalization	The generalization is between a source use case and a target use case. The generalization specifies that the contents of the source use case may be added to the target use case. The relationship specifies where the contents should be added (extension point) and the condition that must be satisfied in order to add the source use case. When an instance of the target use case reaches the extension point and the condition is fulfilled, the instance continues according to a sequence that is the result of extending the target use case sequence with the source use case sequence at that point.
<<facade>>	Package	The package only contains references to model elements owned by other packages. It does not contain any model elements of its own. It is used to provide a "public view" of some of the contents of another package.
<<file>>	Component	The component represents a document or file containing source code or data.
<<framework>>	Package	The package consists mainly of patterns (collaborations).
<<friend>>	Dependency	The dependency is between a source element (operation, class, or package) and a target element (operation, class, or package) in a different package. The dependency specifies that the source element may access the target element regardless of the declared visibility of the target element.
<<global>>	Association role end	The corresponding element is accessible because it has global scope within the context in which it is accessed. That is, the instance is accessible throughout the system.

Table 15-1: Standard Stereotypes (continued)

Name	Application	Semantics
<<import>>	Dependency	The dependency is between a source package and a target package. The dependency specifies that the source package receives and may access the public contents of the target package.
<<implementation class>>	Class	The class defines the implementation of another class in some programming language. The class is not a type. An instance may have zero or one implementation classes. But an instance may statically have many general or non-implementation classes, and it may dynamically gain or lose general classes over time.
<<inherits>>	Generalization	The generalization is between a source classifier and a target classifier. This constrains the generalization such that instances of the source classifier may not be substituted for instances of the target classifier. See the "subclass" and "subtype" stereotypes.
<<instance>>	Dependency	The dependency is between a source instance and a target classifier. The dependency specifies that the source instance is an instance of the target classifier.
<<interface>>	Class	The class defines a collection of operations that may be used for defining a service offered by other classes. The class may contain only externally accessible, or public, operations without methods.
<<invariant>>	Constraint	The constraint is attached to a set of classifiers or relationships. The constraint specifies a condition that must hold true for the classifiers or relationships and their instances. See the "precondition" and "postcondition" stereotypes.
<<local>>	Association role end	The corresponding element is accessible because it has local scope within the context in which it is accessed. That is, the instance is a local variable within an operation.

Table 15-1: Standard Stereotypes (continued)

Name	Application	Semantics
<<library>>	Component	The component represents a static or dynamic library. A static library is utilized by a program during development time: the library is linked into the program. A dynamic library is utilized by a program during run time: the library is accessed by the program during execution.
<<metaclass>>	Classifier	The class is a metaclass of some other class.
	Dependency	The dependency is between a source classifier and a target classifier. The dependency specifies that the target classifier is the metaclass of the source classifier.
<<parameter>>	Association role end	The corresponding element is accessible because it is a parameter within the context in which it is accessed. That is, the instance is a parameter variable within an operation.
<<postcondition>>	Constraint	The constraint is attached to an operation. The constraint specifies a condition that must hold true after the invocation of the operation. See the "invariant" and "precondition" stereotypes.
<<powertype>>	Classifier	The classifier is a metatype whose instances are subtypes of another type. That is, the classifier is the type of a discriminator involved in a generalization relationship.
	Dependency	The dependency is between a source set of generalizations and a target classifier. The dependency specifies that the target classifier is the powertype of the source set of generalizations. That is, the classifier is the type of the discriminator involved in the set of generalizations.
<<precondition>>	Constraint	The constraint is attached to an operation. The constraint specifies a condition that must hold true for the invocation of the operation. See the "invariant" and "postcondition" stereotypes.

Extension Mechanisms

Table 15-1: Standard Stereotypes (continued)

Name	Application	Semantics
<<private>>	Generalization	The generalization is between a source classifier and a target classifier. The generalization specifies that inherited features of the target classifier are hidden, or made private, within the source classifier. Instances of the source classifier may not be substituted for instances of the target classifier.
<<process>>	Classifier	The classifier denotes an active class that has a heavyweight flow of control. It is a thread with a representation of control (code), and may be composed of threads. See the "thread" stereotype.
<<query>>	Operation	The operation does not modify the state of the instance. See the "update" stereotype.
<<realize>>	Generalization	The generalization is between a source element and a target element. The generalization specifies that the source element realizes the target element. If the target element is an implementation class, the relationship implies inheritance of operations but not of structure (attributes and associations). If the target element is an interface, the source element supports the operations of the interface.
<<refine>>	Dependency	The dependency is between a source element and a target element. The dependency specifies that the two elements are at different semantic levels of abstraction. The source element refines or is derived from the target element. This may be used between different types of models (analysis, design, and implementation) or between use cases and their implementations. The refinement may be described in a note attached to the dependency.
<<requirement>>	Comment	The note specifies a responsibility or obligation of the element to which it is attached.
<<self>>	Association role end	The corresponding instance is accessible because it is the requester.
<<send>>	Dependency	The dependency is between a source operation and a target signal class. The dependency specifies that the operation sends the signal.

Table 15-1: Standard Stereotypes (continued)

Name	Application	Semantics
<<signal>>	Class	The class defines a signal whose name may be used to trigger transitions. The parameters of the signal are shown in the attribute compartment. The class must not have any operations. It may have generalization relationships to other signal classes.
	Operation	The class accepts and responds to a given signal. The response (operation) is shown using a state machine.
<<stereotype>>	Classifier	The classifier is a stereotype. The classifier is a metamodel class. This is used to model stereotype hierarchies.
<<stub>>	Package	The package is not completely transferred to other packages via generalization relationships. That is, only the public parts of the package are inherited, and the protected parts of the package are not inherited.
<<subclass>>	Generalization	The generalization is between a source classifier and a target classifier. This constrains the generalization such that instances of the source classifier may not be substituted for instances of the target classifier. See the "inherits" and "subtype" stereotypes.
<<subtraction>>	Refinement	The refinement specifies that the target can no longer be refined.
<<subtype>>	Generalization	The generalization is between a source classifier and a target classifier. This indicates that instances of the source classifier may be substituted for instances of the target classifier. This is the default semantic for generalizations. See the "inherits" and "subclass" stereotypes.
<<subsystem>>	Package	The package is a subsystem. It has one or more public interfaces and a private implementation that realizes the interfaces. It must have at least one public interface and must not make any of its implementation publicly accessible.
<<supports>>	Dependency	The dependency is between a source node and a target component. The dependency specifies that the component may reside on the node; that is, the node supports or allows the component to execute on the node.

Table 15-1: Standard Stereotypes (continued)

Name	Application	Semantics
<<system>>	Package	This package denotes a collection of models that describe a system from different viewpoints. Each model shows a different view of the system, including specification and realization views. This package is the root of the package hierarchy. It may be contained only in a system package.
<<table>>	Component	The component represents a database table.
<<thread>>	Classifier	The classifier denotes an active class that has a lightweight flow of control. It is a single path of execution through some representation of control (code). See the "process" stereotype.
<<top level package>>	Package	The package denotes the topmost package in a model. It represents all the nonenvironmental parts of the model. It is at the top of the containment hierarchy in a model.
<<trace>>	Dependency	The dependency is between a source element and a target element. The dependency specifies that the two elements represent the same concept at different levels of semantics or from different points of view. This may be used for tracing requirements or to track changes of model elements.
<<type>>	Class	The class specifies a set of instances together with the operations applicable to the objects. The class may have attributes, operations, and associations, but it may not contain any methods.
<<update>>	Operation	The operation modifies the state of the instance. See the "query" stereotype.
<<use case model>>	Package	The package denotes a model that describes a system's functional requirements. It contains use cases and their interactions with actors. The package may contain only use cases, actors, extends and uses relationships between use cases, communication relationships between use cases and actors, and generalization relationships between actors.

Table 15-1: Standard Stereotypes (continued)

Name	Application	Semantics
<<uses>>	Generalization	The generalization is between a source use case and a target use case. The generalization specifies that the contents of the target use case are included or used in the description of the source use case. The relationship is used for extracting shared behavior.
	Dependency	The dependency is between a source element and a target element. The dependency specifies that the source element requires the presence of the target element for its correct implementation or functioning.
<<utility>>	Classifier	The classifier denotes a named collection of nonmember attributes and operations. All the instance scope attributes and operations have class scope by default.

Properties

Properties (Figure 15-2) are characteristics of an element.

{Property-String, ...}

Figure 15-2: Property

Properties

- Are strings consisting of a comma-separated list of substrings (property strings) enclosed in curly braces. Each substring is a value attached to the element to which the whole property string is attached. These values may include attributes, associations, constraints, and tagged values.

- May be elements within a list of strings. The properties apply to all succeeding elements of the list until another property string list element appears or the end of the list is reached. Properties (applied to a list of elements) are not superseded by property strings attached to individual elements, but may be augmented or modified by them.

- May be associated with a single graphical symbol, where the string

    - Is a property of the single graphical symbol to which it is attached.

    - May follow the name of an element (Figure 15-1).

    - May be placed in a note and attached (using a dashed line) to the graphical symbol (Figure 15-3). If the note is stereotyped, the property need not be enclosed in curly brackets.

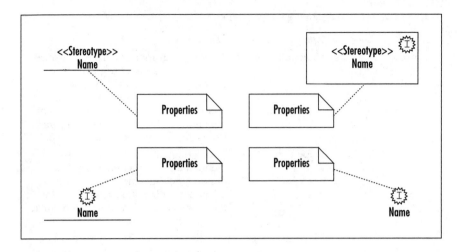

Figure 15-3: Properties for Symbols Using Notes

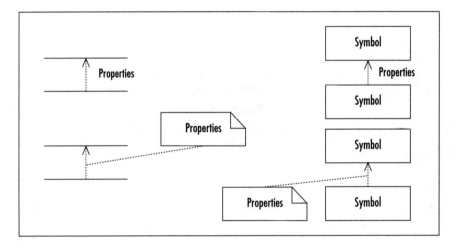

Figure 15-4: Properties between Two Symbols

- May be associated with two graphical symbols (Figure 15-4), where the string

    - Is a property of the two graphical symbols to which it is attached.

    - May be attached to a dashed arrow from one element to the other element. The direction of the arrow is relevant within the property. If the property is a constraint, the direction of the arrow indicates that one element is dependent on another element.

    - May be placed in a note and attached (using a dashed line) to a dashed arrow from one element to the other element. The direction of the arrow is relevant. If the note is stereotyped, the property need not be enclosed in curly brackets.

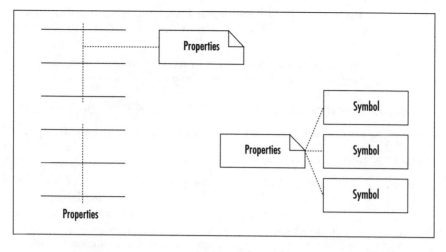

Figure 15-5: Properties between Three or More Symbols

- May be used with three or more graphical symbols (Figure 15-5), where the string

  - Is a property of the three or more graphical symbols to which it is attached.

  - May be attached to a dashed line crossing a set of paths. This indicates that the property applies to the paths the dashed line crosses.

  - May be placed in a note and attached (using a dashed line) to a dashed line crossing a set of paths. If the note is stereotyped, the property need not be enclosed in curly brackets.

  - May be placed in a note and attached (using a dashed line) to three or more graphical symbols. If the note is stereotyped, the property need not be enclosed in curly brackets.

Constraints

Constraints (Figure 15-6) are a mechanism for specifying semantics or conditions that must be maintained as true for model elements.

Figure 15-6: Constraint

Constraints

- Are strings within property strings. Constraint strings specify conditions that must be maintained as true for a model element or elements.

- Must be expressed using a particular language (computer language, human language, or the Object Constraint Language) that is conceptually interpretable or executable.

- May be comments. Comments are text strings written in a human language. The meaning of the string is significant to humans.

Standard Constraints

Table 15-2 shows the standard constraint elements predefined in the UML.

Table 15-2: Standard Constraints

Name	Application	Semantics
abstract	Class	The class has at least one abstract operation and may not be instantiated.
	Operation	The operation provides an interface specification, but no implementation.
active	Object	The object owns a thread of control and may initiate control activity.
add only	Association end	Additional links may be added (the multiplicity is variable), but links may not be modified or deleted. See the "frozen" constraint.
association	Association end	The corresponding instance is accessible via an association.
broadcast	Operation signal	The request is simultaneously sent to multiple instances in an undefined and unspecified order.
class	Attribute	The attribute has class scope. All instances of a class share one value for the attribute. See the "instance" constraint.
	Operation	The operation has class scope. The operation may be applied on the class. See the "instance" constraint.
complete	Generalization	For a set of generalizations, all subtypes have been specified, some may be suppressed or elided, and no additional subtypes are permitted. See the "incomplete" constraint.
concurrent	Operation	The operation may be called from concurrent threads simultaneously, and all threads may proceed concurrently. Concurrent operations perform correctly in the case of simultaneous sequential or guarded access. See the "sequential" and "guarded" constraints.

Table 15-2: Standard Constraints (continued)

Name	Application	Semantics
destroyed	Class role Association role	The model element is destroyed during the execution of an interaction. See the "new," "new destroyed," and "transient" constraints.
disjoint	Generalization	For a set of generalizations, instances may have no more than one of the given subtypes as a type. Derived classes may not have generalization relationships to more than one of the subtypes. This is the default semantic for generalizations. See the "overlapping" constraint.
frozen	Association end	No links may be added, deleted, or moved from an object after the object is created and initialized. See the "add only" constraint.
guarded	Operation	The operation may be called from concurrent threads simultaneously, but only one thread is allowed to commence. Other calls are blocked until the performance of the first call is complete. Guarded operations perform correctly in the case of simultaneous sequential access. See the "sequential" and "concurrent" constraints.
global	Association end	The corresponding instance is accessible because it has global scope within the context in which it is accessed. That is, the instance is accessible throughout the system.
implicit	Association	The association is only notational or conceptual and is not utilized in elaborating the model (manifest).
incomplete	Generalization	For a set of generalizations, not all subtypes have been specified, some may be suppressed or elided, and additional subtypes are permitted. This is the default semantic for generalizations. See the "complete" constraint.
instance	Attribute	The attribute has instance scope. Each instance of a class has its own value for the attribute. See the "class" constraint.

Extension Mechanisms

Table 15-2: Standard Constraints (continued)

Name	Application	Semantics
	Operation	The operation has instance scope. The operation may be applied on instances of a class. See the "class" constraint.
local	Association end	The corresponding instance is accessible because it has local scope within the context in which it is accessed. That is, the instance is a local variable within an operation.
new	Class role Association role	The model element is created during the execution of an interaction. See the "destroyed," "new destroyed," and "transient" constraints.
new destroyed	Class role Association role	The model element is created and destroyed during the execution of an interaction. This is equivalent to the "transient" stereotype. See the "new," "destroyed," and "transient" constraints.
or	Association	From a set of associations, only one is manifest for each associated instance.
ordered	Association end	The corresponding elements form an ordered set in which duplicates are prohibited. See the "unordered" constraint.
overlapping	Generalization	For a set of generalizations, instances may have more than one of the given subtypes as a type. Derived classes may have generalization relationships to more than one of the subtypes. See the "disjoint" constraint.
parameter	Association end	The corresponding instance is accessible because it is a parameter within the context in which it is accessed. That is, the instance is a parameter variable within an operation.
polymorphic	Operation	The operation may be overridden by subclasses.
private	Attribute Operation	The feature (attribute or operation) is not accessible outside its class, and is not accessible by descendants of its class. See the "public" and "protected" constraints.

Table 15-2: Standard Constraints (continued)

Name	Application	Semantics
protected	Attribute Operation	The feature (attribute or operation) is not accessible outside its class, but is accessible by descendants of its class. See the "public" and "private" constraints.
public	Attribute Operation	The feature (attribute or operation) is accessible outside its class, and is accessible by descendants of its class. See the "protected" and "private" constraints.
query	Operation	The operation does not modify the state of the instance. See the "update" constraint.
self	Association end	The corresponding instance is accessible because it is the requester.
sequential	Operation	The operation may be called from concurrent threads simultaneously, but the callers of the operation must coordinate so that only one call to the operation may be outstanding at any one time. See the "guarded" and "concurrent" constraints.
sorted	Association end	The corresponding elements are sorted based on their internal values. This specifies a design decision for implementation.
transient	Class role Association role	The model element is created and destroyed during the execution of an interaction. This is equivalent to the "new destroyed" stereotype. See the "new," "destroyed," and "new destroyed" constraints.
unordered	Association end	The corresponding elements form an unordered set in which duplicates are prohibited. This is the default constraint for association ends. See the "ordered" constraint.
update	Operation	The operation modifies the state of the instance. See the "query" constraint.
vote	Operation Signal	The return value of the request is selected by a majority vote of all the values returned from multiple instances.

Tagged Values

Tagged values (Figure 15-7) are a mechanism for specifying properties of model elements.

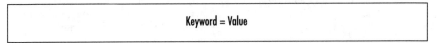

Keyword = Value

Figure 15-7: Tagged Value

Tagged values

- Are keyword-value pairs within property strings. These keyword-value pairs are known as *property specifications*. Keyword-value pairs specify values for model element properties.

- Must have a keyword. Keywords

  - Are called *tags*.

  - Are strings that represent properties of the element to which the keyword-value pair is attached.

  - Must appear only once for a given element.

  - May represent tagged values for a model element. These are attributes defined for the model element.

  - May represent attributes defined by modeling elements. These are attributes defined by the metaclass of the model element.

  - Must be specified if no default value is specified by an element's meta-model class.

- May have an equal sign followed by a value following the keyword. Values

  - Are strings that represent the value of the keyword or property.

  - May be omitted (along with the equal sign) if the property is of type Boolean. When the keyword is present, the property is true. When the keyword is omitted, the property is false.

Standard Tagged Values

Table 15-3 shows the standard tagged value elements predefined in the UML.

Table 15-3: Standard Tagged Values

Name	Application	Semantics
documenta-tion	Element (any modeling element)	The tag value specifies a comment, description, or explanation of the element.
location	Classifier	The tag value specifies the component in which the classifier is located.
	Component	The tag value specifies the node on which the component is located.

Table 15-3: Standard Tagged Values (continued)

Name	Application	Semantics
persistence	Attribute Classifier Instance	The tag specifies that the model element is persistent. If an element is transitory, its state is destroyed when it or its container is destroyed. If an attribute is persistent, its state is not destroyed when it or its container is destroyed, and may be recalled at a later time.
responsibility	Classifier	The tag value specifies a contract by or an obligation of the classifier.
semantics	Classifier	The tag value specifies the meaning of the classifier. That is, it specifies what the classifier represents and its purpose.
	Operation	The tag value specifies the meaning of the operation. That is, it specifies what the operation represents and its purpose.

UML Extension for the Objectory Process for Software Engineering

The UML Extension for the Objectory Process for Software Engineering document registers a process-specific extension to the UML. It includes a set of stereotypes (Table 15-4), various association rules (Table 15-5), and a set of stereotype icons (Figure 15-8) derived from Ivar Jacobson's work.

The objectory process for software engineering involves the following approach:

1. Develop a use case model.
2. Elaborate the use case model into an analysis model.
3. Elaborate the analysis model into a design model.
4. Elaborate the design model into an implementation model.
5. Realize the implementation model.

Because the UML does not dictate a method, this extension only specifies how the UML may be utilized and does not provide more details regarding the above approach.

Table 15-4: Stereotypes for the Objectory Process for Software Engineering

Name	Application	Semantics
<<use case model>>	Model	The model denotes the topmost package in a use case system.
<<analysis model>>	Model	The model denotes the topmost package in an analysis system.
<<design model>>	Model	The model denotes the topmost package in a design system.

Table 15-4: Stereotypes for the Objectory Process for Software Engineering

Name	Application	Semantics
<<implementation model>>	Model	The model denotes the topmost package in an implementation system.
<<use case system>>	Package	The package is the top-level package containing use case packages, use cases, actors, and relationships.
<<analysis system>>	Subsystem	The subsystem is the top-level package containing analysis subsystems, analysis service packages, analysis classes, and relationships.
<<design system>>	Subsystem	The subsystem is the top-level package containing design subsystems, design service packages, design classes, and relationships.
<<implementation system>>	Package	The package is the top-level package containing implementation subsystems, components, and relationships.
<<analysis subsystem>>	Subsystem	The subsystem contains other analysis subsystems, analysis service packages, analysis classes, and relationships.
<<design subsystem>>	Subsystem	The subsystem contains other design subsystems, design service packages, design classes, and relationships.
<<implementation subsystem>>	Package	The package contains implementation subsystems, components, and relationships.
<<use case package>>	Package	The package contains use cases, actors, and relationships.
<<analysis service package>>	Subsystem	The package contains analysis classes and relationships.
<<design service package>>	Subsystem	The package contains design classes and relationships.
<<boundary>>	Class	The class defines objects that lie on the periphery of a system and interface with actors outside the system and objects within the system. The class is an analysis class.
<<entity>>	Class	The class defines objects that are passive and do not initiate interactions on their own. The class is an analysis class.

Table 15-4: Stereotypes for the Objectory Process for Software Engineering

Name	Application	Semantics
<<control>>	Class	The class defines objects that control interactions among a collection of objects. The class usually has behavior specific to one use case. The class is an analysis class.
<<communicates>>	Association	The association denotes a relationship between actors and use cases. The relationship specifies that the actor sends messages to the use case, and the use case sends a message to the actor. One-way and two-way navigation capture the direction of the communication. The stereotype may be omitted since it is the only kind of relationship between actors and use cases.
<<subscribes>>	Association	The association denotes a relationship between a source subscriber class and a target publisher class. The subscriber specifies a set of events, and the publisher notifies the subscriber when one of the events occurs in the publisher.
<<use case realization>>	Collaboration	The collaboration realizes or implements a use case.

Table 15-5: Association Rules for the Objectory Process for Software Engineering

Association	Source	Possible Targets
<<communicates>>	Actor	Boundary
	Boundary	Actor Boundary Control Entity
	Control	Boundary Control Entity
	Entity	Entity
<<subscribes>>	Boundary	Entity
	Entity	Entity

UML Extension for Business Modeling

The UML Extension for Business Modeling document registers a domain-specific extension to the UML. It includes a set of stereotypes (Table 15-6), various association rules (Table 15-7), and a set of stereotype icons (Figure 15-9) derived from Ivar Jacobson's work.

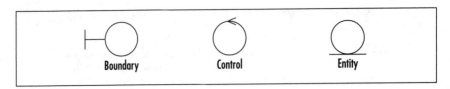

Figure 15-8: Stereotype Icons for the Objectory Process for Software Engineering

Business systems may be characterized by internal models and external models. Internal models are object models that describe the things internal to the business. External models are use case models that describe business processes involved in interactions with external parties.

Table 15-6: Business Modeling Stereotypes

Name	Application	Semantics
<<use case model>>	Model	The model denotes the business processes of a business and interactions with external parties. The model describes business processes as use cases, parties external to the business as actors, and relationships between external parties and business processes.
<<use case system>>	Package	The package is the top-level package containing use case packages, use cases, actors, and relationships.
<<use case package>>	Package	The package contains use cases, actors, and relationships.
<<object model>>	Model	The model denotes the topmost package in an object system. The model describes things internal to the business system.
<<object system>>	Subsystem	The subsystem is the top-level subsystem in an object model containing organization units, classes (workers, work units, and entities), and relationships.
<<organization unit>>	Subsystem	The subsystem is an organization unit of the actual business consisting of organization units, work units, classes (workers and entities), and relationships.
<<work unit>>	Subsystem	The subsystem contains one or more entities. The objects form a task-oriented view to end users.

Table 15-6: Business Modeling Stereotypes (continued)

Name	Application	Semantics
<<worker>>	Class	The class defines a human that acts within the system. Workers interact and manipulate entities while participating in use case realizations.
<<case worker>>	Class	The class defines a worker who interacts directly with actors outside a system.
<<internal worker>>	Class	The class defines a worker who interacts with other workers and entities inside a system.
<<entity>>	Class	The class defines objects that are passive and do not initiate interactions on their own. These classes provide the basis for sharing among workers involved in interactions.
<<communicates>>	Association	The association denotes a relationship between two instances that interact. The relationship specifies that the instances interact by sending and receiving messages. One-way and two-way navigation capture the direction of the communication.
<<subscribes>>	Association	The association denotes a relationship between a source subscriber class and a target publisher class. The subscriber specifies a set of events, and the publisher notifies the subscriber when one of the events occurs in the publisher.
<<use case realization>>	Collaboration	The collaboration realizes or implements a use case.

Table 15-7: Business Modeling Association Rules

Association	Source	Possible Targets
<<communicates>>	Actor	Case worker Work unit
	Case worker	Actor Case worker Entity Internal worker Work unit
	Entity	Entity Work unit

Extension
Mechanisms

Table 15-7: Business Modeling Association Rules

Association	Source	Possible Targets
	Internal worker	Case worker Entity Internal worker Work unit
	Work unit	Actor Case worker Entity Internal worker Work unit
<<subscribes>>	Entity	Entity
	Internal worker	Entity Work unit
	Work unit	Entity Work unit

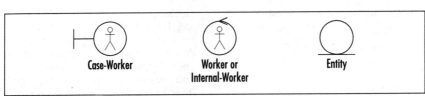

Figure 15-9: Business Modeling Stereotype Icons

CHAPTER 16

The Object Constraint Language

The Object Constraint Language (OCL) is a language for expressing constraints on model elements. OCL expressions specify rules in the form of conditions and restrictions attached to model elements. This includes expressions specifying invariants or constraints attached to model elements, preconditions and postconditions attached to operations and methods, guard conditions, and navigation between model elements.

Expressions

Expressions are strings that evaluate to a value of a particular type. Expressions

- May be attached to model elements. These expressions specify conditions that must be maintained as true for all instances of the model elements.

- May be attached to operations. These expressions specify conditions that must hold true for the invocation of an operation (preconditions), or conditions that must hold true after an operation finishes (postconditions).

- May specify guard conditions attached to model elements. These expressions specify conditions that are attached to trigger messages, loops, and transitions.

- Are expressed in the context of an instance of a specific type. The "self" keyword

  - Refers to the instance to which the expression is attached. This instance is called the *contextual instance* since it provides the context in which an expression is evaluated. The type of the "self" keyword is the associated class to which the expression is attached, or the class enclosing or which owns the operation or guard condition.

  - Must start with a lowercase character.

  - May be omitted in an expression.

- Are evaluated from left to right. Each part (subexpression) of the overall expression results in a specific value or object of a specific type. The object

OCL

243

may be a single item or a collection of items. Based on the type or class of the object, a feature (attribute and operation) may be applied to the object to derive the next value or object. Associations of the object may also be used, or navigated, to reference associated objects and association objects. The evaluation of an overall expression starts with the "self" keyword to derive an object and continues with the application of features on intermediate objects from left to right until the complete expression is evaluated.

- May utilize basic values and types. Basic types are predefined by the OCL. Basic values are values of predefined basic types. These types include Boolean, Integer, Real, and String. Basic values evaluate to a single item.

- May utilize collection values and types. Collection types are predefined by the OCL. Collection values are values of predefined collection types. These types include Collection, Set, Bag, and Sequence. Collection values evaluate to a single item that is a collection containing items.

- Are evaluated in accordance with the following precedence order (from highest to lowest):

  - Dot (".") and arrow ("->")

  - Unary "not" and unary minus ("-")

  - Multiplication ("*") and division ("/")

  - Addition ("+") and subtraction ("-")

  - Logical "and," "or," and "xor"

  - Logical "implies"

  - Logical "if then else endif"

  - Logical comparison operators "<", ">", "<=", ">=", and "="

  Parentheses ("( )") may be used to change the order in which an expression is evaluated, where expressions are evaluated from innermost to outermost parentheses.

- May include comments. These are denoted using two dashes. Everything after the two dashes up to and including the end of line is a comment.

- May refer to model classes and their features, and associations and their features. All classes within a model are types within OCL expressions attached to the model elements. Features (attributes and operations) of objects are called *properties* within the OCL. Operations used within these expressions must be stereotyped using the "query" keyword; that is, operations must not have any side effects (or modify their containing class or association class). For postconditions, the value of a property represents the value it has upon completion of the operation. Within postconditions, properties may be postfixed with the at sign followed by the keyword "pre" ("@pre") to reference the value of the property at the start of an operation.

- May reference queries that are undefined. In such a case, the whole expression is undefined. However, subexpressions adhere to the following rules:

  - The value true ORed with any other value results in true.

  - The value false ANDed with any other value results in false.

Object Properties

Object properties are features of model elements defined in class diagrams.

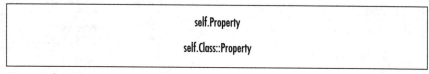

self.Property

self.Class::Property

Figure 16-1: Object Properties

Object properties

- May be referenced using the "self" keyword (Figure 16-1). This is expressed using the "self" keyword followed by a dot and the property name or string. The expression results in the value of the property.

- May reference properties using pathnames. This is used to resolve ambiguity when two properties have the same name within the same object. For example, one class may inherit a property with the same name as an existing property. Selecting one of the properties is expressed by specifying the class or superclass name followed by two colons (":") and the property name.

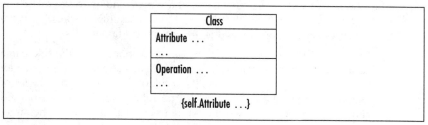

Figure 16-2: Attribute

- May reference attributes (Figure 16-2). This is expressed by specifying the property string as the attribute name. The result of the expression is the value of the attribute, and the type of the result is the type of the attribute.

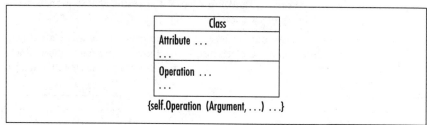

Figure 16-3: Operation

- May reference operations (Figure 16-3). This is expressed by specifying the property string as the name of the operation followed by parentheses containing an argument list consisting of a comma-separated list of arguments passed to the method. The result of the expression is the value returned from the operation, and the type of the result is the return type of the operation. The "result" keyword may be used to reference the result of the operation. The arguments must match the order, number, and types specified in the formal parameter list of the operation.

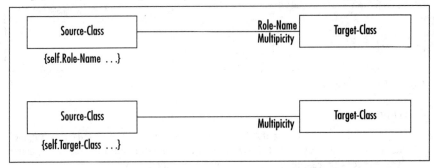

Figure 16-4: Associated Classes

- May be used to navigate associations to reference other target classes and their properties (Figure 16-4). This is expressed by specifying the property string as the role name or class of the target element.
  - If the multiplicity of the association end corresponding to the role name has a maximum multiplicity value of 1, the result of the expression is the associated object, and the type of the result is the target class.
  - If the multiplicity of the association end corresponding to the role name has a maximum multiplicity value of more than 1 and is not adorned with the "ordered" keyword constraint, the result of the expression is the set of associated target objects attached to the role name that are associated with the source objects, and the type of the result is a Set of the target class. This type is denoted as "Set (Target-Class)."
  - If the multiplicity of the association end corresponding to the role name has a maximum multiplicity value of more than 1 and is adorned with the "ordered" keyword constraint, the result of the expression is the set of associated target objects attached to the role name that are associated with the source objects, and the type of the result is a Sequence of the target class. This type is denoted as "Sequence (Target-Class)."
  - If the role name is omitted, the name of the class at the association end, starting with a lowercase character, is used as the role name. Fundamentally, the same target class name is utilized; however, the first character is converted to lowercase.

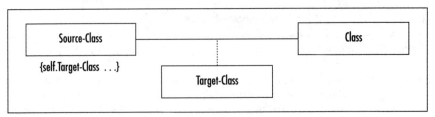

Figure 16-5: Association Classes

- May be used to navigate or reference association classes (Figure 16-5). This is expressed by specifying the property string as the name of the association class starting with a lowercase character. The result of the expression is the set of association objects that associate the source objects, and the type of the result is a Set of the target class.

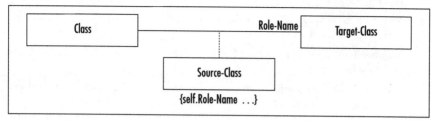

Figure 16-6: Associated Classes

- May be used to navigate from association classes to reference the classes that participate in the association (Figure 16-6). This is expressed by specifying the property string as the role name of the target element. If the role name is omitted, the name of the class at the association end, starting with a lower-case character, is used as the role name. The result of the expression is the associated object, and the type of the result is the target class.

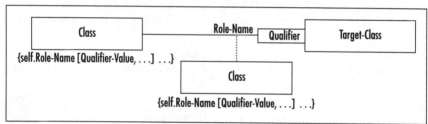

Figure 16-7: Qualifiers

- May be used to navigate through qualified associations (Figure 16-7). This is expressed by specifying the property string as the role name of the target element followed by a comma-separated list of qualifier values enclosed in square braces. The qualifier values and square braces may be omitted, in which case the results will be all objects on the association end.

Collections

Collections are groups of objects or elements that may result during the evaluation of an expression.

self. ... -> Property

Figure 16-8: Collection Property

Collections

- Must have their properties referenced by using an arrow "->" followed by the name of the property (Figure 16-8). The arrow may also be applied to a single item, in which case the single item behaves as if it were a collection containing one item.

- May be Sets. Sets are groups of objects that do not contain duplicate elements and are unordered.

- May be Bags. Bags are groups of objects that may contain duplicate elements and are unordered.

- May be Sequences. Sequences are groups of objects that may contain duplicate elements and are ordered.

Set {Value, . . .}

Bag {Value, . . .}

Sequence {Value, . . .}

Figure 16-9: Set, Bag, and Sequence Literals

- May be specified by a literal (Figure 16-9). This is expressed by specifying the type of collection followed by curly braces containing a comma-separated list of values. When Integers are specified, a multiplicity expression may be used (Chapter 6).

- Must not be nested. That is, all collections of collections are automatically flattened so that the elements of both collections are combined into a single collection.

Iterator-Value : Type | Iteration-Expression

Figure 16-10: Iteration Expression

- May be projected from existing collections (Figure 16-10). That is, for each element in an existing collection, an iteration expression is evaluated. Based on the result of the evaluation, the element may be included in the result collection. This applies to the "select," "reject," "collect," "forAll," and "exists" features of collections. Iteration expressions

  - May have an iterator variable name or identifier string that is enumerated over all the elements in the collection.

  - May have a colon followed by a type expression that indicates the type of the iterator variable. If no iterator variable is specified, no type expression is used and the colon is omitted.

  - May have a comma-separated list of iterator variables and types. This enables the iteration expression to utilize multiple iterator variables.

  - Must have an iteration expression that indicates the expression to evaluate for each element in the collection. If an iterator variable name is used, a vertical bar precedes the iteration expression, and the expression may utilize the iterator variable.

- For the "select" feature, the iteration expression specifies a Boolean expression that must evaluate to true for an element in order for the element to be selected into the result collection.

- For the "reject" feature, the iteration expression specifies a Boolean expression that must evaluate to false for an element in order for the element to be selected into the result collection.

-> collect (Property)

. Property

Figure 16-11: "Collect" Shorthand Notation

- For the "collect" feature, the result is the collection of the results of all the evaluations of the iteration expression over elements in the original collection. If the expression is simply a property, a shorthand notation may be used, in which the "collect" feature is suppressed and only the property name is specified (Figure 16-11). In general, when a property is applied to a collection, it will automatically be interpreted as a "collect" over the members of the collection with the specified property.

- For the "forAll" feature, the iteration expression specifies a Boolean expression that must evaluate to true for all the elements in the collection in order for the expression to result in a value of true. If the Boolean expression is false for one or more of the elements in the collection, the complete expression evaluates to false.

- For the "exists" feature, the iteration expression specifies a Boolean expression that must evaluate to true for at least one element in the collection in order for the expression to result in a value of true. If the Boolean expression is false for all the elements in the collection, the complete expression evaluates to false.

Iterator-Variable : Type ;

Accumulator-Variable : Type = Accumulator-Expression |

Iteration-Expression

Figure 16-12: Iterate Expressions

- May be accumulated from existing collections (Figure 16-12). That is, for each element in an existing collection, an iteration expression is evaluated. The result of the evaluation is accumulated in another collection. This scheme of evaluating the expression is used by the "iterate" feature of collections. This is a very generic operation that may be used to define the "select," "reject," "collect," "forAll," and "exists" features of collections. Iterate expressions

  - Must have an iterator variable name or identifier string that is enumerated over all the elements in the collection.

- Must have a colon followed by a type expression that indicates the type of the iterator variable.

- Must have a semicolon followed by an accumulator variable name or identifier string that specifies a collection in which the result will be accumulated.

- Must have a colon followed by a type expression that indicates the type of the accumulator variable.

- Must have an equal sign followed by an expression that specifies the initial value for the accumulator variable.

- Must have a vertical bar followed by an iteration expression that indicates the expression to evaluate for each element in the collection. Within this expression, the results are accumulated or added to the accumulator variable.

Standard Types

The OCL defines a set of basic types (Boolean, Integer, Real, and String) and collection types (Collection, Set, Bag, and Sequence) that are related and supplemented with other fundamental OCL types (Figure 16-13). These types are organized in a type hierarchy adhering to the following rules:

- All types defined in a model or within the OCL have a type that is an instance of the OCL type OclType.

- The OclAny type is the supertype of all types in a model.

- The OclExpression type is the type of all OCL expressions.

- The Real, String, Boolean, Enumeration, and Collection types are subtypes of the OclAny type.

- The Integer type is a subtype of the Real type.

- The Set, Bag, and Sequence types are subtypes of the Collection type.

- Each instance of a given type may be substituted for an instance of its supertypes. This is a transitive rule. That is, if T1 is a supertype of T2, and T2 is a supertype of T3, an instance of T3 may be substituted for an instance of T1 or T2. Collection instances may be substituted in accordance with this rule if they are collections of element types that adhere to the rule.

The features of these types are depicted using the standard UML notation and are described in the following sections. Operations of these types are declared using parentheses for their parameters as the standard UML notation specifies, but OCL operations that are depicted as operators do not use parentheses to enclose their arguments when used in expressions. That is, the declaration "I + (I2 : Integer) : Integer" is actually used in the expression "I + I2," and not "I + (I2)," where "I2" is of type Integer and the result is of type Integer. Those operations that do use parentheses when used in an expression are indicated.

OclType Type

The OclType type is the type of all the OCL predefined types and the types defined in a model. The OclType allows access to the meta-level of the model.

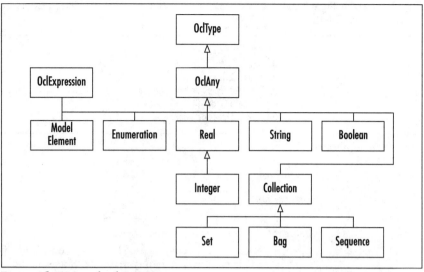

Figure 16-13: Standard OCL Types

The features of the OclType type are depicted in Figure 16-14 and described in Table 16-1, where *T* represents the instance on which the feature is applied.

```
T.name : String
T.attributes : Set (String)
T.associationEnds : Set (String)
T.operations : Set (String)
T.supertypes : Set (oclType)
T.allSupertypes : Set (OctTypes)
T.allInstances : Set (T)
```

Figure 16-14: OclType Type Features

Table 16-1: OclType Type Features

Feature	Description
allInstances	Returns a set of all instances of T and all its subtypes.
allSupertypes	Returns a set of all supertypes of T.
associationEnds	Returns a set of names of the navigable association ends of T.
attributes	Returns a set of names of the attributes of T.
name	Returns the name of T.
operations	Returns a set of names of the operations of T.
supertypes	Returns a set of all direct supertypes of T.

OclAny Type

The OclAny type is the supertype of all types in a model. All classes in a model inherit the features defined by the OclAny type. The features of the OclAny type

OCL

are depicted in Figure 16-15 and described in Table 16-2, where *O* represents the instance on which the feature is applied.

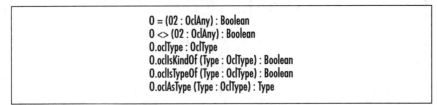

```
O = (02 : OclAny) : Boolean
O <> (02 : OclAny) : Boolean
O.oclType : OclType
O.oclIsKindOf (Type : OclType) : Boolean
O.oclIsTypeOf (Type : OclType) : Boolean
O.oclAsType (Type : OclType) : Type
```

Figure 16-15: OclAny Type Features

Table 16-2: OclAny Type Features

Feature	Description
=	Returns true if O is the same object as O2.
<>	Returns true if O is not the same object as O2.
oclAsType	Returns O, but of the specified type. The result is undefined if the type of O is not the specified type or one of its subtypes.
oclIsKindOf	Returns true if the specified type is a supertype of the type of O.
oclIsTypeOf	Returns true if the specified type is the same as the type of O.
oclType	Returns the type of O.

OclExpression Type

The OclExpression type is the type of all OCL expressions. This type only has one feature: "E.evaluationType : OclType," where *E* represents the instance on which the feature is applied, and the feature returns the type of the object that results from evaluating E.

Real Type

The Real type represents the mathematical concept of real numbers. These are numbers with fractional parts expressed following a decimal point. The features of the Real type are depicted in Figure 16-16 and described in Table 16-3, where *R* represents the instance on which the feature is applied.

Integer Type

The Integer type represents the mathematical concept of integer numbers. The features of the Integer type are depicted in Figure 16-17 and described in Table 16-4, where *I* represents the instance on which the feature is applied.

String Type

The String type represents a sequence of ASCII characters. As a literal, a string is enclosed in single quotes. The features of the String type are depicted in Figure 16-18 and described in Table 16-5, where *S* represents the instance on which the feature is applied.

```
R + (R2 : Real) : Real
R - (R2 : Real) : Real
R * (R2 : Real) : Real
R / (R2 : Real) : Real
R.abs : Real
R.floor : Integer
R.max (R2 : Real) : Real
R.min (R2 : Real) : Real
R = (R2 : Real) : Boolean
R <> (R2 : Real) : Boolean
R > (R2 : Real) : Boolean
R <= (R2 : Real) : Boolean
R >= (R2 : Real) : Boolean
```

Figure 16-16: Real Type Features

Table 16-3: Real Type Features

Feature	Description
+	Returns the sum of R and R2.
-	Returns the value of subtracting R2 from R.
*	Returns the value of multiplying R and R2.
/	Returns the value of dividing R by R2.
abs	Returns the absolute value of R. If the value is negative, its positive counterpart is returned.
floor	Returns the largest integer that is less than or equal to R.
max	Returns the maximum of R and R2.
min	Returns the minimum of R and R2.
=	Returns true if R is equal to R2.
<>	Returns true if R is not equal to R2.
<	Returns true if R is less than R2.
>	Returns true if R is greater than R2.
<=	Returns true if R is less than or equal to R2.
>=	Returns true if R is greater than or equal to R2.

Boolean Type

The Boolean type represents the values true and false. The features of the Boolean type are depicted in Figure 16-19 and described in Table 16-6, where *B* represents the instance on which the feature is applied.

Enumeration Types

Enumeration types (Figure 16-20) specify the values an object of the type may be assigned. An Enumeration type is expressed by specifying the keyword "enum" followed by curly braces containing a comma-separated list of values that an object of the type may be assigned. When a specific value is referenced, it is expressed with an additional "#" symbol. The features of the Enumeration type are

```
I + (I2 : Integer) : Integer
I + (R2 : Real) : Real
I - (I2 : Integer) : Integer
I - (R2 : Real) : Real
I * (I2 : Integer) : Integer
I * (R2 : Real) : Real
I / (I2 : Integer) : Real
I / (R2 : Real) : Real
I.abs : Integer
I.div (I2 : Integer) : Integer
I.mod (I2 : Integer) : Integer
I.max (I2 : Integer) : Integer
I.min (I2 : Integer) : Integer
```

Figure 16-17: Integer Type Features

Table 16-4: Integer Type Features

Feature	Description
+	Returns the sum of I and I2. The result is of type Integer.
+	Returns the sum of I and R2. The result is of type Real.
-	Returns the value of subtracting I2 from I. The result is of type Integer.
-	Returns the value of subtracting R2 from I. The result is of type Real.
*	Returns the value of multiplying I and I2. The result is of type Integer.
*	Returns the value of multiplying I and R2. The result is of type Real.
/	Returns the value of dividing I by I2. The result is of type Real.
/	Returns the value of dividing I by R2. The result is of type Real.
abs	Returns the absolute value of I. If value is negative, its positive counterpart is returned.
div	Returns the number of times that I2 fits completely within I.
max	Returns the maximum of I and I2.
min	Returns the minimum of I and I2.
mod	Returns the remainder after the number of times that I2 fits completely within I, that is, the value of I modulo I2.

```
S.size : Integer
S.concat (S2 : String) : String
S.toUpper : String
S.toLower : String
S = (S2 : String) : Boolean
S <> (S2 : String) : Boolean
S.substring (Lower : Integer, Upper : Integer) : String
```

Figure 16-18: String Type Features

depicted in Figure 16-21 and described in Table 16-7, where *E* represents the instance on which the feature is applied.

Table 16-5: String Type Features

Feature	Description
concat	Returns the concatenation of S2 to the end of S.
size	Returns the number of characters in S.
substring	Returns the substring of S starting at the character number specified by the "Lower" argument, up to and including the character number specified by the "Upper" argument. This feature requires the use of parentheses when used in an expression.
toLower	Returns S with all uppercase characters converted to lowercase characters.
toUpper	Returns S with all lowercase characters converted to uppercase characters.
=	Returns true if S contains the same characters in the same order as S2.
<>	Returns true if S does not contain the same characters in the same order as S2.

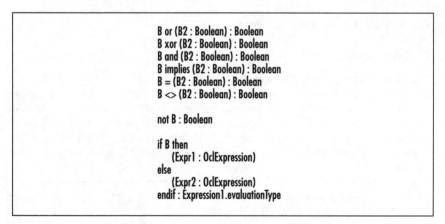

```
B or (B2 : Boolean) : Boolean
B xor (B2 : Boolean) : Boolean
B and (B2 : Boolean) : Boolean
B implies (B2 : Boolean) : Boolean
B = (B2 : Boolean) : Boolean
B <> (B2 : Boolean) : Boolean

not B : Boolean

if B then
     (Expr1 : OclExpression)
else
     (Expr2 : OclExpression)
endif : Expression1.evaluationType
```

Figure 16-19: Boolean Type Features

Table 16-6: Boolean Type Features

Feature	Description
and	Returns true if both B and B2 are true.
if then else endif	Returns the result of evaluating expression-1 if B is true; otherwise, returns the result of evaluating expression-2.
implies	Returns true if B is false, or if B is true and B2 is true.
not	Returns true if B is false, and false if B is true.
or	Returns true if either B or B2 is true.
xor	Returns true if either B or B2 is true, but not both.
=	Returns true if B is equal to B2.
<>	Returns true if B is not equal to B2.

OCL

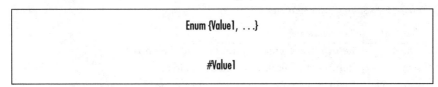

Figure 16-20: Enumeration Types

Table 16-7: Enumeration Type Features

Feature	Description
=	Returns true if E is equal to E2.
<>	Returns true if E is not equal to E2.

E = (E2 : Enumeration) : Boolean
E <> (E2 : Enumeration) : Boolean

Figure 16-21: Enumeration Type Features

Collection Type

The Collection type is the abstract supertype of all collections in the OCL. An object within a collection is called an *element*. The Collection type is a template with a "T" parameter denoting the type of the collection. A concrete collection type substitutes a type for the "T" parameter of the Collection type and is denoted as "Set (T)," "Bag (T)," or "Sequence (T)." The features of the Collection type are depicted in Figure 16-22 and described in Table 16-8, where *C* represents the instance on which the feature is applied.

```
C->size : Integer
C->includes (Object : OclAny) : Boolean
C->count (Object : OclAny) : Integer
C->includesAll (C2 : Collection (T)) : Boolean
C->isEmpty : Boolean
C->notEmpty : Boolean
C->sum : T
C->exists (Iteration-Expr : OclExpression) : Boolean
C->forAll (Iteration-Expr : OclExpression) : Boolean
C->iterate (Iterate-Expr : OclExpression) : Iterate-Expr.evaluationType
```

Figure 16-22: Collection Type Features

Table 16-8: Collection Type Features

Feature	Description
count	Returns the number of times the object occurs in C.
exists	Returns true if the expression evaluates to true for at least one element in C. This feature requires the use of parentheses when used in an expression.

Table 16-8: Collection Type Features (continued)

Feature	Description
forAll	Returns true if the expression evaluates to true for each element in C. This feature requires the use of parentheses when used in an expression.
includes	Returns true if the object is an element of C.
includesAll	Returns true if C contains all the elements of C2.
isEmpty	Returns true if C has no elements.
iterate	Iterates over C. This feature requires the use of parentheses when used in an expression.
notEmpty	Returns true if C has at least one element.
size	Returns the number of elements in C.
sum	Returns the sum of all elements in C. The elements must be of a type supporting addition (Integer or Real).

Set Type

The Set type is a subtype of the Collection type in which the group of objects does not contain duplicate elements and is unordered. The features of the Set type are depicted in Figure 16-23 and are described in Table 16-9, where *S* represents the instance on which the feature is applied.

```
S->union (S2 : Set (T)) : Set (T)
S->union (B2 : Bag (T)) : Bag (T)
S->intersection (S2 : Set (T)) : Set (T)
S->intersection (B2 : Bag (T)) : Set (T)
S - (S2 : Set (T)) : Set (T)
S->including (Object : T) : Set (T)
S->excluding (Object : T) : Set (T)
S->symmetricDifference (S2 : Set (T)) : Set (T)
S->select (Iteration-Expr : OclExpression) : Set (T)
S->reject (Iteration-Expr : OclExpression) : Set (T)
S->collect (Iteration-Expr : OclExpression) : Bag (Iteration-Expr.oclType)
S->count (Object : T) : Integer
S->asSequence : Sequence (T)
S->asBag : Bag (T)
S = (S2 : Set) : Boolean
S<> (S2 : Set) : Boolean
```

Figure 16-23: Set Type Features

Table 16-9: Set Type Features

Feature	Description
-	Returns the elements of S that are not in S2.
asBag	Returns the bag that contains all the elements in S.
asSequence	Returns a sequence that contains all the elements in S in random order.

Table 16-9: Set Type Features (continued)

Feature	Description
collect	Returns the bag of elements that results from applying the expression to every member of S. This feature requires the use of parentheses when used in an expression.
count	Returns the number of occurrences of the object in S.
excluding	Returns the set containing all elements of S without the object.
including	Returns the set containing all elements of S plus the object.
intersection	Returns the intersection of S and S2. The result is of type Set. The result set contains all the elements that are in both sets; elements in only one set are not in the result set.
intersection	Returns the intersection of S and B2. The result is of type Set. The result bag contains all the elements that are in both collections; elements in only one collection are not in the result set.
reject	Returns the set of elements of S for which the expression is false. This feature requires the use of parentheses when used in an expression.
select	Returns the set of elements of S for which the expression is true. This feature requires the use of parentheses when used in an expression.
symmetricDifference	Returns the set containing all the elements that are in S or in S2, but not in both.
union	Returns the union of S and S2. The result is of type Set. The result set contains all the elements in either set.
union	Returns the union of S and B2. The result is of type Bag. The result bag contains all the elements in either collection.
=	Returns true if S and S2 contain the same elements.
<>	Returns true if S and S2 do not contain the same elements.

Bag Type

The Bag type is a subtype of the Collection type in which the group of objects may contain duplicate elements and is unordered. The features of the Bag type are depicted in Figure 16-24 and described in Table 16-10, where *B* represents the instance on which the feature is applied.

Sequence Type

The Sequence type is a subtype of the Collection type in which the group of objects may contain duplicate elements and is ordered. The features of the

```
B->union (B2 : Bag (T)) : Bag (T)
B->union (S2 : Set (T)) : Bag (T)
B->intersection (B2 : Bag (T)) : Bag (T)
B->intersection (S2 : Set (T)) : Set (T)
B->including (Object : T) : Bag (T)
B->excluding (Object : T) : Bag (T)
B->select (Iteration-Expr : OclExpression) : Bag (T)
B->reject (Iteration-Expr : OclExpression) : Set (T)
B->collect (Iteration-Expr : OclExpression) : Bag (Iteration-Expr.oclType)
B->count (Object : T) : Integer
B->asSequence : Sequence (T)
B->asSet : Set (T)
B = (S2 : Bag) : Boolean
B<> (S2 : Bag) : Boolean
```

Figure 16-24: Bag Type Features

Table 16-10: Bag Type Features

Feature	Description
asSequence	Returns a sequence that contains all the elements from B in random order.
asSet	Returns the set that contains all the elements from B with duplicates removed.
collect	Returns the bag of elements that results from applying the expression to every member of B. This feature requires the use of parentheses when used in an expression.
count	Returns the number of occurrences of the object in B.
excluding	Returns the bag containing all elements of B apart from all occurrences of the object.
including	Returns the bag containing all elements of B plus the object.
intersection	Returns the intersection of B and B2. The result is of type Bag. The result bag contains all the elements that are in both bags; elements in only one bag are not in the result bag.
intersection	Returns the intersection of B and S2. The result is of type Set. The result bag contains all the elements that are in both collections; elements in only one collection are not in the result set.
reject	Returns the bag of elements of B for which the expression is false. This feature requires the use of parentheses when used in an expression.
select	Returns the bag of elements of B for which the expression is true. This feature requires the use of parentheses when used in an expression.
union	Returns the union of B and B2. The result is of type Bag. The result bag contains all the elements in either bag.
union	Returns the union of B and S2. The result is of type Bag. The result bag contains all the elements in either collection.

OCL

Table 16-10: Bag Type Features (continued)

Feature	Description
=	Returns true if B and B2 contain the same elements the same number of times.
<>	Returns true if B and B2 do not contain the same elements the same number of times.

Sequence type are depicted in Figure 16-25 and described in Table 16-11, where *Q* represents the instance on which the feature is applied.

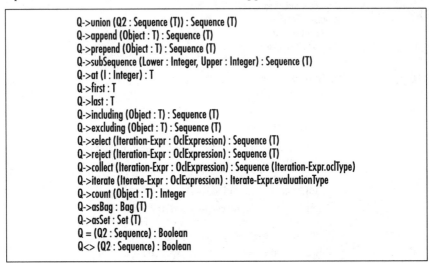

```
Q->union (Q2 : Sequence (T)) : Sequence (T)
Q->append (Object : T) : Sequence (T)
Q->prepend (Object : T) : Sequence (T)
Q->subSequence (Lower : Integer, Upper : Integer) : Sequence (T)
Q->at (I : Integer) : T
Q->first : T
Q->last : T
Q->including (Object : T) : Sequence (T)
Q->excluding (Object : T) : Sequence (T)
Q->select (Iteration-Expr : OclExpression) : Sequence (T)
Q->reject (Iteration-Expr : OclExpression) : Sequence (T)
Q->collect (Iteration-Expr : OclExpression) : Sequence (Iteration-Expr.oclType)
Q->iterate (Iterate-Expr : OclExpression) : Iterate-Expr.evaluationType
Q->count (Object : T) : Integer
Q->asBag : Bag (T)
Q->asSet : Set (T)
Q = (Q2 : Sequence) : Boolean
Q<> (Q2 : Sequence) : Boolean
```

Figure 16-25: Sequence Type Features

Table 16-11: Sequence Type Features

Feature	Description
append	Returns the sequence consisting of all elements in S followed by the object.
asBag	Returns a bag that contains all the elements from Q, including duplicates.
asSet	Returns the set that contains all the elements from Q with duplicates removed.
at	Returns the *i*-th element in Q.
collect	Returns the sequence of elements that results from applying the expression to every member of Q. This feature requires the use of parentheses when used in an expression.
count	Returns the number of occurrences of the object in Q.
excluding	Returns the sequence containing all elements of Q apart from all occurrences of the object. The order of the elements is not changed.
first	Returns the first element in Q.

Table 16-11: Sequence Type Features (continued)

Feature	Description
including	Returns the sequence containing all elements of Q plus the object added as the last element.
iterate	Iterates over Q. The iteration will be done from the first element to the last element in the order of the sequence. This feature requires the use of parentheses when used in an expression.
last	Returns the last element in Q.
prepend	Returns the sequence consisting of the object followed by Q.
reject	Returns the sequence of elements of Q for which the expression is false. This feature requires the use of parentheses when used in an expression.
select	Returns the sequence of elements of Q for which the expression is true. This feature requires the use of parentheses when used in an expression.
subSequence	Returns the subsequence of Q starting at the element number specified by the "Lower" argument, up to and including the element number specified by the "Upper" argument. This feature requires the use of parentheses when used in an expression.
union	Returns the sequence consisting of all elements in S followed by all elements in Q2.
=	Returns true if Q and Q2 contain the same elements the same number of times in the same order.
<>	Returns true if Q and Q2 do not contain the same elements the same number of times in the same order.

APPENDIX A

References

This section contains references to notable resources on the World Wide Web and various books.

World Wide Web Resources

The Object Management Group (*http://www.omg.org*) is the main source for the formal UML documentation.

The Object Management Group's UML Revision Task Force (*http://uml.system-house.mci.com*) is the main source for clarifications and revisions to the UML specification.

Rational Software Corporation (*http://www.rational.com/uml*) offers a complete resource center, including the formal UML documentation.

International Business Machines Corporation (*http://www.software.ibm.com/ad/ocl*) offers information on the Object Constraint Language (OCL).

The Centre for Object Technology Applications and Research (COTAR) (*http://www.csse.swin.edu.au/cotar/OPEN*) offers information on the Object-oriented Process, Environment and Notation (OPEN) and the OPEN Modeling Language (OML).

Recerca Informàtica (*http://www.recercai.com*) offers information on the Universal Object Language (UOL).

ObjecTime Limited (*http://www.objectime.com*) offers information on the use of the UML for real-time systems.

Project Technology Incorporated (*http://www.projtech.com*) offers information on the use of the UML with the Shlaer-Mellor method.

The Cetus Team (*http://www.cetus-links.org*) offers various links on object orientation.

Scott Ambler (*http://www.ambysoft.com*) offers information on object orientation and the UML.

Brad Appleton (*http://www.enteract.com/~bradapp*) offers various links on object orientation.

Alistair Cockburn (*http://members.aol.com/acockburn*) offers information on object orientation, use cases, risk management, and human factors in software development.

Desmond F. D'Souza (*http://www.iconcomp.com*) offers information on object orientation and the UML.

Richard T. Dué (*http://ourworld.compuserve.com/homepages/rtdue*) offers various links on object orientation.

Paul Evitts and Dion Hinchcliffe (*http://www.objectnews.com*) offer various links on object orientation.

Martin Fowler (*http://ourworld.compuserve.com/homepages/Martin_Fowler*) offers information on object orientation, analysis and design, patterns, and the UML.

Robert Martin (*http://www.oma.com*) offers information on object orientation and the UML.

Doug Rosenberg (*http://www.iconixsw.com*) offers information on object orientation and the UML.

Kendall Scott (*http://softdocwiz.com/UML.htm*) offers the UML Dictionary.

Jeff Sutherland (*http://jeffsutherland.org*) offers information on object orientation.

Books

Grady Booch. *Object-Oriented Analysis and Design with Applications* (Addison-Wesley Object Technology Series). Benjamin/Cummings, 1994.

Grady Booch. *Object Solutions: Managing the Object-Oriented Project* (Addison-Wesley Object Technology Series). Addison-Wesley, 1995.

Grady Booch and Ed Eykholt. *The Best of Booch: Designing Strategies for Object Technology.* SIGS Books & Multimedia, 1996.

Grady Booch, James Rumbaugh, and Ivar Jacobson. *Unified Modeling Language User Guide* (Addison-Wesley Object Technology Series). Addison-Wesley (in press).

Eugene E. Brussell. *Webster's New World Dictionary of Quotable Definitions.* Prentice Hall, 1988.

Don Firesmith, Brian Henderson-Sellers, and Ian Graham. *The OML Reference Manual.* SIGS Books, 1997.

Ian Graham, Brian Henderson-Sellers, and Houman Younessi. *The OPEN Process Specification.* Addison-Wesley, 1997.

Brian Henderson-Sellers, Tony Simons, and Houman Younessi. *The OPEN Toolbox of Techniques.* Addison-Wesley, 1998.

Ivar Jacobson. *Object-Oriented Software Engineering: A Use Case Driven Approach* (Addison-Wesley Object Technology Series). Addison-Wesley, 1994.

Ivar Jacobson, Grady Booch, and James Rumbaugh. *The Objectory Software Development Process* (Addison-Wesley Object Technology Series). Addison-Wesley (in press).

Ivar Jacobson, Martin Griss, and Patrik Jonsson. *Software Reuse: Architecture Process and Organization for Business Success.* Addison-Wesley, 1997.

James Rumbaugh, Michael Blaha, William Premerlani, Frederick Eddy, and William Lorensen. *Object-Oriented Modeling and Design.* Prentice Hall, 1991.

James Rumbaugh, Ivar Jacobson, and Grady Booch. *Unified Modeling Language Reference Manual* (Addison-Wesley Object Technology Series). Addison-Wesley (in press).

Object Constraint Language Specification 1.1. Rational Software Corporation and IBM Corporation, 1997.

Unified Modeling Language Summary 1.1. Rational Software Corporation, 1997.

Unified Modeling Language Notation Guide 1.1. Rational Software Corporation, 1997.

Unified Modeling Language Semantics 1.1. Rational Software Corporation, 1997.

Unified Modeling Language Extension for Business Modeling 1.1. Rational Software Corporation, 1997.

Unified Modeling Language Extension for Objectory Process for Software Engineering 1.1. Rational Software Corporation, 1997.

—

Index

A

Abstract class, 61–62, 80
Abstract operation, 54
Abstract use case, 162
Abstraction
    characteristics, 49–50
    levels of, 66, 120–121, 126
Accessibility
    attribute, 54–55, 61
    operation, 54–55
    type, 57
Action
    action clause, 201
    deferred event, 200–201
    send clause, 202–203
    types, 203–204
Action flow, 103, 205, 208
Action state, 103, 188, 205, 207
Activation, 85, 170–172
Active class, 141
Active object, 53
Active state, 101, 188
Activity, 36, 89, 96, 189
Activity diagram, 102–104, 118,
    205–206
Actor, 160–161
Ad hoc polymorphism, 62
Aggregation, 58–59, 76
Analysis phase, 24–25, 126

Anonymous object, 84
Architectural element, 29
Architectural view, 31–33, 116–118
Architecture
    characteristics, 28–30, 111–114
    subordinate, 29
Architecture-centric, 30
Architecture-centric process, 121
Artifact, 36
As-is situation, 17
Association, 58, 75, 77, 112–113,
    149–152
Association class, 149–150
Association end, 149
Association role, 94, 180–182
Asynchronous communication, 63, 91,
    174, 185
Atomic operation, 201–202
Attribute
    characteristics, 142, 148
    class, 54, 57, 78
    object, 52, 54, 57, 245
Auxiliary Elements package, 116

B

Bag type, 248, 259
Base class, 220
Becomes relationship, 218
Behavioral diagram, 124

Implementation inheritance, 60
Implementation model view, 33, 118, 124, 211
Implementation phase, 25, 126
Import dependency, 137
Inception development phase, 23, 125
Inclusion polymorphism, 62
Incremental process, 122
Industrialization period, 13
Information hiding, 51
Inheritance, 60–61, 77
Initial state, 99, 190–191
Initializer operation, 55
Input parameter, 43
Integer type, 252–254
Interaction, 64, 168
Interface, 144–145
Interface inheritance, 60
Internal transition, 189
Is-a-kind-of relationship, 59, 77
Iteration cycle, 22, 24–25, 125–126, 175
Iteration expression, 248–250
Iteration phase, 22, 24, 126
Iterative process, 122

J

Jacobson, Ivar, 4

K

Keyword, 133–134, 236, 245–246
Keyword-value pair, 108, 236
Knowledge, as a probelm-solving element, 19

L

Label, 133
Language, 34
Levels of abstraction, mechanism, 120
Life cycle
  characteristics, 20–22
  class, 55–56, 61
  development phase, 21–24
  iteration phase, 22, 24–25
Lifeline, 85, 169–170
Line segment, 131
Link, 57–58, 82, 112, 154–156

Link end, 155
Link time, 212
List, 134
Live activation, 172
Local invocation action, 204
Localization, 51
Logical view. *See* Structural model view

M

Management phase, 24
Mechanism, 118–121
Message, 172–176
  asynchronous, 174
  branching, 175
  characteristics, 182
  iteration, 175
  noninstantaneous, 175
  recurrence clause, 183
  return list, 183–184
  sequence expression, 183
  simple, 173, 184
  synchronous, 173–174, 184
Message exchange, 63–64, 85, 94, 167–168
Metaclass, 66
Meta-metamodel, 112
Metamodel, 31, 66, 112–116, 219
Metamodel layer, 112
Metatype, 66
Method, descriptive/prescriptive, 17
Method level, 120
Method wars, 10
Methodology, 17
Model, 30–31, 111
Model layer, 113
Model Management package, 116
Model view, 32–33
Modeling element, 31, 220, 243
Modeling language, 7
Multiple classification, 55
Multiplicity, 76, 83, 112, 134–135, 150–151, 169, 246
Multi-role, 181–182
Mutator operation, 56

N

Name, 131–132

Name compartment, 147
Nested state diagram, 189, 198
Node, 130, 216–217
Noninstantaneous message, 175
Notation Guide, 8–9
Note, 106, 135

O

Object, 52–53, 68, 112, 147–148
Object attribute, 52, 54, 56
Object Constraint Language, 9,
    107–108, 113
  collections, 248–250
  expressions, 243–244
  object properties, 245–247
  standard types, 250–261
Object diagram, 82–85, 117, 123, 140
Object factory, 54
Object flow, 103, 205, 208–209
Object Management Group, vii
Object model, 81–82
Object Modeling Technique, 4–6,
    11–12
Object operations, 54
Object Process for Software
    Engineering
    Extension, 237–240
Object property, 245–247
Object-oriented paradigm, 35
  and world view, 39–42
  characteristics, 46–49
  summary, 66–67
  variations, 65–66
Object-Oriented Software
    Engineering, 4–6, 11–12
Occurrence, in real world, 42
OCL. See Object Constraint Language
OclAny type, 251–252
OclExpression type, 252
OclType type, 250–251
OMG. See Object Management Group
OMT. See Object Modeling Technique
One-level system, 65
OOSE. See Object-Oriented Software
    Engineering
Operation
  characteristics, 142–144
  class, 53–56, 78
  expressions, 243

object, 53–56, 245–246
virtual, 62
Organization, 51
Output parameter, 43
Overloading, 61
Overriding, 62

P

Package
  characteristics, 136–138
  model element, 105–106
Paradigm
  characteristics, 35
  comparison of, 47–49
  component-oriented, 67
  data-driven, 45–46, 66
  function-driven, 44–45, 66
  object-oriented, 46–47, 66
Paradigm element, 35
Parameters
  class, 55
  operations, 143
  procedural construct, 43
Parametric polymorphism, 62
Passive class, 141
Passive object, 53
Path, 130–131
Pathname, 132, 245
Pattern (parameterized
    collaboration), 179–180
Persistent object, 53
Perspective, mechanism, 119
Phases, life cycle
  cessation, 22
  conception, 20
  development, 21–24
  evolution, 21
  iteration, 22, 25
Physical view. See Environment model
    view
Polymorphism, 61
Powertype, 153
Predecessor specification, 182
Prescriptive aspect of method, 17
Private accessibility, 55
Private visibility, 78, 132
Problem, 15, 25–26, 122
Problem solving, 15–19, 34–35, 124
Procedural construct, 43, 66

About the Author

Sinan Si Alhir has breadth and depth in all phases of the systems development life cycle. With experience in high-level and low-level project work, and his broad and deep knowledge of technology and methodology, he focuses on delivering quality solution-oriented results within various application domains using a multitude of technologies and methods.

While tremendously enjoying his profession, Sinan Si Alhir also enjoys being intellectually and artistically active by reading and writing poetry and philosophy and listening to music, and he enjoys being physically active—walking and jogging. Furthermore, it is the works of Edgar Allen Poe, Leo Tolstoy, Rene Descartes, Georg Hegel, Immanuel Kant, Sigmund Freud and others that galvanize his perpetual discovery of the mystery we call life. But above all, it is his family that keeps him balanced, fulfilled, content, and makes it all worthwhile.

Colophon

Our look is the result of reader comments, our own experimentation, and feedback from distribution channels. Distinctive covers complement our distinctive approach to technical topics, breathing personality and life into potentially dry subjects.

The animal on the cover of *UML in a Nutshell* is the domestic short-hair cat (*Felis catus*). Cats have been kept as pets for thousands of years, originally for their skill in ridding homes of mice and rats; domestic cats are descended from the European wildcat (*Felis silvestris*). While cats make excellent pets, they are not as obedient as dogs, as their social structure in the wild is not based on submission to a leader. They are most closely related to fellow carnivores hyenas and mongooses. Cats spend about two-thirds of their time napping or sleeping.

Domestic cats have much in common with their wild relatives. Cat bodies are engineered for supremely efficient hunting: excellent balance, silent paws, sharp claws and teeth, sensitive whiskers, flexible muscles and skeletons. Their sight is especially attuned to moving objects, but they do need a small amount of light to see at night. It's not true that cats always land on their feet; it is true that given enough distance, they usually can orient their bodies correctly using their tails as counterweight. Science has not yet determined exactly why or how cats purr.

Cats have been both revered and feared throughout history. Ancient Egyptians worshipped them, adorned them with jewelry, and mummified them; the Egyptian goddess Bastet had the head of a cat, and was associated with beauty, grace, and fertility. During the Middle Ages, though, they were believed to be associated with witches and the devil.

Paula Carroll served as production coordinator. Argosy provided editorial and production services. Megan Morahan created the illustrations using Macromedia FreeHand 7; Robert Romano coordinated the art program. Mike Sierra provided FrameMaker technical support.

Edie Freedman designed the cover of this book, using a 19th-century engraving from the Dover Pictorial Archive. The cover layout was produced with Quark XPress 3.32 using the ITC Garamond font. Whenever possible, our books use RepKover™, a durable and flexible lay-flat binding. If the page count exceeds RepKover's limit, perfect binding is used.

The inside layout was designed by Nancy Priest and implemented in FrameMaker 5.0 by Mike Sierra. The text and heading fonts are ITC Garamond Light and Garamond Book. This colophon was written by Nancy Kotary.

More Titles from O'Reilly

C and C++ Programming

C++: The Core Language

By Gregory Satir & Doug Brown
1st Edition October 1995
228 pages, ISBN 1-56592-116-X

A first book for C programmers transitioning to C++, an object-oriented enhancement of the C programming language. Designed to get readers up to speed quickly, this book thoroughly explains the important concepts and features and gives brief overviews of the rest of the language. Covers features common to all C++ compilers, including those on Unix, Windows NT, Windows, DOS, and Macs.

High Performance Computing, 2nd Edition

By Kevin Dowd & Charles Severance
2nd Edition July 1998
466 pages, ISBN 1-56592-312-X

This new edition of *High Performance Computing* gives a thorough overview of the latest workstation and PC architectures and the trends that will influence the next generation. It pays special attention to memory design, tuning code for the best performance, multiprocessors, and benchmarking.

Practical C++ Programming

By Steve Oualline
1st Edition September 1995
584 pages, ISBN 1-56592-139-9

A complete introduction to the C++ language for the beginning programmer and C programmers transitioning to C++. This book emphasizes a practical, real-world approach, including how to debug, how to make your code understandable to others, and how to understand other people's code. Covers good programming style, C++ syntax (what to use and what not to use), C++ class design, debugging and optimization, and common programming mistakes.

Programming Embedded Systems in C and C++

By Michael Barr
1st Edition January 1999
194 pages, ISBN 1-56592-354-5

This book introduces embedded systems to C and C++ programmers. Topics include testing memory devices, writing and erasing Flash memory, verifying nonvolatile memory contents, controlling on-chip peripherals, device driver design and implementation, optimizing embedded code for size and speed, and making the most of C++ without a performance penalty.

Practical C Programming, 3rd Edition

By Steve Oualline
3rd Edition August 1997
454 pages, ISBN 1-56592-306-5

Practical C Programming teaches you not only the mechanics of programming, but also how to create programs that are easy to read, maintain, and debug. This third edition introduces popular Integrated Development Environments on Windows systems, as well as Unix programming utilities, and features a large statistics-generating program to pull together the concepts and features in the language.

Mastering Algorithms with C

By Kyle Loudon
1st Edition August 1999
560 pages, Includes CD-ROM
ISBN 1-56592-453-3

This book offers robust solutions for everyday programming tasks, providing all the necessary information to understand and use common programming techniques. It includes implementations and real-world examples of each data structure in the text and full source code on the accompanying disk. Intended for anyone with a basic understanding of the C language.

O'REILLY®

TO ORDER: **800-998-9938** • order@oreilly.com • www.oreilly.com
ONLINE EDITIONS OF MOST O'REILLY TITLES ARE AVAILABLE BY SUBSCRIPTION AT *safari.oreilly.com*
ALSO AVAILABLE AT MOST RETAIL AND ONLINE BOOKSTORES

How to stay in touch with O'Reilly

1. Visit Our Award-Winning Web Site

http://www.oreilly.com/

★ "Top 100 Sites on the Web" —PC Magazine
★ CIO Magazine's Web Business 50 Awards

Our web site contains a library of comprehensive product information (including book excerpts and tables of contents), downloadable software, background articles, interviews with technology leaders, links to relevant sites, book cover art, and more. File us in your bookmarks or favorites!

2. Join Our Email Mailing Lists

Sign up to get email announcements of new books and conferences, special offers, and O'Reilly Network technology newsletters at:
elists.oreilly.com.
It's easy to customize your free elists subscription so you'll get exactly the O'Reilly news you want.

3. Get Examples from Our Books

To find example files for a book, go to:
http://www.oreilly.com/catalog
select the book, and follow the "Examples" link.

4. Contact Us via Email

order@oreilly.com
For answers to problems regarding your order or our products. To place a book order online visit:
http://www.oreilly.com/order_new/

catalog@oreilly.com
To request a copy of our latest catalog.

booktech@oreilly.com
For book content technical questions or corrections.

proposals@oreilly.com
To submit new book proposals to our editors and product managers.

international@oreilly.com
For information about our international distributors or translation queries. For a list of our distributors outside of North America check out:
http://international.oreilly.com/distributors.html

5. Work with Us

Check out our web site for current employment opportunites:
http://jobs.oreilly.com/

6. Register your book

Register your book at:
http://register.oreilly.com

O'Reilly & Associates, Inc.
1005 Gravenstein Hwy North
Sebastopol, CA 95472 USA
TEL 707-827-7000 or 800-998-9938
    (6am to 5pm PST)
FAX 707-829-0104

O'REILLY®

TO ORDER: 800-998-9938 • order@oreilly.com • www.oreilly.com
ONLINE EDITIONS OF MOST O'REILLY TITLES ARE AVAILABLE BY SUBSCRIPTION AT safari.oreilly.com
ALSO AVAILABLE AT MOST RETAIL AND ONLINE BOOKSTORES

International Distributors

http://international.oreilly.com/distributors.html • international@oreilly.com

UK, EUROPE, MIDDLE EAST, AND AFRICA (EXCEPT FRANCE, GERMANY, AUSTRIA, SWITZERLAND, LUXEMBOURG, AND LIECHTENSTEIN)

INQUIRIES
O'Reilly UK Limited
4 Castle Street
Farnham
Surrey, GU9 7HS
United Kingdom
Telephone: 44-1252-711776
Fax: 44-1252-734211
Email: information@oreilly.co.uk

ORDERS
Wiley Distribution Services Ltd.
1 Oldlands Way
Bognor Regis
West Sussex PO22 9SA
United Kingdom
Telephone: 44-1243-843294
UK Freephone: 0800-243207
Fax: 44-1243-843302 (Europe/EU orders)
or 44-1243-843274 (Middle East/Africa)
Email: cs-books@wiley.co.uk

FRANCE

INQUIRIES & ORDERS
Éditions O'Reilly
18 rue Séguier
75006 Paris, France
Tel: 33-1-40-51-71-89
Fax: 33-1-40-51-72-26
Email: france@oreilly.fr

GERMANY, SWITZERLAND, AUSTRIA, LUXEMBOURG, AND LIECHTENSTEIN

INQUIRIES & ORDERS
O'Reilly Verlag
Balthasarstr. 81
D-50670 Köln, Germany
Telephone: 49-221-973160-91
Fax: 49-221-973160-8
Email: anfragen@oreilly.de (inquiries)
Email: order@oreilly.de (orders)

CANADA

(FRENCH LANGUAGE BOOKS)
Les Éditions Flammarion ltée
375, Avenue Laurier Ouest
Montréal, QC H2V 2K3 Canada
Tel: 1-514-277-8807
Fax: 1-514-278-2085
Email: info@flammarion.qc.ca

HONG KONG

City Discount Subscription Service, Ltd.
Unit A, 6th Floor, Yan's Tower
27 Wong Chuk Hang Road
Aberdeen, Hong Kong
Tel: 852-2580-3539
Fax: 852-2580-6463
Email: citydis@ppn.com.hk

KOREA

Hanbit Media, Inc.
Chungmu Bldg. 210
Yonnam-dong 568-33
Mapo-gu
Seoul, Korea
Tel: 822-325-0397
Fax: 822-325-9697
Email: hant93@chollian.dacom.co.kr

PHILIPPINES

Global Publishing
G/F Benavides Garden
1186 Benavides Street
Manila, Philippines
Tel: 632-254-8949/632-252-2582
Fax: 632-734-5060/632-252-2733
Email: globalp@pacific.net.ph

TAIWAN

O'Reilly Taiwan
1st Floor, No. 21, Lane 295
Section 1, Fu-Shing South Road
Taipei, 106 Taiwan
Tel: 886-2-27099669
Fax: 886-2-27038802
Email: mori@oreilly.com

INDIA

Shroff Publishers & Distributors PVT. LTD.
C-103, MIDC, TTC Pawane
Navi Mumbai 400 701
India
Tel: (91-22) 763 4290, 763 4293
Fax: (91-22) 768 3337
Email: spdorders@shroffpublishers.com

CHINA

O'Reilly Beijing
SIGMA Building, Suite B809
No. 49 Zhichun Road
Haidian District
Beijing, China PR 100080
Tel: 86-10-8809-7475
Fax: 86-10-8809-7463
Email: beijing@oreilly.com

JAPAN

O'Reilly Japan, Inc.
Yotsuya Y's Building
7 Banch 6, Honshio-cho
Shinjuku-ku
Tokyo 160-0003 Japan
Tel: 81-3-3356-5227
Fax: 81-3-3356-5261
Email: japan@oreilly.com

SINGAPORE, INDONESIA, MALAYSIA, AND THAILAND

TransQuest Publishers Pte Ltd
30 Old Toh Tuck Road #05-02
Sembawang Kimtrans Logistics Centre
Singapore 597654
Tel: 65-4623112
Fax: 65-4625761
Email: wendiw@transquest.com.sg

AUSTRALIA

Woodslane Pty., Ltd.
7/5 Vuko Place
Warriewood NSW 2102
Australia
Tel: 61-2-9970-5111
Fax: 61-2-9970-5002
Email: info@woodslane.com.au

NEW ZEALAND

Woodslane New Zealand, Ltd.
21 Cooks Street (P.O. Box 575)
Waganui, New Zealand
Tel: 64-6-347-6543
Fax: 64-6-345-4840
Email: info@woodslane.com.au

ARGENTINA

Distribuidora Cuspide
Suipacha 764
1008 Buenos Aires
Argentina
Phone: 54-11-4322-8868
Fax: 54-11-4322-3456
Email: libros@cuspide.com

ALL OTHER COUNTRIES

O'Reilly & Associates, Inc.
1005 Gravenstein Hwy North,
Sebastopol, CA 95472 USA
Tel: 707-827-7000
Fax: 707-829-0104
Email: order@oreilly.com

O'REILLY®

TO ORDER: **800-998-9938** • *order@oreilly.com* • *www.oreilly.com*
ONLINE EDITIONS OF MOST O'REILLY TITLES ARE AVAILABLE BY SUBSCRIPTION AT **safari.oreilly.com**
ALSO AVAILABLE AT MOST RETAIL AND ONLINE BOOKSTORES